SUCCESSFUL

TURKEY

HUNTING

M.D. JOHNSON
Photos by Julia Johnson

Published by

krause
publications

Please call for our free catalog. Our toll-free number to place an order or obtain a free catalog is 800-258-0929 or please use our regular business telephone 715-445-2214 .

Library of Congress Catalog Number: 2001097830
ISBN: 0-87349-352-4
Printed in the United States of America

Dedication

This book is dedicated to the men and women who proudly served in the United States Armed Forces in Southeast Asia, and to the more than 58,000 who made the ultimate sacrifice. From an artillery captain's son, thank you.

And to Julie, who understands well the 3:30 a.m. wake-ups, the siren song of Spring, and why I do what I do. You are something else. Love you.

Foreword

It's amazing how often you hear someone talking about something other than turkey hunting, but what they say turns out to be a perfect description of the sport. A few years ago I was watching a downhill ski race from Europe on ABC television when the announcer brought on a local commentator to analyze the contest. He was a short, dark, little dude with a single eyebrow over both eyes and a funny little Alpine hat with a feather in it. You could barely understand a word he said. But he plunged ahead anyway. The Italians, he said, skied like men of madness, completely not caring of their own safety. He was asked about the French. They were even worse, he avowed darkly, skiing as if they don't care if they are dying or living. He was asked about the Americans, whereupon his face lit up. Ah, the Americans, he said. They ski as if they *insisted* to die.

Here was a man talking, whether he knew it or not, about turkey hunting. Not from the safety angle, of course. (Turkey hunters are passionate about their personal safety, if only because they are unsure of the exact season dates and regulations in the afterlife.) But the men and women who chase turkeys are not like other hunters, who are people who hunt because they like to, want to, even need to. No. Turkey hunters simply *insist* on chasing their quarry.

I have known men about to be married who, in their last private moments before walking down the aisle, elected to practice their yelps in the privacy of the church coat room. I have seen 80-year-old hunters levitate from a sitting position and sprint the 30 yards to a downed gobbler at speeds that would make an NFL coach grin. And I have watched my own legs perform an arrhythmic version of "Lord of the Dance" as the biggest, strongest, most elusive bird in the North American woods strutted past me on a spring morning.

There is something about the wild turkey that moves certain souls. I have no idea what it is or why. The older I get, the less concerned I am about the meaning of things, whether turkey hunting or life itself. I'll leave that to the guys sitting in dens puffing on pipes. What I crave is to *experience* those things – their taste, touch, sight, sound and smell.

Be forewarned. If you have not already succumbed to Turkey Madness, one of the experiences will be a nearly infernal frustration. The birds will gobble like crazy one day and shut up the next, even though the two days are alike in every respect. The call that works magic one day will fail utterly the following day. An expert hunter comes to know both suffering and ecstasy.

Even the ecstasy of turkey hunting is different. I once tagged along with an elderly hunter in the mountains of southern Virginia. We spent an entire morning working a single bird, one he'd been hunting for three solid years. Every morning in season, the gobbler would fly down to a laurel thicket and visit a succession of hens, never leaving his quarter acre of safety. We talked to him from sunup to the close of business at noon. We moved four times, each time sure we finally had him coming. I'd had my gun up and ready for so long that my arms had turned to mush. And we never saw a feather of that bird.

When it was over, the old guy just lay back in the leaves grinning like an idiot, or so it looked. When I could stand it no longer, I asked just what the hell he was so happy about. "Think about it," he said. "We just spent five hours locked in combat, never fired a shot and I still came away with one of the best hunts of my life. Try that with any other critter in the woods. When you kill a bird, that hunt is over. But a hunt like today, shoot, it goes on forever."

He had a point.

Bill Heavey
Freelance writer, *Field & Stream*
Arlington, Virginia
September 2001

Acknowledgments

Julie and I recently had the honor and the privilege of penning our first book, a – how shall I say – web-footed prelude to this turkey hunting endeavor titled *Successful Duck Hunting: A look into the heart of waterfowling.* To those of you who have read our first attempt, a heart-felt thanks; however, as word of warning to those same folks, I'm about to repeat myself here.

As I've said so many times before: Nothing comes as the result of a solo effort. This is a saying of which I am admittedly quite fond. Yes, it's a cliché, but there really is no "I" in team. And a team is exactly what it takes to put together a book, regardless of the content. Holden Caulfield was an individual, or perhaps a conglomeration of personalities, that Salinger had had the good fortune – or would that be the misfortune? – of meeting. Hell, even Cujo, Stephen King's killer Saint Bernard, had *Myotis lucifugus*, and a rabid bat at that, to thank for his drooling rise to stardom.

As it was with our earlier book, I owe many, many folks a deep debt of gratitude for giving of their time, and more significantly, of themselves in order that I might reach this book-writing rung on the literary ladder. These folks, and there truly have been many over the years, took from their lives, their families, and their businesses so that I could see and learn. Through them and their unselfishness, I've become a different person. One who I'd like to think is a bit more educated. More mature – no laughing! More responsible. But more importantly, a person who is now better able to return the favor to yet another generation of turkey hunters.

That said, I'd like – as Jim Schoby used to say – to give a tip of the ol' hunting cap to:

Walt Ingram, regional director for the National Wild Turkey Federation, currently serving in the state of Ohio, who led me to my first gobbler in 1991. Man, did you have any idea what you were starting that morning in the Wayne National Forest?

Bob "Greenie" Grewell, for proving once and for all that giggling does indeed scare turkeys away. Also for his wonderful photographic contributions to this project. Thanks, Greenie.

Warren H. "Chip" Gross, for serving as my literary mentor and sounding board for all these years. Oh, and for talking me out of joining the circus that time I wanted to quit writing.

Dan Blatt, Sr., who spent 25 years convincing the Washington Department of Fish and Wildlife that wild turkeys *were* a good thing, and who has been instrumental in creating one of the most spectacular turkey hunting opportunities available in the United States – the Washington Mini-Slam.

The Maddy Family of Centerville, Iowa – Stan, Linda, Keane, and Jason. These people opened up their home and their hearts to two turkey hunting strangers-turned-friends. You just don't find better folks.

The National Wild Turkey Federation (NWTF) of Edgefield, South Carolina, without whose hard work and commitment to this incredible wild natural resource, this book – but more precisely, the memories and the photographs, the friendships and the frustrations – would not have been possible.

Mark Drury, Brad Harris, David Hale, Harold Knight, Dick and Chris Kirby, Walter Parrott, Ricky Joe Bishop, Matt Morrett, and to all of the turkey hunting educators, innovators, and instructors – past, present, and future. Yours is a dedication and a passion unequaled. And very much appreciated.

Tony "The Jakeman" Miller, and his wife, Kerri, who both have taken it upon themselves to make sure I stop and smell the foxglove.

My folks, Mick and Sue Johnson, for support, encouragement, and love beyond words.

Julie Johnson, without whose fantastic images – again – this would be nothing more than just a pile of vowels and consonants.

And from Julie to her folks – her dad, Gordon; step-dad, Henry; and Mom, Mary – thanks, each of you, for bringing me up as a child of the outdoors. Because of who you are, you *would* believe the things I've seen. And to her sons – Adrian, Casey, and Robbie – I love you.

Table of Contents

Introduction

Tell me something. Why is it the things that at first seem the simplest ultimately turn out to be the most difficult? If you can relate to that, then you can fully understand the trouble I had with this introduction.

This is supposed to be easy, I told my outdoor photographer wife, Julie. All I have to do is write about turkey hunting. Not the ins and outs, but just about turkey hunting as a whole. It's a chance for me, I told her, to wax nostalgic. To reminisce about all the people and the places I've been over the course of my turkey hunting career, fine world traveler that I am. It's free-writing in its purest form, and yet, for some odd reason, I found this initial step the most difficult.

Part of the reason behind this difficulty lies in what I thought an introduction should be. An introduction, I told myself, simply had to be one's best writing. Done correctly, a 500-word introduction should overshadow everything that rests between Chapter One and The End. It's Aldo Leopold, John Madson, and Archibald Rutledge, all rolled into one. It's eloquence and refinement. Nostalgia. History. Tradition. How can one write so flawlessly? How is it possible to conjure up images as strong and as lasting as those that were hauled – no, forced – to the surface of every reader's soul who even so much as looked at the first page of "A Sand County Almanac?" How do I follow an act like that?

And then it hit me. It isn't necessary that I create, from scratch, all of the images and all of the visuals. They're not mine; they're yours. You saw those three gobblers roosted together last spring. Snow on the oak that was their nighttime hideout, but gobbling to beat the band nonetheless. And you saw the fox squirrel sniff the sole of your boot and the house wren land on your gun barrel. You were the lone witness to the trillium and the foxglove, the heron rookery and the whitetail twins. No, my task here is not to create. It's simply to remind. To refresh. To relearn.

Then I thought…Well, what's my goal here? Or better yet, is there a reason for writing this. Unless your last name is King (as in Stephen) or Grisham (as in John), you can immediately take money and throw it far into the corner of the room. My guess is that no one has ever and no one will ever write a book that centers around turkey hunting solely for the money involved. If that person exists, they most certainly are living in their folks' basement and dining nightly on a menu consisting of pur-

loined fish sticks and ketchup soup. Cold ketchup soup. No, it's not the money.

The fame then. It's got to be the fame. Remember Leopold? Madson? Rutledge? They all wrote about the wild turkey, and in the world of outdoor literature, they're each considered legends. And rightly so. But did these remarkable wordsmiths use the wild turkey simply as a stage, a marquee upon which to thrust their names into the public eye? I don't think so. There was no need to. Back when these men were writing, folks enjoyed the written word for the written word's sake. This was before the seven-head video cassette recorder/player and the interactive compact disc Omega computer simulator, whatever the hell that is. No, back then, peoples' imagination were like kindling, and the words of a Madson or Rutledge, a match. Were they hot? You bet they were hot. (Note to self – Hate yourself for saying that!)

But unfortunately, I still haven't answered the question – what's my goal? What's my reason? To be honest with you, there are a couple answers.

Number one – I want to entertain you. I want this to be the journalistic equivalent of an open-mike night at the local comedy club. An improvisation, but an improvisation based on reality. Because if you think about it, aren't the funniest things those things that we can relate to? Maybe things that we've attempted or even, unfortunately, accomplished ourselves. You fell on the ice. Last one to be picked for the dodge ball team. Went stag to the J-Prom. You have a mother-in-law? If so, then you can relate. And that's what it's all about, being able to relate. Which brings me back to one of my goals. Here, roosted among these 140-some odd pages, it's my hope that there are words, phrases, paragraphs, and images, both provided and self-created, that have you saying things like "I know that" or "I've seen that." Maybe "I've been there." No, I don't take that as an indication that I'm presenting old, often-used, and merely recycled information. Instead, I see it as me hitting a nerve. For when you say "I've been there," then I made you feel. And when I made you feel, I made you see. And all in a light-hearted, conversational tone. Not with flowery language or long-winded tirades discussing the heretos and where-art-thous of many a microphyte community. Just two friends talking over a good, percolator cup of coffee. If, while you read this, you smiled, even once, goal attained.

Number two – I want to educate you. Let me rephrase that. I want to present you with information that you can use to your advantage whenever you step into the turkey woods.

Education. You have to be careful how you use that word. As the offspring of a retired high school biology teacher who did his Master's Thesis on slime molds, some specimens of which were grown – no lie – in his closet, and a newly-retired English teacher with a bachelor's degree in Latin who did her Master's Thesis entirely in Old English, I think I've learned how the word 'education' can affect folks. It all goes back to Number One – entertainment. The secret to education, in part, lies in the ability to provide education disguised as entertainment. Not that such tactics are always necessary nor are they always warranted; still, somewhere among these chapters hide a paragraph or two that will make you close the book, look at the ceiling, and say, "Why didn't I think of that?" There's no shame in that. It's not like you're asking for directions, guys. And when you've said, "Why didn't I think of that?" Well, goal attained.

And finally, there's the sharing. Yes, the sharing. Think about it. Isn't that what experience and the written word are all about? Thanks to this wonderful creature known as the wild turkey, I've seen things – and Julie's seen things – that are just too incredible to keep to ourselves. The little hen that tried her best to strut and gobble. Oregon's snow-capped Mt. Adams, my hand clenched around the long-spurred legs of a beautiful Washington state Merriams. A Texas Rio strutting in a field of blue bonnets and Indian paint brush. Words do it no justice, but I'm going to try.

But because this is a turkey hunting book, some of you may be thinking right about now – "Well, where in the hell is the turkey hunting story? We need a 'Let me tell you about this one nasty gobbler.' Or, 'One morning, years and years ago…'" Truth is, you're right. This is a turkey hunting book. And there should be, first rattle out of the box, a turkey hunting story. Well, here's the best one I know. It even starts out right.

Years ago, when my Grandma Verity was in her mid-70s, I guess, I took her up on the Ridge Road there in Athens County, Ohio. It was Spring, and I wanted G'ma to hear the turkeys gobbling. Excited she was. Made a thermos of coffee and put together a batch of home-made cookies just for the occasion.

It was a glorious morning. Towhees chattered from their hidey-holes in the roadside bushes. Ruffed grouse drummed from every hollow we passed. And the turkeys. Boy, the turkeys gobbled like they were putting on a show just for G'ma. After a while – and I knew I shouldn't – I called a few times on an old box call that I had "just happened" to throw on the truck seat. Did it just to get the birds all fired up. And when they gobbled all the harder, that wonderful lady grinned from ear to ear.

Down the Ridge Road we went. Down to another part of the property and yet another roadside show. Then it was back to our original listening post. And there, right in the middle of the gravel road, right where he should have been, was a huge gobbler. In full strut, he was. Looking good, and in all likelihood searching for that all-too-eager hen he'd heard hollering from up on the ridge earlier in the morning. For a full minute. Maybe two, he spun 'round and 'round. And we had front row seats. Just us. Me and G'ma.

Thinking back, I don't remember what she said. Tell you the truth, I can't remember if she said anything at all. Don't know as though she had to. But I do know she smiled. And I know her heart felt 50 years younger. Me? Well, I felt like a kid again. And as long as I have that picture – her face, just beaming as bright as the sun, and that full-strut gobbler in the middle of that lonely country road – I'll always feel like a kid.

You never forget things like that. We all have them. Or we should. And that's what this book is all about.

Oh, and I guess this is probably a good time to mention something. Unlike those magazine articles and books that transform turkey hunting and turkey calling into some type of indistinguishable hybrid, well, this isn't one of those. It's like I tell folks during the opening couple minutes of our turkey hunting seminars. I tell 'em – "Folks, thanks for coming. But if you've come expecting to hear 45 minutes to an hour of turkey calling, well, you're going to be disappointed." Every time though, just as if I'd had it planned, someone in the audience tentatively raises their hand and asks quietly, "Well, M.D. If you're not going to talk about turkey calling, what are you going to talk about?"

And now's the time I get to deliver my line. Actually, it's not my line. It's actually David Hale's line. That's David Hale of Knight & Hale Game Calls. Several years ago, I had the good fortune of interviewing David for a story that I had titled "There's more to turkey hunting than meets the ear." During our half hour or so on the telephone, David Hale gave me probably THE best thing I've learned about turkey hunting over the course of the last decade. And here, I'm going to share it with you.

What Hale said was this – "M.D.," he said, "only about five to 10 percent of turkey hunting is turkey calling." Five to 10 percent, he said. Well, even with my limited math skills, I could easily figure out that that left somewhere of 90 to 95 percent of something else. This book is all about that something else.

M.D. Johnson
2001

1

Meet The Players: Turkeys Times Five

From where I stood, there in the heart of the Missouri Ozarks, it was hard to believe that there had been a time in this nation's history when a body couldn't step into the woods in the spring and hear what I was at that moment hearing. And what I was hearing could only be described as a cacophony. All around me, a full 360 degrees, there were turkeys. Not just turkeys, but gobbling turkeys. Beside me, my wife and hunting partner, Julie, stood as awestruck as I. "You know," I whispered. "You could close your eyes and spin around in a circle. And anywhere — any direction — you stopped, you could walk that way and be walking in on a gobbler. Cool, eh?"

Her response, though delayed, left no room for discussion. "Quiet," she hissed. "Can't you see I'm listening?" I just smiled. You have to love a girl like that.

Am I telling the truth? Was this a real hunt in the Ozarks? You betcha! It was opening day, late April of 1995. And to be there on that two-track road as the sun airbrushed the horizon in unrivaled combinations of reds and pinks and oranges, it was easy to believe that every gobbler on the planet had decided that, just for a morning, the hills and ridges of the Show-Me State were *the* place to be. It was incredible.

But what's even more incredible — or maybe unbelievable is a better word — is the fact that it wasn't that long ago, 70 or so years, that the gobble of the wild turkey was as rare as diamonds the size of cinder blocks.

How can that be, you ask? After all, today's wild turkey population stands at more than 5 million birds.

This Iowa Eastern weighed 27.2 pounds and sported a 12.25-inch beard – impressive stats regardless of state or subspecies!

Hell, in some states, Iowa for instance, a hunter can harvest two gobblers in the spring and then another two birds of either sex in the fall. What gives? What gives is a story of wealth, greed, and decline, all fortunately followed by a most noteworthy rebirth that can only be described as a resurrection.

Releasing an Iowa-raised Eastern hen in western Washington, part of a National Wild Turkey Federation project co-sponsored by the Lower Columbia River NWTF chapter and the Washington Department of Fish and Wildlife.

The Rise, Fall, And Rise Of The Wild Turkey In America

Long before the first white men ever trod on the soil that would eventually become the United States, the wild turkey was filling the spring woods with gobbles. He also was filling the larders and smokehouses of many of the country's tribes of American Indians, all of whom understood the importance of the wild turkey as both a source of food and a natural resource. But turkeys weren't found nationwide, even in these earliest times. Some states, particularly Western and Northwestern states such as Washington, Idaho, Montana, and California, have only supported populations of wild turkeys in the past 30 to 40 years.

But in those states that did have birds — the Plains, the Midwest, the Southeast, and parts of the Northeast — the first 100 years of this nation's history were indeed a time of plenty. Unfortunately, that time was far too short. As the colonies gained their independence and the push to settle the Great American West grew from gentle surf to tidal wave, the wild turkey, like the whitetail, the beaver, and the snowy egret, was caught in the undertow. Unregulated hunting was justified as a means to feed the new residents of the expanding frontier. It was made logistically simpler thanks to the creation of roads. Easier access into those areas formerly known as wilderness, accounted for much of the decline in wild turkey populations. Habitat loss, a necessary (or so it seemed) part of this westward movement, also played a major role in the decline. Finally by the early 1900s, with its fate seemingly sealed, the last remaining vestiges of this once thriving natural population slipped into hiding into those places where the white man could not, or would not, go. In the rugged, untouched hills of Virginia, the swamps of Florida and Georgia, the Blue Ridge Mountains of North Carolina and the untamed vastness of Texas, turkeys survived.

The Rise

In the opening days of the 20th century, outdoor enthusiasts, hunters in particular, began to wake up. They realized that unless the country's natural resources were managed and, in some cases protected, there would be no natural resources to tend to. The demise of the American bison may have served as one eye-opener, as might the death of the last passenger pigeon. Inconceivably, the last of a population of 5 billion birds died in a Cincinnati zoo in September 1914. In the West, fur trappers were finding fewer and fewer beavers; in the East, whitetail deer, once a major source of food and clothing for the settlers, had become alarmingly scarce. Something, and something major, had to be done.

Something was done. However, these first steps to bolster wild turkey populations were not without their setbacks. Initially, wildlife managers and biologists thought that the answer to revitalizing the nation's wild turkey population was simple — raise turkeys and turn them loose in the woods. Over time, it was thought, these turkeys would both increase in number and revert back to a creature not from but of the wild. The system was good in theory, bad in practice. Quickly, these same good-intentioned managers realized, first, that pen-raised, semi-domestic turkeys weren't all that adept at eluding the many predators still roaming the United States. In short, the country's coyotes and bobcats were eating very well, thanks to members of the various state fish and wildlife agencies. Secondly, those birds that did manage to escape the predators often succumbed to disease or, in some cases, something as simple as the elements. There had to be a better answer. And there was, and still is today. The answer is wild birds.

But while the solution to restocking the country with wild turkeys using wild turkeys seemed elemental, the practice was anything but easy. Fortunately, an innovation known as the cannon net made capturing these less-than-willing subjects not only possible, but relatively simple. The cannon net is essentially a large fishing net that can be propelled using weights launched by a series of cannon-like devices. The birds are netted after being attracted to a target area through the use of bait. Since its first use

The Eastern wild turkey. This particular bird is a big Ohio gobbler.

This Eastern jake (a year-old or younger tom) was seen during a spring outing. Notice the short, protruding beard.

in the field in 1951 in South Carolina, the cannon net has allowed biologists and researchers from all over the country to trap birds in one location and transplant them to another — hence the now-popular name, the trap-and-transfer program. Often, these transplants took place within the borders of the home state. But in recent years trades of species between states — Washington state river otters for Missouri turkeys, for instance — have begun to become a popular, not to mention effective, way of increasing any number of wild populations, while at the same time diversifying and ensuring the health of existing gene pools.

Still, the reintroduction of the wild turkey wouldn't start and end with the invention and advancement of the cannon net. In 1973, the National Wild Turkey Federation (NWTF) was founded. Today, as it did some 29 years ago, the NWTF holds as its mission statement "the conservation of the wild turkey and the preservation of the hunting heritage." And like wild turkey populations across the nation, the NWTF has grown and expanded, increasing in size and scope from a membership of just 1,300 in its inaugural year to an astonishing 315,000 members in 1,800 state chapters and 18 foreign countries in 2001. Oh, and the turkeys? The country's population of wild turkeys in 1973 was estimated at 1.3 million. Currently, their numbers stand at an estimated 5.4 million. Obviously, someone's doing something right.

Today, wild turkeys and turkey hunting seasons can be found and enjoyed in 49 of the 50 states — sorry, Alaska — as well as several of the Canadian provinces and Mexico. Most states offer both a spring and fall season, with several providing additional opportunities for those who might choose to pursue their birds with archery or muzzle-loading equipment. In this new millennium, the mere existence of the wild turkey stands as testimony to the hard work and concentrated efforts of hundreds of thousands of individuals. It is rightfully regarded by many as one of the greatest wildlife management success stories of the 20th century. It would have been unforgivable had we "progressed" to the point of silencing forever that most wondrous of spring sounds, the gobble of the wild turkey. Fortunately, we learned our lessons earlier and wisely decided against such a course of action.

Turkeys Times Five

Personally, it matters not what color a gobbler's tail tips or rump feathers are. Just as long as he increases my heart rate, raises my blood pressure and gobbles a couple hundred times. That said, for me and for many, a turkey is indeed a turkey. However, the fact remains that while these birds, particularly the North American breeds, may appear visually similar, there are differences. Differences are found in the way they look, how they act, and where they live. There are even differences in how they gobble and what it sounds like.

Although looking like hairs, the gobbler's beard is actually comprised of modified feathers. Typically, a tom's beard will grow from 3 to 5 inches per year.

Don't think they can hurt you? Take another look at the spurs on this Iowa Eastern – and be careful.

But before you get to thinking that this turkey "who's who" is akin to a "you-can't-tell'em-apart-without-a-program" type of thing, let me simplify the situation. Basically, there are two species of wild turkey. There's the North American species, of which there are five different subspecies. Then there's the Oscellated species. The Ocellated, not to be confused with the North American Osceola subspecies, is easy to tell apart from the others, thanks to the fact that he resides only on the Yucatan Peninsula, and his blue head is dotted with bright orange warts that look like something out of a Stephen King novel.

With few exceptions, you folks reading this won't have to concern yourself with the Oscellated; therefore, let's spend some time getting to know the five North American subspecies a little bit better. But first...

The Wild Turkey: At First Glance

Generally speaking, all wild turkeys look about the same — head, two wings, and two legs. As with many wild animals, humans included, there are some differences between the sexes. And what better place to start looking at these differences than the names given these individuals: gobbler and hen.

Gobblers (male)

● Larger in size (both height and weight) than the hens, often weighing 20 pounds or more. Some gobblers, particularly the Eastern subspecies, may reach weights in excess of 30 pounds. Many will stand more than 45 inches tall.

● The overall coloration is black. Gobblers have black-tipped breast feathers, and will appear shiny or iridescent, almost metallic, over much of their body.

● Gobblers have a beard. Protruding from a pellicle located on the chest, the beard appears to be a horsetail-esque switch of hair. In truth, it's modified feathers. Beards typically grow 3 to 5 inches per year, and therefore can be used to estimate a gobbler's age. The beard's reason for being, like that of the human appendix, is a mystery.

● They also have sharp, bony hooks, called spurs, on their legs. Spurs, too, can be used to determine the age of a bird.
  ● One year or less — one-half inch or less; rounded or dull point
  ● Two years — one-half to 1 inch; slightly rounded point

12

Julie's first gobbler, a Washington Merriams shown here, sported five beards of differing lengths. Though unusual, multiple beards aren't all that rare.

An excellent example of the patriotic red, white, and blue head of an aroused spring gobbler. It's a sight you'll never forget.

Keane Maddy, my turkey hunting brother, and a true "Limbhanger."

- Three years — 1 inch or more; pointed; may show a slight hook
- Four years — 1 inch or more; very sharp; hooked. In many circles, if a bird possesses spurs that can be hooked over a tree limb and the bird's weight supported entirely, that bird is said to be a "limbhanger" and quite the trophy. But don't let anyone fool you. Any turkey is a fine turkey.

- The color of the head can be a collection of reds, whites, and blues, depending upon the bird's temperament. Colors of the head can and do change quickly. Often, the first thing a hunter notices is a gobbler's pure white head shining, as a friend of mine used to say, "like a light bulb coming through the woods." It's a one-time learning experience. Once you see it, you'll never forget it. Oh, and a gobbler's head has feathers, per se, only these little stubby hair-like things that kind of remind me of long nose hairs. He's a handsome bird to be sure, but there's absolutely nothing pretty about a gobbler's head.

- Gobbling is unique to the wild turkey and, with few exceptions, to the male of the species. Gobbling is used to attract hens, intimidate male competitors, and cause any one of two

A pair of Eastern jakes that came into a spring decoy set-up and would not leave. Again, note the short beards. Oh, and the eyes of the bird behind the pine. They don't miss much!

An Eastern hen. Notice how much more dull her feathers are, a protective coloration which helps camouflage her as she incubates next year's crop of birds.

Bob Grewell photo.

million humans to lose sleep for four to six weeks each spring.

● Male turkeys strut as a courtship dance. Many males, including humans, make themselves appear larger, louder, and more handsome than they actually are in hopes of attracting a mate.

● Gobblers produce a low-pitch, low-volume, sympathetic sound that you feel as well as hear. It's called spitting and drumming or simply drumming, and is made by a gobbler in strut. Creating the sound involves an exhalation of air and a vibrating of feathers complemented by a dragging of wing tips along the ground. Drumming is thought to be part of the courtship process; however, it may also be used to intimidate lesser gobblers or same-age rivals.

● Jakes are year-old gobblers, hatched the spring prior to your hunt.

Hen (female)

● An adult hen is approximately half the size of an adult gobbler. Most hens will weigh from 8 to 12 pounds, depending upon subspecies —

Bob Grewell photo.

An Eastern gobbler in full strut. Note the striking contrast between the jet black body feathers and the black-and-white barring on the wings.

Easterns, more; Osceolas, less — and other variables such as habitat and food availability.

● The bird's overall coloration is brown or buff. A hen's breast feathers will be tipped in brown or buff and, like the majority of avian females, her overall appearance will be much duller — a camouflage necessity designed by Mother Nature to help hide the hens while on the nest.

● Whereas a gobbler's head will be devoid of feathers, hens will have progressively smaller and daintier feathers running up the back of the neck. The hen's head, too, will be a bluish-gray color and won't show the patriotic hues of the gobbler's.

● Spurs, none. Beard, none. Gobble, none. Strut, none. Spit and drum, none; HOWEVER, hens, both wild and domestic, of all four North American subspecies, have been found with both spurs and beards and have been seen to strut, gobble, and drum. Though uncommon, bearded hens, like antlered whitetail does, certainly do exist. Typically, hens' beards are thin, rudimentary things; however, I've personally seen a wild Eastern hen in western Iowa that sported a paintbrush-thick beard every bit of 10

inches long. Very few hens, however, will grow anything more than small bumps, if they have "spurs" at all. And as for the gobble, strut, and drum — well, I've seen it and heard it, both in the wild and in our domestic Eastern Bronze varieties. Why? Perhaps the bird is searching for an alternative lifestyle. It may have something to do with dominance, as the pecking order is as strong within the ranks of the hens as it is among gobblers; still, I'm not sure that anyone knows for sure.

● Jennies are the hen equivalent of the gobbler's jake — a year-old hen.

The Eastern
Meleagris gallopavo silvestris

For many turkey hunters, their introduction into the sport comes courtesy of the Eastern subspecies. The reason is simple. Of the nation's current population of more than 5 million wild turkeys, 3 million are Easterns. So numbers play a part here. So, too, does the Eastern's widespread distribution, a range that currently and somewhat roughly encompasses the whole of the United States east of a line drawn from the northeastern corner of North Dakota south to just north of Houston, Texas. Minus, that is, central and south Florida, and extreme southern Louisiana. I say 'roughly' here because the Eastern subspecies, thanks to the aforementioned trap-and-transfer and agency trade programs, can also be found, alive and well, in such out-of-the-way and non-traditional places as western Washington and northwest Oregon. The land surrounding Idaho's Dworshak Reservoir also harbors an increasing Eastern population, as do several of the Canadian provinces.

One of the largest of the wild turkey subspecies, it's not unusual to hear of an Eastern gobbler weighing between 25 and 30 pounds; however, 18- to 22-pounders are much more common. Growing up as an Ohio turkey hunter, I believed in our standing rule of thumb that any bird over 20 pounds was a trophy. Come 1997 and our relocation to Iowa, I was to learn that Hawkeye State eyebrows don't even perk up until the scales tip to 25 or 26 pounds. Kill a 27-pound tom in Iowa, and you're getting closer. A 28-pounder like the one that hunting partner Dave Fountain tagged on his first-ever turkey hunt in the spring of 1999 — Oh, sorry. That would be 28.3 pounds! — will definitely get noticed. Got a 30-pounder? Now you're talking a trophy Iowa longbeard. Need more? At present, three of the top-10 heaviest Eastern gobblers recorded in the NWTF ledgers were taken in Iowa, including the No. 3 gobbler that weighed an incredible 33.75 pounds, and the No. 8

The Rio Grande. Home for the Rio is Texas and the western U.S., including Washington, Oregon, and California.

bird, an equally impressive longbeard that dropped the scales to 32 pounds, even. Story has it that the 32-pounder was one of four gobblers that came into a decoy set-up, but, as the hunter claims, he wasn't the biggest of the four. What would the biggest bird have weighed? The world may never know.

The Eastern's scientific name, *silvestris*, translates into "forest turkey," which is a reasonably accurate description of the bird's most frequented habitat. Easterns are set apart visually from the other subspecies by a chocolate brown or darker buff coloration on both the rump feathers and the tips of the tail feathers. The wing feathers will show equal amounts of black and white barring, and the bird will appear proportionate in size (leg length to body mass) overall.

The Rio Grande
Meleagris gallopavo intermedia

The Rio Grande, or simply Rio, takes its Latin name, *intermedia*, from the fact that the bird appears to fall somewhere between the Eastern and the Merriams in terms of looks. So this "in the middle" moniker certainly does make sense.

Second only to the Eastern in terms of population size with a current flock numbering some 700,000 birds, the Rio, like the Merriams, is a bird of the wide open country. Texas, home to some 600,000 Rio Grande turkeys, is the nation's best bet for those seeking an audi-

ence with this remarkable Western big game bird. Other states with excellent Rio populations include Kansas and Oklahoma; however, increasing numbers can also be found in eastern Washington, central Oregon, Idaho, Montana, California, and of all places, Hawaii.

Similar in size to the Eastern, the Rio differs in two ways. First, the birds have disproportionately long legs, a feature difficult to notice on a gobbler in strut, but very obvious in both toms and hens when the birds are walking or standing. Secondly, where the Eastern's tail tips and rump feathers will be a dark brown, the Rio will show a lighter buff or tan color. It is almost a caramel or butterscotch hue. It's a noticeable difference in most cases; however, in those instances where Easterns and Rio Grandes have the ability to intermingle, in the state of Kansas for instance, the resulting hybrids can be difficult, if not impossible, to tell apart.

The Merriams
Meleagris gallopavo merriami

A true inhabitant of the West, the Merriams subspecies was named in honor of C. Hart Merriam, the first chief of the U.S. Biological Survey. This subspecies is, for lack of a better phrase, a bird of the mountains, moving up and down in elevation following the snowline in both spring and fall, much in the way of big game animals such as mule deer, western whitetails, and elk. Like the Rio, the Merriams is somewhat of a long-distance, nomadic wan-

Texan John Bagley, left, and the author admire Bagley's first bird, a fine Blanco County, Texas, Rio Grande.

For many turkey hunters, the Merriams, pictured here, epitomizes the Wild, Wild West.

derer; he leads a sort of "here today, gone tomorrow, back again the next day" lifestyle.

If I were to choose one subspecies as my "favorite," it would have to be the Merriams. The reasons are many. First, he's an extremely handsome bird, with his snow-white rump feathers and tail tips set off in a startling contrast to an overall black background. Secondly, he's eager to gobble. Merriams not only gobble frequently, but it would seem at all hours of the day and sometimes well past dark. Finally, on more than one occasion, Merriams gobblers have demonstrated a willingness to come long distances to a call or decoy set-up. While the reasons behind these marathons are uncertain, my theories include the vastness of the Merriams' historical habitat, that being the big country territories of Colorado, Arizona, and New Mexico, as well as the availability of receptive hens. These gobblers apparently often find it necessary to travel great distances in order to locate their next date. In contrast, all an Iowa or Ohio Eastern gobbler has to do to find his next girl is peek around the closest tree trunk or hop down to the next limb.

Today, some 200,000 Merriams inhabit not only their original range, but have been successfully transferred to a host of other states including South Dakota, Nebraska, Washington, Oregon, and Idaho.

The Osceola
Meleagris gallopavo Osceola

You want an Osceola? Well, you have three choices — Florida, Florida, and Florida. True, some hybridization between Osceolas in northern Florida and southern Georgia has been rumored and may actually be happening. You see, turkeys don't differentiate between species. To an Osceola gobbler, an Eastern hen is just another pretty girl. If it's a pure-strain Osceola gobbler that you're wanting for the picture album, then you'd best be thinking about plane tickets to the central or southern portions of the Sunshine State. That is, unless you're fortunate enough to already be a resident.

The least numerous of the four better-known North American subspecies, the Osceola, with a current population of around 80,000 birds, is also the smallest in size and weight. Gobblers of the subspecies will typically weigh less than 20 pounds; hens, between 8 and 10 pounds. Named after the great Seminole chief, the Osceola is a long-legged thing. The bird is leggy, in some cases, to the point of being odd-looking. Though similar in appearance to the Eastern, the Osceola, also known as the Florida turkey, is more black overall, even down to the wing feathers, which show only a fraction of the contrasting white markings commonly found in the other subspecies. Rump feathers and tail tips are often Eastern-like, though the tails tips often may be much more narrow than on the

Avid turkey chaser, Steve Puppe, glasses the Black Hills of South Dakota, a favorite haunt of the Merriams subspecies.

Oregon's spectacular Mt. Hood provides an incredible backdrop for the author's wife and hunting partner, Julie, and her '96 Washington state Merriams.

The most sought-after and some would say, the most elusive, member of the North American Big Four, Florida's Osceola.

Eastern. Another characteristic of the Osceola gobbler is the long, sharp spurs, which can reach lengths of up to two inches. It's thought that these dagger-like spurs are due in part to the absence of rocks or other natural grinding materials that often can work to wear down the spurs of toms found elsewhere in the country.

The Goulds
Meleagris gallopavo mexicana

The Goulds, sometimes called the Mexican turkey, traditionally makes his home in the mountains of northern Mexico. I say traditionally because in recent years, wildlife officials in the states of New Mexico and Arizona have been working diligently to reintroduce this tremendous game bird in their respective states. And they are apparently doing so with good to moderate success on all fronts.

Due in large part to his "foreign" residence, the Goulds is the least-known of the five subspecies. A big bird, a Goulds gobbler will often weigh in excess of 20 pounds, with occasional birds — the NWTF record currently stands at 28.5 pounds — pushing the 25-pound mark.

Visually, the Goulds, with its white rump coverts and tail tips, resembles the Merriams; however, the white of a Goulds is much more pure. This South of the Border bird will also have longer legs and larger feet than any of its cousins to the north.

...and finally, the Ocellated

Let's face it. The Ocellated turkey (*Meleagris ocellata*) is just flat strange looking. Even under the worst of conditions, there's no mistaking this creature for any of the North American subspecies. It could perhaps have been a figment of the late Dr. Seuss' imagination, but it certainly cannot be confused with an Eastern or a Merriams.

Little is actually known about the habits of this bird. It does make its home on the Yucatan Peninsula. By all accounts the males make no sounds even approaching what North American hunters recognize as a gobble. The male of species does not sport a beard, but toms do possess remarkably long spurs, some up to or exceeding 2 inches in length. Both sexes are an iridescent bronze-green color overall. The birds have red legs and teal-blue heads accentuated with orange growths called nodules. And let's not forget the bright red eye-ring. Such coloration set these birds off from all but the occasional macaw or peacock, to which, they were originally thought to be related. Small birds, Ocellated hens will weigh a mere 6 to 7 pounds, while gobblers push to reach 12.

Personally, I have never seen an Ocellated turkey in the wild; however, I'd wager 100 to 1 that 99.98 percent of all American turkey hunters haven't either. Luckily, I do have a dear friend in Washington state who has seen them. In his younger days, Tony Miller traveled to South America with a group of similarly focused 20-somethings. Missionary work, he says. An avid hunter, he spent a goodly amount of his time talking the natives out of their taped-up single-shot shotguns, .22 rimfires, and small stashes of ammunition. Armed as such, he tells of calling in these wary jungle turkeys using his voice to mimic the birds'

Julie took this beautiful Osceola in Florida in '98 as the first step in her successful quest for the coveted Wild Turkey Grand Slam. Note the relative absence of white barring on the wings, a very distinctive Osceola characteristic.

high-pitched and strange, as he described it, whistling call. Now a fanatical hunter of Merriams, Rios, and Easterns, Miller says that the jungle birds weren't much of a challenge to hunt, though — big smile — they were awfully good to eat. Seems that these birds have a little more in common with our U.S. turkeys than one might think!

2

Turkey Vocabulary: Speaking The Language

The gobble. It's what we all want to hear. And this bird's giving it his all!

I have a confession to make. I am, without a doubt, the world's worst goose caller. And I'll tell you why. Simple. I have no idea what I'm saying to geese. For years, while I thought I was hollering, "Hey, goose. Come here," I was, in fact, screaming — "Hey! There's a guy. No, wait. There's two guys down here who want nothing more than to shoot you and take you home." That type of talk is not conducive to getting Canada geese, even dumb ones, to land in your decoys.

Such is the case with turkey calling. You see, learning turkey — to talk turkey that is — is really no different than learning any other language for that's exactly what it is, another language. In order to speak any language, it's vital first to know how to make those sounds which make up the whole of the language and what the individual words that make up the language mean.

Let's say you've decided to travel abroad. This summer you're going overseas to, say, Germany. So you go, armed with your English-to-German dictionary and trust

Hens, like this little one photographed in southern Ohio, are the finest instructors when it comes time to learn turkey vernacular.

that volume and gestures will help get your point across. This first trip, you discover, is relatively language un-intensive. In fact, all you need to know are four things — (1) how to find the bathroom; (2) how to get back to your hotel; (3) where to get a pizza; and (4) where to find a beer. They're all pretty simple and straight-forward questions. Truth is, I know many a man who has lived a full and very satisfying life knowing only the answers to these four questions; however, I digress.

Now let's say that it's two years later, and you've decided to return to Germany to see those things that you missed because of all the beer and pizza. This time, though, you want to know a little bit more about what's going on around you. You want more detail. This time, you want to know — (1) where is the nearest and the cleanest bathroom; (2) how to hail a taxi in order to return to your nice hotel; (3) where to order a pizza with mushrooms, pepperoni, and sausage; and (4) where to find a cold beer, not that room-temperature stuff that looks like watered down axle grease. Sure, the questions may lack some refinement, but the bottom line is what matters. You've become more fluent in German. On this second trip, you're asking not only questions, but requesting specific answers to those questions. Surprise! You're well on your way to becoming a conversationalist.

Such is the case with turkey calling. The more fluent you become, the better your chances are of carrying on a detailed and very pointed conversation. Must you speak as well as the natives? Certainly not; however, the more

you understand about the language, the more likely you'll be to sweet-talk that reluctant longbeard into doing exactly what it is you'd like him to do. That is you want him to walk over and stop within 35 yards of you.

Let's take a look at wild turkey vernacular. As we do, I would like you to keep one thing in mind. While researchers and biologists have identified more than two dozen different turkey sounds, this does not mean that you have to be skilled in the use of all of them. Even if you understand only a little more each time you step into the field, that's certainly better than, "no habla turkey." You know what I'm saying?

Yelp — This is the "the" of the turkey's vocabulary. Every sound a turkey makes, with a couple of exceptions, begins with the yelp. For the most part, it's the yelp that hunters try to imitate in order to lure a lusty gobbler into range. Therefore, it's the yelping of the hen with which hunters are most familiar. Some might not know that gobblers also yelp. It is a different sounding yelp, much lower in pitch and slower in cadence or rhythm; still, it's a yelp nonetheless.

There are actually several different types of yelps, each made according to a bird's mood or, in some cases, what that bird hopes to achieve by making that particular sound. Most of these call types are separated by variables such as volume, duration, cadence, intensity, and situation. These variables are but human-forged guidelines, any one or all of which may change depending upon which turkey you ask; still, the list of basic yelps would include —

Plain yelp — An everyday communication sound. Turkeys use the plain yelp as they "talk" amongst themselves in the flock, or, as they're prone to do, talk to themselves as they go about their daily routine. Some yelps are soft; others are higher in volume. Some are issued as single notes, while in other cases, a yelp sequence, or run, may contain a dozen or more separate calls.

Assembly yelp — Mama turkeys will use this call to collect their young, called poults, in the event they get separated from one another. Fall hunters often hear this yelp following the scattering of a flock of birds as the adult hen or hens begin calling, trying to assemble — get it! — their broods.

Lost yelp — Sometimes called a lonesome yelp. This is a plaintive call, often made by single birds just looking for a little company. Gregarious and very social creatures, turkeys, particularly hens and young birds, don't take well to being alone. The lost yelp is typically heard as a monotone series of calls with neither rise nor fall, and can include 20 or more separate yelps.

Bob Grewell photo.

There's nothing noisier than a group of jakes, and much can be learned simply by listening. Are you taking the time to listen?

Tree yelp — A very soft, quiet call made by hens still on the roost. Imagine yourself just waking up in the morning. You're stretching, working out the overnight kinks, and thinking about that first cup of coffee. Those little unintelligible back-of-the-throat noises you make? Those are tree yelps.

Breeding yelp — This yelp, made by a willing and receptive hen, translates into — "Come here, big boy. It's time we got to know each other a little better!" Typically made by an adult or dominant hen, the breeding yelp is a coarse series of damn-near irritating calls that leave little to the imagination. Few toms find them irritating, however.

Phonetic translation: The yelp is actually a two-note call blended to sound as though it were one. Spelled out, the yelp might appear as *kee-yolk*, or *keouk, keouk, keouk*.

Cluck — For those of you who can "click" your tongue against the roof of your mouth, you're well on your way to imitating a wild turkey's cluck. Similar to the common barnyard chicken's cluck, the turkey's sound of the same name is most often heard coming from birds who are not alarmed or worried and are just going about their business. It could perhaps be described rather accurately as a "busy" type of call that turkeys make when they're just, well, wandering around. Because they denote calm, clucks

are a fantastic low-key, low-volume confidence call and can be extremely effective on late-season gobblers that have been exposed to just about every hideous noise capable of being produced by a human being. Soft cluck-yelp combinations, too, can prove a hot ticket, especially in blind-calling situations.

Phonetic translation: I'd like to be more specific, but the name — *cluck…cluck, cluck* — really says it all.

Purr — Like the cluck, the purr is another relatively self-explanatory wild turkey sound, and one used under an identical set of conditions; that is, when everything in the bird's world is going well. When things are calm and collected, and there's not a dark cloud on the horizon, turkeys will purr. You know that cat that purrs simply because he's happy and content? A turkey's the same beast, only without the fur. The cluck, the purr or cluck-and-purr combination can often be used successfully to entice pressured gobblers who have heard all the yelping, cutting, and cackling they can handle.

Phonetic translation: Just like it sounds — *purr…..pppp-puuuurrrrr*. Inflection plays a big part in setting one purr apart from another. Some are short and abrupt; others may carry a melodic rise and fall, while another may build gradually before tailing off into a quick, but quiet yelp or two.

Mama turkeys, like this Eastern hen, talk to their little ones constantly – even before the poults are hatched. Do they know their Mama's voice? You bet they do!

Fighting purr — I'd probably be remiss if I failed to mention another type of purr, the fighting purr. As is the case with a fox squirrel's bark and a rooster pheasant's cackle, this angry, back-of-the-throat trilling growl, once heard, isn't likely to be forgotten. The fighting purr is made by a gobbler as a vocal form of intimidation. Over the years, I've often heard this sound being made by adult gobblers approaching a jake-and-hen decoy set-up, presumably to convince the young bird — yes, he's plastic, but the tom doesn't know that — that it's best if he vacate the premises immediately. In many cases, the fighting purr is a prelude to a wing-beating, knock-down, drag-out rumble. For this reason, it can be an effective calling tactic, particularly when it's combined with other elements such as flapping a prepared turkey wing or aggressively slapping your hat or gloved hand against your leg. After all, everyone enjoys watching a good fight. And it's true of gobblers, too.

Cutt — Cutts, or cutting as it's often called, present some confusion, especially to new callers who sometimes have a difficult time differentiating this sound from the traditional cluck. Think of it this way. If a cluck was a butter knife, a cutt would be a fillet knife. Confounded now? There's really no need to be. A cutt is nothing more than an aggressive cluck. Add a bit more volume, and sharpen the edges of the sound a bit — I mean really pop it out there — and you'll find yourself cutting in no time.

Unlike clucks and clucking, which are contented, "nothing happening here" sounds, cutting is an excited,

energized, and demanding type of sound delivered in an almost stuttering, machine-gun style. What's it all mean? In some cases, it's the hen's way of letting off steam, perhaps at members of her flock. Other times, it's a sure-fire way of getting that old longbeard's attention.

Phonetic translation: Take absolutely all the "lazy" out of your clucks, and put them together like — *cutt...cutt...cutt-CUTT...cutt-CUTT-cutt...cutt-cutt...CUTT*. The best way to think about it, and yes, I am repeating myself but it's a worthwhile repetition, is like a machine-gun. Use single shots, then three-round bursts, then a long burst. Then go back to singles, then three-rounds, then singles, then another long burst. Mix in an aggressive yelp or two every now and then, and you have all the makings of a sequence that even old, hard-of-hearing gobblers can't resist. How do you know when you're trying hard enough? You show me a turkey caller who can run through an excited cutting sequence in the field without a whole lot of body English, and while standing flat-footed, and I'll show you someone who's not trying hard enough.

Cackle — The cackle is another call that sometimes flusters folks. Not its slow start building to a rapid-fire crescendo sequence, mind you, but rather its individual notes or sounds. The cackle — yes, I can see a resemblance to the traditional witch's laughter — probably would fall somewhere between the soft-edged cluck and the sharper-edged cutt in terms of presentation, volume,

Box calls are just one of the many different instruments that hunters use to reproduce a wide variety of turkey sounds.

Like box calls, friction calls like this Primos pot-and-peg are popular because of their authentic sound capabilities and the simplicity with which they're used.

and intensity. I think it could be accurately described as being a combination of the two; however, it's easier to understand and then reproduce a wild hen's cackle when you know that there are at least a couple different types of cackles, including:

The fly-down cackle — Made by the hens as they prepare to and then finally do fly down from their nightly roost, usually at first light. The fly-down cackle starts out with soft, widely-spaced clucks — *cluck......cluck......cluck-cluck.* At this point, hunters sitting near a roost may hear a sound like that of a drop of water falling into a container of water from quite a distance, a kind of *poink......poink......poink.* Although it may read strangely, this clear, bell-like call is immediately recognizable. In time, this clucking and poinking will turn more toward a cutt — *cutt...cutt-CUTT...cutt-CUTT.* Eventually, the hen, still cutting, will spread her wings and break into a cackle. Phonetically, though I've never seen an accurate version of it spelled out, a cackle might look something like —*poink...poink...cluck-cluck...cluck-cutt...cutt...cutt...cutt-CUTT...cutt-CUTT...CUTT...CUTT...CUTT-CUTT...CUTT-CUTT-CUTT-CUTT-CUTT-CUTT.* Hunters will often duplicate this cackling cadence, complementing the illusion by flapping a dried turkey wing or a hat in an effort to say, "Hey there, big fellow. I'm on the ground

now. Why don't you come on over?"

The fly-up cackle — Similar to the fly-down cackle — surprise! — only with less lead-in. Once on the roost, it's not uncommon for a hen to cluck, purr, or *poink* a few times, just to get it out of her system before bedtime.

The ground cackle — Seldom do I hear hens cackle on the ground during the course of the day. I can't say I've never heard it, though I think that when it has occurred, it was the result of a cutting hen forgetting herself and lapsing into a half-hearted cackle before she even knew what she was doing. Regardless of the fact that the sound is heard infrequently, it often does do the trick on tight-lipped gobblers. Personally, I think it's a clear-cut case of avian hormones being unable to resist a hen that's so willing as to cackle at 10 o'clock in the morning. Thus, we are left with a fine example ——and there are many, many of them in the realm of turkey hunting — of not knowing why something works, only that it does.

Spit and drum — I really do wish I could remember the turkey hunter who told me in regards to the spit-and-drum of the gobbler, "If you can hear that, man, you better sit down 'cause he's close. Real close." In actuality, it's amazing just how far this low-pitched, feel-it-in-your-

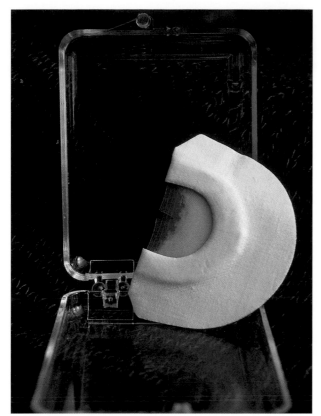

Give a kid a diaphragm call, and you'll get results; give one to an adult, and you'll likely get frustration.

Non-yelping turkey sounds such as the spit-and-drum demonstrated here by turkey calling veteran, Mark Drury, should also be included in your vocabulary.

chest sound can travel; however, the man who told me this was right. If you're hearing it, you better be "sat down" and have the gun up, because something's going to happen soon.

As the name implies, the spit-and-drum is two separate sounds made during the strutting process. The first, the spit, is often compared to a tire rapidly losing air — *pfitt!* Most folks have already made this noise, perhaps unintentionally. If you haven't, simply put your upper teeth over your bottom lip and say the word FIT. Add a little bit of a hiss behind it, and you've got it. How the gobbler actually makes this sound is a mystery. Some people believe it comes from inside, a quick exhalation of air; others claim that it's the result of the gobbler's body feathers suddenly being raised as he goes into strut. Either way, the fact remains if you hear this sound, he's in strut, and he's in close.

The source of the drumming sound, likewise, is unknown. Is it a low moan from inside? Or is it caused by feathers vibrating against one another? Only the bird knows for sure. What we do know is that the sequence, spelled out as…*pfitt! Oooommmmmm…*, is used by a breeding gobbler both as an attractant (hens) and as a deterrent (other gobblers). Hunters will often mimic the spit-and-drum, either with their natural voice or by using an artificial device such as the aptly-name Lohman "Spit-n-Drum" call, as a sort of challenge, a strategy that can be particularly effective on hesitant or hung-up toms.

Gobble — Come on, now. Do I really need to explain this? This is it. This is the mother of all natural sounds. This is why we get up at 3 a.m. for six straight weeks, and wobble into the woods, saying under our breath or, better yet, to the slightly aromatic individual who's spent the past 40 days in our company, "I … just … gotta … hear … it … one … more … time." This wonderfully wild sound makes exhausted men run and strong men weep. It is a sound so frustrating that it would make a nun curse the Pope, and so fulfilling as to make Lucifer himself attend a good, old-fashioned revival. The gobble. It's why we do what we do.

Putt (a.k.a. alarm putt) — This is a bad sound to hear, unless you're a turkey. And then it's still a bad sound, as the putt means there's trouble afoot and we, the turkeys, that is, had best be leaving the immediate vicinity — quickly.

The putt, which not surprisingly sounds just exactly as the word might indicate — *putt! putt!* — might be best described as a hard-edged or sharpened cluck. And like the whitetail's snort, the fox squirrel's bark, or the hen mallard's repetitious *quack…quack…quack…quack…* the wild turkey's putt is a sound of warning. Hear it, and you can rest assured that the bird in question has seen something that he or she doesn't care for and is letting the world, and you, know. Or, the bird in question *thought* he saw something, and simply due to his constantly paranoid condition has decided to let the rest of the woods in on his

Again, the gobble. Even photographs of the act in progress are enough to give a seasoned turkey hunter the shivers.

discovery. Either way, the jig's up, and chances are, you're now faced with a decision: Shoot, if a clean and responsible shot presents itself in the few seconds before the bird disappears or flies into the sunset, or, as is often the case following a *putt*, get to your feet, slap your leg with your hand — go on, get it over with — and start looking for another turkey.

Oh, and for what the *putt* truly sounds like in the wild? Not to worry. You'll hear it soon enough.

Kee kee (a.k.a. kee-kee run, whistle) — The kee-kee, or kee-kee run as it's often referred to, is the sound that a young and very lost turkey, jake or jenny, makes as it tries to re-establish contact with its mama and the rest of the flock. Those who hunt turkeys in the fall are very familiar with this clear, high-pitched whistling sound, as it's frequently heard after a flock is scattered and the individual members of the broken flock call back and forth in an attempt to regroup. The sound is commonly reproduced with a diaphragm call, although it can, with practice, be copied quite accurately using a box or friction-style call. The kee-kee is the primary tool in the arsenal of the November turkey hunter; however, its inclusion during a spring calling sequence can also be surprisingly effective.

Why? Although often heard after a disturbance, the kee-kee is also used by these very gregarious birds simply as a way of locating one another from a distance; therefore, because it is a common sound among turkeys and groups of birds, it can help lend an air of realism and confidence to a calling set-up, regardless of the time of year. Some folks — myself included — believe that the high pitch of the kee-kee run can sometimes pry a gobble from a tight-lipped tom, even after locator calls and more traditional spring turkey sounds have failed to draw a response.

Phonetic translation: The instructions that come with most diaphragm calls recommend hunters use the words 'pee-pee-pee' combined with a goodly amount of tongue-to-reed pressure when attempting to mimic the wild turkey's high-pitched kee-kee run. And it's worthwhile advice as the call itself — *kee-kee…kee-kee* — does sound quite similar to the "P" word; however, the kee-kee run is not all kee-kee. In the wild, a young turkey will often combine the kee-kee with adolescent — think of a 15-year-old boy's voice cracking — yelps. The end result is a pleading, plaintive — *kee-kee…kee-kee…kee-kee-kee-yelp…kee-kee-kee-yelp-yelp…kee-kee* — sound that, with a little bit of practice and some body English, is a relatively easy sound to make.

3

The Well-Dressed Turkey Hunter

*"The secret to camouflage is simple.
There is no such thing as an insignificant detail."*

Let me think. If I remember correctly, my Old Man was wearing a brown canvas duck hunting coat and a matching pair of brush pants. He had olive-drab Northerner boots at one end, and a forest green Hunt Ohio baseball hat at the other. I wasn't much better, what with my military surplus paratrooper jump pants —one color, green — and Woodland camo sweatshirt. Our headnets and gloves? Homemade the night before by my very talented Aunt-turned-short-deadline-seamstress, Kay, out of mosquito netting, burlap, and wire from a couple coat hangers. Hell, I can't even remember what I had on my feet. Boots, I think. Brown boots. I do know that our shotguns, neither of which had ever seen minute one in front of a patterning board, were as naked as the day we pulled them out of their respective Remington boxes. A camouflage-intensive, traditional turkey hunt? Not hardly.

Still, the Good Lord found it fitting to smile on two simple minds that April morning in Athens County, Ohio, by delivering what had to have been the most short-sighted, testosterone-riddled wild turkey gobbler in a five-state area. For 40 minutes, the big longbeard, the first we'd ever seen in the field, strutted and pranced. All puffed up, he was, spitting and drumming, though at the time, we had no idea what that — how did my Old Man describe it, "booming and dragging?" — hollow sound was. What I did know was what I had read. I shouldn't call a lot. And I shouldn't move. Never, not even once, did I think about the fact that dressed as we were, that cagy old gobbler should have taken one very, very short look and walked the other way.

Occasionally these days, I'll lay those faded pictures of my Pop's first gobbler alongside photographs of our subsequent springtime adventures. Man, I tell you. What

Of Julie's photographs showing camouflage in action, this is my favorite. Matching the terrain, the use of shadows, attention to detail – this one has it all!

As Iowa's Andy Bowers demonstrates, that old stand-by – Woodland Camo – still has its place…and a successful place at that!…in today's turkey woods.

Despite the jovial atmosphere here in Florida, camouflage is no laughing matter to turkey devotees Julia Johnson and Steve Puppe. Nor to the fine Osceola hanging over Johnson's shoulder.

a difference. Gone are the Northerners, long replaced by LaCrosse packs and Rocky snake boots. Absent, too, is my Old Man's brown canvas ducker. Oh, it still sees use during the fall. Just not in the spring. Today, it's a head-to-toe kind of deal with camo hats, store-bought headnets and gloves. An X-tra Brown shirt, Forest Floor pants, and, if the weather's cool, an All-Purpose jacket. Belts, guns, socks — shoot, even my boot laces are made in a multicolored, camouflage pattern. I'm hiding now. We're invisible. In fact, there's so much depth to my camouflage ensemble that I figure you ought to be able to reach right through me. Yes, sir, I've got it all. Including those most wonderful memories of that old Ohio longbeard. It was truly a camouflage-indifferent lovesick bird that proved without a doubt that clothes don't make you a turkey hunter. *Turkeys* make you a turkey hunter.

Camouflage: A (Very) Brief History

There was a time, not too very long ago, when wearing camouflage clothes in public was a sure-fire way of getting noticed. Would camo make you stand out in a crowd back then? As they say in Minnesota —You betcha!

Today, however, camouflage has made the transition from military to modern. There are camouflage shorts and camouflage swimwear. Camouflage throw rugs and tablecloths. There are camouflage boats, camouflage trucks.

Hell, I even owned a pair of camouflaged high-top Chuck Taylor tennis shoes once. The only things that set them apart from all the other camouflage "stuff" that the kids back in Newton Falls, Ohio, were wearing at the time were the words "right" and "left" written on the corresponding rubber toes. Great conversation starter; however, that's an entirely different story (thank goodness).

Camouflage in this modern world has become — and I almost hate to say it —trendy. In fact, it's pretty cool — there's another of those words — in this day and age to show up at a function, even a wedding, dressed from head to toe in camouflage. Tailored camo, of course, but camo nonetheless. This popularity, however, did not come without a price. For as camouflage became not only accepted but was transferred by society from the work clothes category into a list under the heading, Fashion Statement, it also grew more and more confusing. Or more precisely, the choices as to which camouflage to use for what occasion — wedding, funeral, bar mitzvah, turkey hunting, duck hunting, deer hunting, and so on — became more difficult. Fact is, there's been more than one hunter driven to the point of madness simply by walking into the camouflage clothing and accessories section of the local Gander Mountain store. Trust me, it's not a pleasant sight.

Remember Woodland camouflage? That very effective conglomeration of dark green, light green, tan, brown, and black — well — blotches? It was, of course, pre-Photo Realism. Still, it worked just fine. Then came the late 1960s,

Now you see him. Now you don't. Here, an example that camouflage is just one part of the equation. Success often has to do with where you sit. Or where you don't.

Vietnam, and the tiger stripes. From there, the chronology reads like a "who's who" of camouflage — Jim Crumley and Trebark, Bill Jordan's Realtree, and Toxey Haas' Mossy Oak. It was a time no longer of lights and darks, but of shadows and illusions. Camouflage clothing had entered an entirely new dimension, a third dimension to be so very specific. Camouflage now had depth. It had leaves and rocks, corn stubble and cattails. It was oak trees — yes, with acorns — and bare branches. This was no longer camouflage; it was art. "Laid my gun down," the story/rural legend goes, "and I couldn't find the damn thing again. Good camouflage, eh?" And we all just ate it up.

Okay, so there's a lot to choose from. What's it all mean? Why is this pattern better than that pattern? Or is it? Real-this and shadow-that. How's a body to make a decision when it comes to camouflage and turkey hunting? Actually, it's quite easy. First, remember those nine words with which I began this chapter — *there is no such thing as an insignificant detail.* Secondly, keep reading.

A Crash Course In Camo

Ready? At the risk of being elemental, here's how camouflage works.

A camouflage pattern, whether it's the traditional blobs and blotches or a three-dimensional photographic image, is nothing more than a series of lights and darks and shapes of different sizes intended to transform a two-dimensional image into a three-dimensional image by providing visual depth. It is an optical illusion. Period.

The most classic example of this process, and one which deer hunters are familiar with, is the style of camouflage known as blaze orange camo. Deer, as hunters know, are color-blind, and therefore see blaze orange, as well as the world around them, in varying shades and degrees of gray; however, large expanses of solid color, such as which results when a 350-pound deer hunter dons a blaze orange hunting coat, simply are not natural in the wild setting. Therefore, years ago, it was determined that this solid shape, despite being blaze orange, could be distorted and blended into the natural setting simply by adding distracting shapes, also known as the aforementioned blobs and blotches. Field research proved this theory a success, and since its inception, the concept of blaze orange camouflage, though an oxymoron, has evolved into the realm of the three-dimensional.

Too much? Think of the theory behind camouflage, then, like a plain white sheet of notebook paper on a sandy beach. It's pretty hard not to see the paper; however, if a handful of sand is thrown over the sheet — not covering it entirely, but merely breaking up or distorting the solid visual image — then the paper becomes more difficult to see, and more importantly, more difficult to recognize for what it really is. Which brings us to a most vital point, that the best camouflage in the world cannot be effective if the individual wearing that camouflage can't sit still.

Mix and match camouflage. Browns or "dirt" on the bottom, greens or "leaves" on the top. Again, it's a matter of choosing the proper set-up location.

Camo Tips And Tactics

WARNING! Cliché ahead. It's been said that clothes make the man; however, as I mentioned earlier, camouflage clothing does not a hunter make. In fact, there are instances where quite the opposite might be true, that being that camouflage and camo clothing can actually provide a false sense of security. Make that a false sense of invisibility; almost as if that thin layer of material was a brick wall behind which the hunter could stand — hell, for that matter, could dance around behind — with nary a thought of being seen by his or her quarry. In this case, that quarry is carrying two of the sharpest eyes in the woods. No, camouflage is much more than simply slipping into a 'neat' set of pants and a long-sleeved shirt and becoming — drum roll, please — Stealth Man. For instance:

1. Camouflage doesn't make you invisible. Certainly it can help you blend into the natural environment, but it does not erase your presence in what is essentially this bird's living room. The world's finest camouflage, for instance, coupled with a poor set-up often spells failure. As does said camouflage and over-calling. Or insufficient scouting. Maybe it's easier to think of camouflage not as a total concept, but instead as just one piece in the puzzle which is concealment. That's it right there.

2. Camouflage needs confidence in order to work. This is really a no-brainer and requires little if any explanation as the same concept holds true for your shotgun, your calling abilities, and your choice of hunting locations. Confidence is the placebo that allows humans to get within effective shotgun range of wild turkey gobblers. Luck has nothing to do with it.

3. Match the hatch. Just like the fly-angler who chooses his fly based on the species of insect hatching at the time of his outing, so too should the turkey hunter try to match as closely as possible his or her camouflage to both the environment and to the time of year. Does it have to match exactly? Is it necessary to buy a different camouflage outfit and pattern for each week of the spring season? Certainly not, though the camouflage manufacturers might see that as a good plan; still, a cornfield pattern in a lily pond is going to stand out like a Styrofoam cup in a coal bin. Just come as close as possible. 'Nuff said.

4. Mix and match your patterns. Dirt on the bottom, leaves and greenery on the top. That's the recipe that I try to impress upon folks, regardless of where they're hunting, and when. Most hunters, myself included, have at least one set of early season or predominantly green camo clothing, as well as a second late-season outfit that incorporates the darker browns, tans, grays, and blacks. Often, I'll wear a combination such as Mossy Oak's Forest Floor on the bottom — it's all in the name, eh? — and Realtree's X-tra Brown on top. As the season progresses and the foliage begins to come on strong, I may switch to a straight green X-tra Brown or Full Foliage-esque pattern. Either way and the particular pattern notwithstanding, my goal is to match Mother Nature as best I can. I can't be invisible simply because I don't belong there, but I can come close.

5. Use real shadows. Something I see in the field far too often has to do with the correlation between camouflage, shadows, and visual depth. Far too many hunters don't take advantage of those shadows that Mother Nature provides free of charge. Sure, today's photo-image camo patterns try to incorporate shadows into their make-up, this being the manufacturer's attempt to achieve this so-called depth or dimension. These natural shadows complement a camouflage pattern, emphasize the highs and lows, and help to soften or distort the hard-line edges and borders which humans introduce into the natural world. The bottom line? Choose your set-up location carefully, and remember that shadows are your friend.

Many hunters overlook the areas around the eyes, as well as that void between their headnet and their hairline. Remember – there is no such thing as an insignificant detail.

6. Face first. Noey Vineyard, scout/sniper with the United States Marine Corps stationed at Quantico, Virginia — "Cover every inch of your body in the camo pattern you choose. Many hunters forget things like parts of their face and the underside of their neck. When you raise your head, it's like waving a flag at a turkey. If you decide on traditional face paints instead of the more common headnet, remember this rule: Light on low, dark on high. The effect you are trying to achieve is the opposite that women are trying for when they put on makeup. They're trying to get their features to stand out; you're trying to flatten yours. Apply your darker colors to the higher parts of your face such as your nose, cheek bones, and forehead. Use the lighter colors on your lower features such as under your eyes and under your mouth. And black, white, red, yellow, orange, purple, or blue, this rule applies regardless of your skin color."

The Buddy System

Here's one that I always mention in our seminars. It's easy to tell those folks who have, unfortunately, experienced this first-hand as they're the ones with the "Please don't pick me" looks on their faces. Or, better yet, they're hiding behind their programs. Either way, they've done it, and hopefully, they've learned something. It goes something like this.

You've finally worked that big gobbler into 60 yards, but he's slowing down. He's really taking his time. He hasn't seen your decoys yet, but you've seen him now for the past 15 minutes. Then, suddenly, he breaks into the open. "He's coming," you whisper to yourself. Fifty yards. Then 45. Now 40. "Just a few more steps." Without warning — PUTT! — and you get to see him run away. "What the …" You can't figure it out. You didn't move. You had him pegged. A done deal. It's then you notice the sock. In your rush to sit down, you didn't notice that as you did, your pant leg hiked up. And there it was, right between the top of your boot and the cuff of your new camo pants. Four inches of pure, snow-white, turkey-scaring tube sock. Scientific testing? No, I haven't done any, but I'm reasonably sure that gobblers aren't at all attracted to white tube socks. Or hairy legs, for that matter.

Embarrassing? Yep. Costly? Perhaps, and in more ways than one; still, it's a mistake that I see turkey hunters, young and old, make all across the country. And it's one that goes right back to those insignificant details that we talked about earlier. Wouldn't it be nice if there were a way that you could find and address situations such as the aforementioned white tube sock debacle *at home* before going into the field? Well, there is. It's called the Buddy System.

The Buddy System — no, we don't call it the BS for short. There's enough of that among turkey hunters! — is very simple. So simple, in fact, that there's really no reason

We'll often photograph our camouflage outfits in order to evaluate their overall appearance. Silly? Perhaps; still, such "extremes" often lead to one very important factor – confidence.

not to do it. Each spring, prior to the opener, I'll outfit myself in full turkey hunting garb. It's important that you do this just as if you were going into the field. Include all of your pants, shirts, undershirts, belts, boots, hats … anything you would wear. The same goes for non-clothes items such as shotguns, seats, decoy bags, and blinds. Now, sit down with your back against your favorite brown reclining chair. Put the gun up — action open, finger off the trigger— in your typical ready-position, whatever that might be. Now, here's where the Buddy comes in. Have a partner look for what I'll call "chinks" in your camouflage suit of armor, things such as —

    a. Do your pants hike up and your socks show?

    b. When you put your gun up, do your shirt sleeves roll back and expose your watch? Or bare arms? A bracelet or other non-natural item?

    c. Your eyes. Do you need to incorporate camo make-up or face paint around your eyes?

    d. If you turn your head, does your headnet still completely cover your neck and the side of your face?

    e. What color are the soles of your boots?

    f. Do any of the light-colored tops of your strikers show? How about the brass bases of your shotshells?

    g. White tags or clothing labels? Remove them.

Essentially, my rule of thumb when it comes to determining whether or not an object or a potential oversight ranks as "significant" or "insignificant" is pretty simple. If I have to question whether or not it might — key word: MIGHT — make a difference when that old gobbler is standing out there at 45 yards, his dark brown eyes boring a hole right through my very soul, then I tend to it. In other words, if a portion of your camouflage is important enough to question, it's important enough to check. And double-check.

You want an insignificant detail camouflage story? Here's a good one. A couple years ago, I had the pleasure of hunting with Brad Harris, long-time head hunting guru for Lohman Game Calls, on a wonderful — no, make that exquisite — piece of hardwood timber property in the Missouri Ozarks. As we made ready to seat ourselves at the junction of two woods roads where the night before we had roosted precisely 4.72 million gobblers, Harris looked at me and said in paraphrase, "We'll set up right here. Cameraman over there." He then turned, but quickly turned back and added, with, I might add, no room left for discussion, "And cover that up." End of conversation.

"That," to explain, was approximately 4 square inches, if that, of plastic Ziploc baggie that I had hanging exposed from the left front pocket of my turkey vest. How it got there, I don't know; what I do know was that Harris wanted it covered up. And covered up now. You see, Brad Harris believes in tending to insignificant details. And that, in part, is why he's so good at what he does.

Accessories And Today's Turkey Hunter

It's like Noey Vineyard, USMC, says — "Cover every part of your body with the camouflage pattern that you've chosen." The way Vineyard puts it, there's nothing left for debate there. Truth is, he's right.

Accessories are to the turkey hunter as the .44 Magnum was to Clint Eastwood's immortal character, Dirty Harry Callahan. What's more, and ever since camouflage earned itself "cool" status, there's been very little left that hasn't received a coat or covering or dipping of one pattern or another. And most with good reason, for if turkey hunters are indeed going to adhere to my "no insignificant detail" credo, well then, camouflage toilet paper certainly isn't out of the question; however, I digress.

Hat down, headnet up but not interfering with the shooter's forward or peripheral vision. Here's where you want to be.

Accessories

Headnets — First, always carry at least two headnets. Why? You will lose one. Or, at the very least, your hunting partner for the morning will have lost or forgotten his. Either way, just carry two. They're light. Basically, headnets have but two criteria. First, they should be long enough to completely cover your neck, particularly when you turn your head from side to side. In the shadows, the flash of an exposed portion of white flesh can have a strobe-like effect, and can be cause for an unpleasant "I thought I saw a gobbler's white head" situation. Check it out at home. Secondly, the headnet you choose should not interfere with either your direct or your peripheral vision. Some of the better masks, such as The Bandito by Quaker Boy, sew a reasonably stiff piece of wire into what I'll call the eyeframes. This wire can be bent and actually molded to the wearer's face, totally eliminating any blockage to the side. Regardless of the manufacturer, be sure to test-drive that new headnet before heading afield. Better yet, take a few minutes while you're on the shooting range and actually shoot a target or two while wearing your headnet. Remember, it's better to discover the problem at home than it is... You know the rest.

Gloves — Likewise, always carry two pairs of gloves. If

today I were to have delivered to my home, every camouflage glove I've left in the turkey woods over the past 10 years, I'd have enough material to sew a quilt the size of Rhode Island. Years ago, I began carrying two pairs of gloves into the field with me — one, a heavier insulated pair, and the other, a lightweight cotton twill. Occasionally, I'll include a third pair made of mesh, for those hunts when the weather's scheduled to be particularly warm. And again like headnets, gloves come with two criteria. One, make sure the cuffs are long enough so that they hide your wrists even when you raise your shotgun to your shoulder and your shirt sleeves slide back. And two, practice shooting with your gloves on prior to the season. In fact, just humor me and put your headnet and your gloves on while you're at the range, and shoot a half dozen targets dressed so. Oh, and fingertips. Personally, I remove all the fingertips in each pair of my field gloves. Two reasons. First, I feel that I can operate a friction call more proficiently when I can actually "feel" the material under my fingers. And second, when I'm shooting, I feel more comfortable and confident having direct flesh-to-metal contact between my fingertips and both the safety and the trigger. Quirks, perhaps, but these tiny details help boost my confidence level, and in this game, confidence can be everything.

Hats — I carry two. Actually, I wear one and carry a sec-

I always remove the fingertips of my gloves so as to better feel and control my pot-and-peg calls; some hunters don't. You decide.

Two hats – one camo, and one blaze orange – are included in my turkey gear on every outing. Changing at the gobble only takes a heartbeat. Accidents last a lifetime.

ond. The first, a solid blaze orange cap, is worn whenever I'm walking into or out of the field, and any time I'm walking from one location to another, such as when I'm walking and calling in hopes of striking or locating a gobbler. My second hat, a favored GERBER Legendary Blades cap in X-tra Brown, is secreted inside my shirt or, if it's chilly, inside my coat. At the gobble, it takes but a split-second to swap the orange for the camo. My headnet goes up, I sit down, and I'm ready to go. In most cases, I'll lay my blaze orange cap, right-side up so as to hide the white inner lining, behind me and to the rear of my set-up location. This knowledge that my backside is now somewhat protected — not armored, but protected — gives me a warm, fuzzy feeling.

Socks and belts — Currently, my belt is a brown camouflaged unit from Knight & Hale that sports the bronze buckle from my father's web gear which we wore in Vietnam in 1965. Though dulled through time and often covered by a shirt, coat, or both, the buckle nonetheless wears a one-inch by one-inch patch of camouflage duct tape. Just in case. My socks? White or gray tube variety; however, I'm not concerned about them showing because of the style of hunting boots I'm currently wearing. If your particular clothing decisions make socks an issue, then by all means address the issue. Camo socks are available. Or you can simply blouse your trousers, tucking

A head-to-toe example, including the footwear. This particular Texas hunt required snake boots, and Julie's knee-highs from Rocky came through the week-long ordeal unscathed. As did Julie!

them into the tops of your boots so your socks cannot show. Regardless — and here we go again — check it out at home.

Footwear — For the past several years, I've worn one of a couple pairs of 15-inch camouflage snake boots made by Rocky Shoes & Boots of Nelsonville, Ohio. Originally, I purchased the first pair for a spring trip to south Texas; however, in the seasons since, I've discovered that these boots are just downright perfect for turkey hunting, bad snakes or no bad snakes. They're waterproof, comfortable, and provide all the ankle and instep support I'd ever want or need, and then some. All this and protection from vicious serpents. Well, here in Iowa, make that barbed wire, sawgrass, multiflora rose, and the occasional garter snake. One of the nicest things about the boots, however, is their height. At 15 inches, I don't have to worry — ever — about my socks showing; still, the same holds true for an old pair of Rocky camouflaged rubber knee-highs that I'll wear on occasion. In the long run, make, model, manufacturer, even height don't matter as much as (a) comfort and (b) the boots' effectiveness as part of the whole camouflage scheme.

Miscellaneous - Successful camouflage techniques for turkey hunting involves as much the placement of colors or patterns as it does the elimination of certain colors or patterns. Take handkerchiefs, for instance.

Florida required a different kind of boot; in this case, rubber knee-highs. It's best to match your boots to the type of terrain you expect to hunt most often, and then get the best your pocketbook can handle.

Julie adjusts her Hunters's Specialties 'Gun Rest,' a camo – of course! – accessory she'd be less likely to leave at home than she would her calls.

Not what we think of when we think full turkey camo; however, the love-starved longbeard in this chapter's opening lines didn't seem to mind my father's lack of camouflage fashion sense.

Many folks, myself and my father included, always carry a hankie in our back pocket opposite our wallet. Most days, that hankie will be red or blue, or in my father's case, white; however, come turkey season, the patriotic red, white, and blue are replaced by a simple green cloth. Should we want to get fancy, we'll invest in a three-pack of camouflage — yep, they're available — handkerchiefs. In part, this color-change decision has roots in our quest to attain a 100 percent camouflage rating, so to speak. It's also a safety issue, and one that becomes quite clear in the chapter on turkey hunting safety.

4

A Look Inside The Turkey Vest

Turkey hunters are a lot like fishermen in that we are a "stuff" people. Not stuffy, at least not for the most part, just stuff-oriented. Like comedian George Carlin, who was always looking for a place to put his stuff, turkey hunters suffer from a similar problem.

At first, turkey hunters didn't have any place to put their stuff. Truth is, they really didn't need anything even remotely resembling a field bag. A box call in a coat pocket and a couple of shotgun shells, and it was time to hit the trail. There were no padded seats. No titanium slate calls. No collapsible water bottles. And certainly no Global Position Systems, unless you consider a good sense of direction the mid-20th century version of a GPS. No, times were simpler way back when. But then again, so was turkey hunting.

Today, turkey hunting is anything but simple. Sure, some folks — myself included — try each season to go back to a less equipment-intensive time. And, thank goodness, some folks — myself not included — succeed. Armed only with a box call and a couple diaphragms, after all they're small and don't take up much space, these enterprising hunters go forth to do battle. Naked they are, by many turkey hunters' accounts. In most cases, it's a visual that none of us really need.

Still, the fact remains. The modern turkey hunter carries an array of equipment and gear into the field that rivals, and in some cases bests, the field pack of even the most well-equipped World War II foot soldier. But short of a wheelbarrow or a camouflaged Hefty bag, how does all this gear, not to mention the person packing the load, get into the field? Better yet, how does a body keep all this gear organized and ready for action at the slightest notice?

Enter — the turkey vest. While I have no concrete

My Pop, Mick, with the contents of my turkey vest, including a very nice Iowa longbeard that made the mistake of parading around in front of his Remington 11-87.

The turkey hunter's catch-all, a good vest handles everything from gobblers to goodies. And then some.

evidence, I'm certain that it was a manufacturer of turkey hunting-related items who first conceived the notion of a turkey vest. The thought, I'm sure, was that given more pockets, even the most disciplined turkey addict — Is there any such thing as a disciplined turkey addict? — could not resist the temptation to fill each and every fabric-rimmed orifice with the latest field technology. Over time, this team of diabolical vest creators began to design units with item-specific pockets, thus instilling a need to house a box call in a box call pocket, a striker in a striker pocket, and a decoy stake... Well, you get the picture.

But for all the sales and marketing know-how that went into the creation and evolution of the turkey vest, there is a definite plus to having what can perhaps be best described as a camouflaged filing cabinet. The turkey vest is a junk drawer with shoulder straps. Whatever you call it, though, a glimpse into the interior of a woodsman's turkey vest is as revealing an experience as you can have. If the eyes are the windows to a man's soul, then the turkey vest is the portal to a turkey hunter's mind. Or what there is of it.

I thought it might prove interesting to take a look and see what folks actually do carry with them into the field. As this chapter unfolded over the course of the weeks devoted to this project, a couple different things became clear. First, there are those things — calls and shotgun shells, or at the very least some type of projectile with which it is hoped a turkey will meet his end — that all hunters include in their list of field gear. They're the can't-do-without things. Things like extra gloves and headnets, indispensable pieces of camouflage equipment which become even more vital when it's discovered that you've lost your original set, or left them on the seat of the truck which at the moment is way too far away. Water and snacks are also at the top of the list; however, the methods used to get the water into the field and the manner in which the snacks are obtained often differ from person to person.

Some of these things you'll recognize. Some though, like Ernie Calandrelli's red-socked jake decoy, might make you sit up and take notice. If nothing else, it may serve simply as another addition to an item of hunting paraphernalia already bulging at the seams... a piece of clothing known affectionately as The Turkey Vest. Here's a look at the contents of a few hunting vests. The names have not been changed to protect the innocent.

Ernie Calandrelli, public relation/sales, Quaker Boy Game Calls:

- Innertube seat
- Three Delta decoys: one jake with a red sock on his neck, one Alert hen, one Feeding hen with a MotoMagnet
- Alligator clips zip-tied to vest straps to hold diaphragm calls
- Two pairs of gloves
- Two face masks
- Push Pin Easy Yelper
- Walnut Masters Series slate call
- Three strikers: heavy maple, carbon, carbon with tape added on end for weight
- Tube call
- Crow call
- 100-grit sandpaper and one large piece of Scotchbrite scrubbing pad
- Insect repellent
- Twenty to 50 mouth calls
- Binoculars
- Pruning shears
- Small camera
- On the way out, sometimes a dead gobbler

The red sock, says Caladrelli, often works to infuriate a gobbler. He learned this trick from friend and fellow Turkey Trot Acres guide, Mark Zizzi, and claims that color "plays everything in bringing a gobbler to a decoy." Calandrelli also adds that he rarely uses a decoy in tight or thick cover, but rather wants the gobbler to come looking for the hen that's making all the racket. A bird that gobbles in thick cover, he says, gives away his location with every sound, and helps a hunter keep track of the bird's movements.

Marty Eby, wildlife conservation officer, Iowa Department of Natural Resources:

- Portable blind
- Jake and hen decoy
- Tree clipping shears
- Assorted box, mouth, and slate calls
- Fighting purr call
- Water
- Shotshells
- Extra gloves and headnet
- Blaze orange game carrier from Hunter's Specialties
- Gallon Ziplock bags
- Nylon material — 18" long and 6" wide
- Owl hooter
- Coyote howler
- Peacock call
- Elk bugle
- Snacks
- Compass
- Waterproof matches

Eby uses the nylon material to simulate the sound of a hen flying down from her roost. "Snapped tight, it sounds just like a turkey wing flapping," he says.

Chris Kirby, president, Quaker Boy Game Calls:

- Four or five mouth calls
- Easy Yelper
- Quaker Boy Boat Paddle
- Single slate
- Triple Threat slate style call
- Two headnets (in case someone forgets)
- Two pairs of gloves
- Compass
- Small first aid kit
- Lightweight rain gear
- Clippers
- Sandpaper and chalk
- Binoculars
- Small camera

"There are no downsides to carrying a big call like the Boat Paddle," says Kirby. "Still, if you prefer, the Mini Boat Paddle is very compact." And what about the Boat Paddle's unique, high-pitched tones? According to Chris, it all comes with an understanding of sound in general. "The farther sound travels," he explains, "the more that sound's consistency or tone is broken down. In other words, while the Boat Paddle may seem scratchy and high-pitched at two steps, it holds together at 300 yards. I don't need to call to a bird at 25 yards, but I do need him to gobble at 300 yards. Therefore, I need a call — like the Boat Paddle — that will hold its sound together at longer distances, yet still give me the option of toning down the sound as needed."

Scott Bestul, full-time freelance outdoor writer from Wisconsin:

- Three decoys and stakes (one hen and two new dekes to experiment with)
- MAD Aluminator
- One slate, one ceramic, one glass call
- Six strikers of different woods and materials, many homemade
- One big box call
- Three diaphragms (minimum)
- One new call for experimentation and entertainment purposes
- One custom call worth more money than the vest and everything in it
- Primos shaker-type gobble tube
- Sandpaper, chalk, brillo pad, MAD call conditioner
- Shotshells
- Mini-flashlight
- Two pair gloves, two headnets
- Pruning shears
- Binoculars
- Compass, matches, knife
- Cabela's packable silent rain gear
- Snack food, water
- Extra clothes
- Mosquito/tick repellent
- Paperback book, westerns and war stories are great
- Waterproof vinyl "wallet" for licenses, tags, or other paperwork

"I used a Browning vest for many years," says Bestul, "but this year went to a Cabela's model that's beautifully made but too darn roomy. I fill up whatever space I have, and I'd hate to guess what this year's vest would tip the scales at. Sometimes I feel less like a turkey hunter and more like a pack mule!"

Insect repellent was among the many common denominators carried by several of the folks brave enough to reveal the contents of their turkey vests to the general public.

Outdoor writer Phil Bourjaily, the same man who includes juice drinks and candy "borrowed" from his young sons among his turkey vest items.

Philip Bourjaily, shooting editor for Field & Stream:

- Bucklick Creek vest with built-in chair ("Very important," says Bourjaily)
- Rohm Bros. walnut box call, signed by Robby Rohm
- MAD Titanium slate
- Metal striker and Hunter's Specialties' acrylic striker
- Quaker Boy call care kit
- Call Caddy for diaphragm calls by Hunter's Specialties
- Primos Woodpecker call
- My Dad's old P.S. Olt crow call
- Camp's Callers owl hooter
- Fiskars clippers
- Chocolate chip granola bars and juice boxes stolen from my children
- Extra gloves and headnet
- Morel mushroom bag
- Knit watch cap
- Decoy bag containing Feather Flex jake and hen decoys
- Hunter's Specialties portable blind
- Mini-Leatherman and Mini Mag Light on my belt

Dale Garner, forest game research biologist, Iowa Department of Natural Resources:

- Decoy and stake
- Calls (box, slate, glass, diaphragm)
- Three different strikers for slate and glass calls
- Ammunition
- Pen
- Hunting license and turkey tag
- Pruning shears
- Crow call
- Peacock call
- Flashlight and whistle
- Water bottle
- Insect repellent
- Knife
- Small length of cord
- Plastic and paper bags
- Trail money a.k.a. toilet paper
- Several folded paper towels
- Wet wipes
- Latex gloves
- Disposable (one-use) camera
- Compact binoculars
- Blaze orange back sack for carrying turkey out
- Rain gear (sometimes)
- Granola bars

A huge fan of fidgeting, Bourjaily claims that the use of a lightweight portable blind "keeps me sitting in one place longer. That way I don't get bored and wander off. Too, I can lie down and dust, and the turkeys won't see me." On a slightly more serious note, however, the writer does say that the blind allows him to hide more effectively in low-cover situations such as on field edges, or in cases where he's using hand-operated calls like box or slate-style calls.

"A peacock call is just another toy to help elicit a gobble when other toys won't work," states Garner. "It's not necessarily the peacock call, per se, that elicits the gobble, but rather the loud sound. A car horn often works just as well, but a car takes up more room in your vest!"

Ah, yes. Morels. No turkey hunter worth his or her salt goes afield without at least one Ziplock or bread bag; however, in a pinch, your shirt will make a wonderful mushroom tote.

New York's Glenn Sapir takes a breather during a South Dakota Merriams hunt. Where's your goose call, Glenn?

Gene Murray, editor, The Big River Outdoors:

- One to three decoys
- Stakes for all, including one extra
- Two spare shotshells
- Binoculars
- Two slate-style calls, one of which will work in the rain
- Assorted strikers
- Box call
- Diaphragms
- Water, dried fruit, and/or granola bars
- Small bottle of 100 percent DEET
- Small bottle of Absorbine Jr. for warding off gnats
- Camera
- Small notebook and pen
- Crow call
- Pruning shears and occasionally, a folding saw
- Mushroom bag

Glenn Sapir, outdoor writer and author of "Secrets of the Turkey Pros":

- Hunter's Specialties Strut and Rut Dual Season vest
- Two hen decoys and one jake decoy by Feather Flex
- Mossy Oak rain suit
- Three sets of decoy stakes
- Toilet paper, surgical gloves, soap, wet-wipes, band-aids, anti-bacterial cream
- Gallon-size Zip-Locs to cover box or slate calls in rain
- Trail Mix, Peach Rings, Rice Krispie treats, pouch drinks
- Bug repellent
- Camo gloves
- Lohman Wing Thing
- Chemical handwarmers
- Five Winchester Supreme shotshells — 3-inch, #5
- Crow call, goose call, owl hooter, gobble shaker
- Knight & Hale's Ol' Yeller slate-style call
- Quaker Boy's Walnut Masters Series slate-style call
- Two wooden strikers and one plastic striker
- Note pad, pen, knife, pocket knife, Mini-Mag flashlight, camo handkerchief

"One thing I've added this year," says Murray, "is a piece of ¾-inch dowel about four inches long. There's a hole drilled in the middle with a loop of heavy cord. Put this over your bird's feet to help carry him over your shoulder. I haven't even used it yet, but loaned it to a guy who thought it was the greatest invention since toilet paper. It's a lot easier to hold on to than those spurs."

Sapir says of his choice of a goose call as a locator call. "We often have geese fly overhead in the Hudson (New York) Valley, even if no bodies of water are very near. They feed in many of the same fields the toms strut in, and they fly over the same woodlands that the turkeys inhabit. Goose calls are very loud and abrupt, and on a few occasions, especially when other geese are calling, I've raised a gobble with one."

My blood brother, Keane Maddy, with an incredible Iowa Eastern. Comparatively speaking, Maddy travels pretty light in terms of turkey gear.

Keane Maddy, marketing director, Bug-Out Outdoorwear, Centerville, Iowa:

- Strut Seat from Hunter's Specialties
- MAD Calls' Super Aluminator, Custom Crystal, Custom Ceramic
- MAD Calls' Mini Master and Cherry Bomb box calls
- Cherry crow, owl, and coyote calls, also from MAD
- Variety of diaphragm calls
- Rosewood, carbon, and Magic Wand strikers (Hunter's Specialties)
- Three FeatherFlex decoys — 2 hens, 1 Bubba half-strut gobbler.
- Bug-Out suit
- Mushroom bag (a requirement for all Iowa and Missouri turkey hunters)
- Extra gloves and headnet
- Small first-aid kit
- Extra decoy stakes
- Gerber clipper/pruners
- Mini-Mag flashlight
- Pentax compact binoculars

Here's more hocus-pocus for you. "As a superstition, I carry spent shotgun shells from other hunts. I put the date, weight, and beard length on each shell, put them in a special pocket in my vest, and carry them all season," says Maddy.

Rob Keck, CEO of the National Wild Turkey Federation:

- Two sets of camouflage gloves
- Two camouflage face masks
- Glass call in brown single-action fly fishing reel case
- Aluminum call in black case
- Four strikers
- Key chain flashlight
- Two turkey totes (one for a partner)
- Piece of string for hanging turkey while cleaning or for tagging
- Crow call
- Box call in sheepskin-lined holster
- Block of brown railroad chalk in plastic bag for box calls
- Zuni Fetish
- Trumpet yelper
- 20-gauge shotshells, five of them
- Turkey permits
- Tube call and extra latex
- Ratchet cutters
- Diaphragm calls
- Chapman Chair seat
- Toilet paper and paper towels
- Pocket knife
- Insect repellent
- Bug-Out suit
- Binoculars

Possibly out of curiosity — I, personally, am afraid to do this — Keck weighed the vest he wears into the field and found that it tipped the scales at an even 10 pounds. Not too bad given the amount of gear he transports. As for the Zuni fetish (fetish — n. any object believed to have magical power), Keck was presented the piece, which is in the shape of a small grizzly bear, in 2000 by the Medicine Man of the Zuni tribe. Its powers represent strength and the ability to kill on the hunt. A superstitious group, turkey hunters often and sometimes secretly carry good luck charms into the field with them. I carry into the field a Canadian $2 piece, a SmarteCarte token from the Portland, Oregon, airport, and the center, with emblem, of a 1965 Ford 500 Custom hubcap. Go figure.

Gary Roberson, owner of Burnham Brothers Game Calls:

- Bucklick Creek Turkey Lounger with built-in seat
- Burnham Brothers DTC-4 diaphragm
- Cody slate call
- "Hustling Hen" box call by Billy White or a Burnham Brothers box
- Mini Coyote Howler by Burnham Brothers

Along with his Mini Coyote Howler, Roberson wouldn't think of leaving for the field without his Bucklick Creek vest. "If you've never hunted with one," he says, "you don't know what you're missing. With this, I can be comfortable sitting flat on the ground without any back support. This is very important when hunting my country for a lot of my turkey hunting is done in areas where there are no large trees to hide under or sit against."

Lipke uses the deer grunt call for those times when he accidentally makes too much noise walking into the field. "It's the same principle," he says, "as using a cow elk chirp out West if you should snap a stick while slipping through the dark timber." Lipke is also a huge fan of Will Primos' Real Wing. "Flapping the cadence of the wing-beats as if a turkey were flying down is excitingly authentic and irresistible. After some initial soft purring and tree yelps early in the morning, the rhythm of the Wing is the perfect complement to those calls. It says, 'Nap time's over, boys. I'm landing right over here.'"

"What I did," said Bishop, "was to take a piece of copper wire about 6 inches long and curled the top into a circle. Then I tied fishing line to that circle, and about 12 inches from that, I tied a ¾-inch washer. You pull that through the decoy, and you have 3 or 4 feet sticking up through the top of the decoy. You just roll this whole thing up and put it in your bag. Then when you get to where you're going to hunt, if you're going to do a quick set-up, you just unroll it, tie the top part to an overhanging limb, and then just take that copper wire and push it in the ground. That decoy will sit there, and if you get a little gust of wind, it'll move. You get a lot more movement out of it. And actually, you'll get a little "bounce" movement out of it, too."

Calling champ, Ricky Joe Bishop, plays a tune on his own creation, the Pump Action Yelper. Make sure you check out Bishop's decoy tip. It's a good one.

Keller likes Hunter's Specialties' 'Lil Strut (compact) box call for several reasons — it's small, and therefore doesn't take up much room in his otherwise hefty vest. The call also comes with a unique peg-and-hole "Silencer Plus" system that prevents the call from squeaking and squawking unintentionally. Finally, and most significantly perhaps, is the fact that the call's high-pitched tones provide all the distance or reach out and touch 'em capabilities that Western turkey hunters often find necessary.

"Out West," says Keller, who has spent most of his formative years in and around the Montrose, Colorado, area, "you need a call that will carry a long way and cut through our spring winds."

Kevin Howard, president, Howard Communications (outdoor public relations):

- Diaphragm calls
- Slate, aluminum, and box calls
- Call care kit
- Gobble tube
- Face mask and gloves
- Compass and hand-held GPS
- Gerber clippers
- Decoys
- Binoculars
- Crow call and coyote howler
- Extra shotshells
- Flashlight
- Bug spray
- Suntan lotion
- Blaze orange safety bag
- Knife
- Drinking water
- Portable blind

Currently residing in Missouri, Howard, who has more than 25 years of turkey hunting savvy under his belt, often guides outdoor writers and photographers in exotic locations such as New York, Pennsylvania, Illinois, Mississippi, Texas, and Montana. His is a vest filled to overflowing, which is why, he says, there are times when he has to carry a small backpack as well as his vest into the field. Not to break away from the overall theme of the chapter here, but in many cases, a small yet sturdy backpack or fanny pack is all that a body needs; however, the downside with a backpack comes in the lack of an integral game bag. The solution? One of Hunter's Specialties' blaze orange turkey bags, complete with shoulder straps and cinch string. It is a wonderful piece of convenience that serves double-duty as safety equipment.

Jody Hugill, original Lohman Gold Staff team member (1983) and turkey camp funny-man:

- Lots of calls
- Binoculars
- Everything else
- One aluminum hunting arrow, cut into two equal halves

One cut-up aluminum arrow? Apparently, Hugill uses the arrow, cut in two so that it can easily fit into his turkey vest, as a decoy stake. Taking a Lohman Model 865-G gun-mount push-pin call which he has altered by drilling a hole completely through it perpendicular to the line of the pin, he slips the call onto the arrow. A balled-up rubber band serves as an adjustable-height stopper for the call. Hugill then operates the call from his set-up location using monofilament fishing line spooled onto an old fishing reel. "It works great," he says. Oh, and as for the funny-man part, let me just add that if Hugill can't make you laugh, you're dead. And I seriously think he's working on solving that problem.

Stan Maddy, art teacher, football coach, avid turkey hunter, and walleye fisherman:

- Bucklick Creek turkey vest in Advantage camo
- MAD crow call and owl hooter
- Pileated woodpecker call
- Red-tailed hawk call
- MAD Super Aluminator and #313 Custom Crystal
- Woods Wise Slate/crystal call and carbon Black Mystic box call
- Gobble shaker
- Lohman Pump Action Yelper with triple reed diaphragm
- Three mouth diaphragm calls
- Five strikers, including wood, carbon, and hand-carved hedge (osage orange)
- Several pieces of coarse sandpaper
- Small bottle, Parker's Anti-fogging eyeglass solution and cleaning cloth
- Pruning shears
- Pentax compact binoculars
- Small bag of Tootsie Roll midges
- Compass
- Packable raincoat and pants, Realtree Pattern
- Extra sweatshirt
- Sharpie permanent marker
- Bug-Out mosquito head-net
- Plastic mushroom bag
- Four, 3-inch 20-gauge shotshells, #5 shot
- Pair of prescription sunglasses in amber tint
- Motorola Talk-About radio
- Toilet paper
- Mini-Mag flashlight and small Gerber lock-blade knife
- Extra face mask and gloves
- Feather Flex decoys — two hens and one jake, with home-made wooden stakes

Jason Maddy, co-owner, Maddy Brothers Guide Service, Centerville, Iowa:

- Bucklick Creek turkey vest
- MAD Mini-Master box call
- Maddy Brothers original box call
- MAD Custom Crystal, Aluminator, and slate calls
- Three strikers — hedge (osage orange, purple heart, carbon)
- Sandpaper and roughing stone
- Mouth calls, including MAD Shippwreck and SS Special
- Crow call and coyote yelper
- Pruning shears
- Extra cushions
- Compass
- Hunting log and pen
- Hunter's Specialties Portable Blind (when guiding clients)
- Mini-Mag flashlight and small Gerber lock-blade knife
- Toilet paper
- Raincoat, extra face mask and gloves
- Two hens and one jake decoys from Delta and Feather Flex
- Leatherman tool
- Motorola Talk-About radio

One of the most patient turkey hunters I've ever had the pleasure of spending field time with, Jason currently uses a decoy set-up consisting of both Delta and Feather Flex brand decoys. "Because I'll hunt many of the same fields and openings several times throughout our season, I use different types of decoys so that the toms don't get used to seeing the same thing every day. And I don't put the (Delta) breeding tom on top of the hen like you're supposed to. Instead, I put him in front of the hen, just like he was going to strut for her. And I put a stick inside

That's Stan "Daddy" Maddy on the left, proud to have led Bob Wells to his first spring gobbler.

the decoy sideways to make him look like he's all puffed up," says Maddy. To add a final touch of realism to his "spread," Maddy chooses Delta's feeding hen decoys. "They're great confidence decoys. In this feeding position with their heads are down its a relaxed posture. Not upright in an alert position like many decoys."

As for me, I typically start out each season with my vest weighing in the neighborhood of 14.23 tons; however, by season's end, that weight has decreased considerably to where it now can be comfortably carried by three small children, a Saint Bernard, and an old man with a ox cart. My list goes something like this:

- Old-style Hunter's Specialties vest in X-tra Brown
- Two pairs of gloves, one mesh and one cotton (fingertips removed)
- Two headnets, one mesh and one cotton
- Four strikers — rosewood, hickory, Knight & Hale's Super Striker, acrylic
- Extra rosewood and hickory strikers
- Four shotshells — Federal 3-inch, 2 ounces of #6 shot
- MAD Cherry Bomb box call
- Coyote howler
- Pruning shears
- Two compasses, one pin-on bubble style and one military
- Two Call Caddies by Hunter's Specialties with an assortment of diaphragms

Another of the Maddy boys, Jason is a huge fan of black powder for both bucks and birds; that is, when the gun goes off.

That's me, proof that even a sightless squirrel will occasionally find an acorn.

- Compact binoculars in camo pouch on right vest/chest strap
- Primos Titan 2000 Titanium call in camo pouch on left vest/chest strap
- Black Magic aluminum call
- Call conditioner, chalk, sandpaper
- Owl hooter and crow call
- One jake and two hen decoys by Feather-Flex, with stakes
- Ziplock containing length of rawhide, bandages, safety pin, cotton swabs
- Pen
- Temple Fork flexible canteen
- Bunsaver seat cushion
- 35mm SLR camera with built-in flash and film in waterproof pouch
- Bug-Out bug suit
- Mini Mag-lite on my belt

I carry a lot of stuff into the field, so it's incredibly important that I know where everything is at all times. Each item has a place in the vest, and is returned to that place every time it is used. That way I can find anything, big or small, without having to search or dig or even turn my head to look. Eyes closed, pitch dark — it doesn't matter. Over the years, this type of organization, although seeming excessive, has been instrumental in allowing me to quickly get into position and set up correctly with little or no fumbling around. If that gobbler's on his way immediately after his first response, he's not going to wait for me to rifle through my vest to find this call or that glove.

5

The Modern
Turkey Gun

Want to start an argument? That's easy. Walk into the shotgun section of any major sporting goods dealer and say in a loud, clear voice, "The (fill in the name of your favorite shotgun) is the best turkey gun on the market today, and I'm here to tell you exactly why!" Chances are that within seconds, you'll have a line forming to your front consisting of avid turkey hunters just dying to explain in detail why you're wrong.

The search for the "perfect" turkey gun has been going on nearly as long as has the debate over whether or not the 6mm centerfire rifle cartridge is acceptable for the whitetail deer. What's the reason behind this apparent lack of reason? It all lies in that one word — perfect.

For example, the mere existence of an autoloading shotgun that can, without hesitation or stutter step, cycle 2¾-inch, 3-inch, and 3½-inch ammunition should not lead one to the assumption or conclusion that this is the perfect shotgun. True, such a piece might prove a versatile firearm. But is it perfect?

Choosing a shotgun for the purposes of turkey hunting then becomes not a search for perfection, but rather a quest combining personal preference, ability and a short list of what we'll call common denominators, all of which, when taken together, can create something close to perfect. In no particular order, these common denominators include:

Simplicity

Simple is often better. And so it is the case with shotguns. The very last thing you want to have happen in the spring turkey woods is for one of your shotgun's 1.4963 million parts — you know, that metal clip thingy that's under the silvery lever lifter — to malfunction. Now I'm not saying that intricate is synonymous with inoperative, only that simplicity often breeds reliability, familiarity, and

A Beretta 390AL, the gun that tagged Julie's Grand Slam in '98, and a fine choice for an all-round shotgun.

Some of the favorites. From left to right – Benelli Super Black Eagle, Benelli Nova, Remington 11-87, Mossberg 500, and a Beretta 390AL. The best? That's not my call.

confidence. You see where I'm headed here? Besides, don't you already have enough to worry about, what with out-witting that walnut-brained turkey gobbler? Do you really want to worry about whether or not your shotgun is going to go "boom" every time you pull the trigger?

Reliability

Ideally, each day of turkey season is going to dawn with a bit of a chill. These wonderful days will warm ever so slightly before cooling down 'round about nightfall. Well, welcome to La-La Land. True, it's nice to hunt under such conditions, but Mother Nature often throws us turkey hunters a climatic curve ball in the form of ice, rain, and snow. And that's just the stuff that falls. Add some cold, a little mud, and an ever-swirling maelstrom of dust, sand, weed seeds, cottonwood fuzz, and 1,001 other less-than-pleasant things, and you have all the makings for a gun-stopper. Equip yourself with a reliable shotgun, and these things become just another physical test of strength and endurance for you, not the gun.

But how do you determine if a shotgun is reliable? Certainly you can conduct such research through the trial-and-error method; that is, you can purchase your next turkey gun, shoot 1,000 rounds through it under all types of weather conditions, and then decide for yourself based on your observations whether or not the gun lives up to your standards of reliability. Good in theory, but that's a lot

of time, effort, and money you're talking about spending. Fortunately, there are several avenues the gun buyer can take when attempting to ensure this reliability factor.

1. Buy a reputable name from a reputable dealer. Chances are, if you've hunted much at all with a shotgun, you're by now familiar not only with the brands which are available, but those brands, makes, and models that are the most popular or commonly seen in the field. In the world of shotguns, there's much to be said for a maker's name. That's not to say that a good name can't make a poor piece; however, poor pieces don't survive long in the rough-and-tumble world of shotguns. Stick with a recognized name, and you'll be well on your way to a good buy.

2. Do your homework. In other words — research, research, research. This day and age, there's absolutely no reason not to know everything there is to know about a shotgun long before you ever start reaching for your wallet. Today, most major manufacturers maintain industry Internet websites, many of which are filled to overflowing with the latest photos and shotgun specs. Some even offer prospective buyers the opportunity to ask questions about particular firearms via e-mail. And let's not forget the telephone. Do you have a question? Call the folks at Remington, Winchester, Mossberg or any of the others. They're in the business of making and selling shotguns, and it's in their best interest to answer all questions you have about their product.

3. Recognize the difference between a bargain and a good buy. I hate to use the cliché, but it's true — you do get what you pay for. Expecting a $100 over-the-counter piece to function and perform like a $1,200 Benelli Super Black Eagle is silly. If it happens, fantastic; however, chances are, you're going to be disappointed and frustrated In the long run you may be wishing you had that $100 back as a down-payment on a better shotgun. My point is this — shop around. Plan a turkey shotgun purchase in advance, and don't make any ill-informed, snap decisions. Remember, the manufacturers are in competition with one another. So it's very possible that you can and will get a good buy on a good gun. A bargain, on the other hand…well, let's just say that I've seen some really poor bargains. Think of it this way. A piece of junk at any price is still a piece of junk.

4. Understand personal preference and peer pressure. These last two items might sound strange, especially in a discussion about shotgun purchases. But peer pressure and personal preference have a lot to do with shot-

Interchangeable choke tubes are just one of the variables to be considered when you're looking to piece together the ultimate turkey gun.

Many modern guns can accept shotshells ranging from 2¾ to 3½ inches; however, it's up to you to determine whether or not such versatility is *really* necessary.

gun selection. Shotgun selection, as we know, leads to the other variables, most significantly, confidence. There's nothing wrong with being the only kid on the block shooting a pump-gun while the other kids are all swinging autoloaders. Single-shot? Not a problem, if you've done your homework on and off the shooting range and understand and can abide by the limitations of such a piece. Once you've done your homework, the final decision concerning the purchase of your new turkey gun is based entirely — yes, entirely — on personal preference. Okay, there are the financial elements, of course, but it's 95 percent personal preference. Are you happy with it? Better yet, are you comfortable and confident with this new shotgun? That's all there is to it.

Versatility And Adaptability

A turkey gun should be versatile and adaptable. Now what's that supposed to mean? Well, it's like this. What's the very first thing that a man does when he gets home from the dealership with his new pickup truck? He starts changing it. First, it's the little trinkets and bobbles inside. Then it's fancy wheels. A canopy. Fog lights. Oh, and a high-tech CD player with multi-disk changer behind the seat. Essentially, he makes it his own. It's kind of a nest-building thing, only, men don't call it that. We call it customizing.

A turkey gun is no different. True, there are those

shotguns that, right out of the box, prove themselves tremendous sporting arms. They pattern well. They fit right. Hell, they even look good. But, as nice as such ready-to-use shotguns are, they're actually in the minority. Most turkey guns — good turkey guns — are the result of shooters twisting this and tweaking that. A choke tube here. A set of sights there. Another set of sights. And another choke tube. Wait. Let's back up and try another brand of ammunition.

Whew! Confused? Just think of turkey hunters and their shotguns like alchemists or mad scientists. What they're looking for is the secret, almost magical, combination that will transform this hunk of steel and wood into a golden gobbler gun. In order to do that, the original hunk of steel needs to be such that it can be transformed. These transformations might include:

Choke tubes — Can the gun accept interchangeable choke tubes? Is a specialized turkey choke tube — Super Full, Extra Full, Super Extra Full, whatever — available for the piece?

Chamber — Will the shotgun accept 2¾ and 3-inch shotshells? What about 2¾, 3-inch, *and* 3½-inch? Such shotshell versatility can prove significant, particularly if the gun isn't equipped with interchangeable choke tubes. Guns without choke tubes are rare today, but patterns and performance can often be

This Mossberg Model 500 has been fitted with Tru-Glo fiber optic sights – a good choice for some, but an option nonetheless.

improved simply by experimenting with different types (brands, shot sizes, shot charges, powder charges, velocities) of ammunition.

Sights — Can the gun be fitted with after-market sights, such as Williams' lock-on iron sights or Tru-Glo's fiber optics? How about a no-drill/no-tap saddle-style scope mount from the folks at B-Square? And what kind of scope? Or maybe a Red Dot, Aimpoint, or HOLOSight? Just what is involved in sighting this particular make and model of shotgun? That's the question.

Camouflage — Is the gun already outfitted in a camo pattern? If so, good. If not, what will it take to camouflage it? Don't want to paint your new Super Black Eagle? How about a gun sock? Or perhaps some of the new leaves-no-goo camo tape?

Slings — I think that if I had to choose between my choke tubes and my sling, I'd choose the sling. There's just nothing better nor more convenient for the turkey hunter, particularly the successful turkey hunter who's trying to extract gear, bird, and gun from the field. The versatile turkey gun will come from the factory with sling studs and swivels. At the very least, the gun will come drilled and tapped so that the installation of such hardware is quick and easy.

Familiarity And Confidence

These two go hand in hand, and are really no more complicated or as involved as they at first might seem. In essence, the translation here is that the more familiar you are with your turkey gun, the more confidence you will have in the gun and your abilities. For instance, I've shot the same Remington Model 11-87 for the past 14 years. During that time, I've made no changes at all. I use the same choke tube (Remington Extra Full Turkey), same 28-inch barrel, same shotshells (Federal, 2 ounces of copper-plated #6 shot). Today, I know exactly what the gun will do in terms of pattern and performance each time I pull the trigger. I know this at 40 yards and I know this at 4 yards. Still, every spring prior to turkey season, Julie and I will take this 11-87 to the firing range and shoot it a dozen or so times at different ranges. Each year, the gun performs as well as it did the spring before. A waste of ammunition, you ask? Not at all. You see, this annual ritual serves two very important purposes. It lets me know that the sight-altering gremlins that abound in every closet, gun cabinet, and storage locker in the country haven't gotten to my turkey gun and changed things while I wasn't looking. These patterning days also give me something more vital to my success in the field than mere evidence. They give me the confidence that I need to know without question that when the hammer on my 11-87 falls — well,

To scope, or not to scope. That is the question. I tried it, and personally didn't care for it; however, some shooters would have nothing but.

John "Bags" Bagley and his Texas Turkey Gun, a Savage 3-inch 12-gauge/.223 over-under. Longbeards and wild hogs alike have learned to fear this piece.

Julie with a great Iowa tom and a Knight MK-86 muzzleloading shotgun, a potent tool *if* one puts the time in behind the stock.

that bird's day is off to a pretty poor start. And if that's not enough for you, then think of it this way. If, in that split second before you pull the trigger on the longbeard of a lifetime, you have to stop and think — "What's this gun going to do?" — well, friend, you might as well point that shotgun skyward or in any other safe, responsible direction and let the hammer fall. Why? Because the results are likely to be just about the same.

Gauge: Does Size Matter?

Up to this point, I've said next to nothing about the subject of what gauge a so-called turkey gun can or should be. I'll tell you exactly why. It's because turkey hunters across the nation, myself included, naturally assume that when someone's talking modern turkey guns, they're speaking either of a 12-gauge or one of the big 10s. Certainly, the chamber dimensions of the 12 may differ from gun to gun and person to person, but the fact — and I'm guessing for the record here — remains that at least 95 percent of America's turkey hunters are taking either a 12 or a 10 into the field. Sure, there's some margin for error here in my percentage estimation. The truth is, there's probably also some room for argument; still, if this number, this 95 percent, were wrong, I think I'd be safe in saying that it's incorrect on the light side. Not 95? Maybe 97 is closer. But before I ramble further, let me just make this

Young Jake Coffman took this Hawkeye State gobbler, his first, with a hard-hitting over-under, a rather uncommon piece in today's single-barrel turkey woods.

elemental statement: There's a whole bunch of 10s and 12s out there.

It's relatively easy to understand this abundance of 10s and 12s. Part of the reason stems from what I'll call the "big bird-big gun" syndrome. This condition, also exhibited by many goose hunters, is not without its justification — to an extent — and it does make sense. Ideally, a hunter, regardless of whether he's chasing longbeards or lions, tries to match his firearm to the game being pursued. Too much gun, and it's a case of overkill, Too little and you're undergunned. In such a case unless the situation nears perfection, you run the risk of a crippling loss. There is, of course, some leeway to one side or the other, but — well, you don't shoot #2 shot in a dove field, now do you?

Turkeys are big birds and can in some situations require heavier loads be used. Unlike goose hunting, this isn't so much a case of needing heavier charges of larger-sized shot, but rather heavier charges of moderately sized pellets. The latter is a combination that translates into pattern density. As you'll see in the next chapter under the section called Patterning, these dense patterns are being directed at the turkey's head and neck area. This is a relatively small target and there is a need for larger capacity shotshell cases — say, 10s and 12s — that are capable of containing the number of pellets necessary to achieve pattern density at reasonable ranges.

A second factor I'm sure contributes to the overwhelming number of 10s and 12s in the turkey woods has to do with the fact that many of these shotguns are seeing double duty. The guns are used both in the spring of the year for gobblers and in the fall for ducks and geese. Sometimes it's as simple as replacing the modified choke tube used for waterfowl with an after-market specialty turkey tube. Other times the transformation from duck gun to turkey tool might necessitate the purchase of a shorter (21- to 24-inch) barrel *and* an after-market choke tube. This one gun-two seasons routine is seen quite often. And why not? It's practical, it's effective, and it's a hell of a lot less expensive than buying another shotgun specifically for turkey hunting. That is, unless that's your intent…wink, wink.

Finally, there are the variables of availability and options. Today, most major American shotgun manufacturers, as well as many foreign makers, concentrate their efforts on the 12-gauge market. For them, it's a sound business decision based purely on numbers sold. This business decision also helps the buyer because this focus on the 12-gauge translates into increased choice, increased availability, and increased options. With everyone and his brother making 12s, the level of competition between the various manufacturers, both foreign and domestic, is elevated. The results? Reasonable prices on high-quality guns.

Like the shotguns, ammunition choices are often made based on availability and options. As an example of the availability aspect, try this. Go into the smallest general store in the smallest town located in the most remote part of your home state. In the showcase that serves both as a counter and a lecturer's pulpit, you will likely find a box of 180-grain soft-point centerfire rifle cartridges in caliber .30-06, and a box of 12-gauge, 2¾-inch #4s. If you need them, there they are; if you don't, just pay for your Moon Pie and RC Cola, and be on your out-of-town way. The locals are waiting for you to leave so they can talk about you. My point here is this: Some things are just more common than others, and consumers tend to gravitate to what's common. With the 12, for example, you can take your pick, depending on what your particular gun likes best, from 2¾-, 3-, or 3½-inch shotshells, any of them containing from 1½ to 2½ ounces of lead, copper-plated lead, or any one of several new exotic metallic combinations. It's a kid-in-a-candy-store type of situation, and, when it comes to developing an effective gun-load-choke combination, it is a pretty good situation.

But does that mean that you won't run across something other than the Top Two while diddy-bopping around the spring woods? Certainly not, especially if you travel down to southern Iowa — the town of Centerville, to be exact — and cut the trail of Stan Maddy — football coach, art teacher, father, grandpa, and 20-gauge devotee.

"Years ago, I had an old Stevens Model 77M 3-inch magnum that I tried to hunt turkeys with," said Maddy. "It had a 30-inch barrel, full choke, the whole works. I just got tired of carrying that big gun around, and so several years ago, I started hunting ducks with a little 20-gauge. I just liked it better. It was lighter, and wasn't so heavy to carry around. My oldest boy, Keane, bought me a turkey choke for that little 20, and so I decided I'd give it a try. We patterned it out in the yard with some 3-inch #5s that I had, and I took it out and killed my first turkey with it."

Maddy said he doesn't remember how long ago it was that he made the switch, but he's staying with the 20-gauge. "I never pick a 12-gauge up," he said. "I never use a 12-gauge. I have two or three of them, but I'll just stay with my little 20-gauge."

Currently, Maddy's pet turkey gun is a Remington Model 870 pump. Capable of handling 2¾- and 3-inch shotshells, the shotgun has been equipped with a Kicks Competition turkey choke, which sits inside a traditional 28-inch ventilated-rib barrel. He also added a sling and a homespun paint job, complete with natural oak leaf stencils — "I don't like that sticky tape," said Maddy — to create one hell of a good-looking turkey gun. But can it shoot?

"I tried some 3-inch 1¼-ounce #5s out of this little gun, and they seem to pattern as well as anything I've ever shot out of it," said Maddy. "I shoot the gun every year before I go out just to make sure that I'm confident that it's shooting in the right place — and it's always shot in the right place"

Still, he knows there are some limitations associated with a firearm that some might incorrectly term "a popgun" that simply due to physics, can't be overcome.

"Don't try to shoot him too far away," said Maddy. "I decide where I'm going to set my decoys and how far out my decoys are. And I'm only setting the decoys out, say, 10 to 12 yards. And then, well, I would really hesitate to shoot at anything that was 30 yards away. I know some people come back and say that they shoot birds at 50 and 60 yards. Well, first of all, I personally feel it's more of a challenge to get a shot at him when he comes in close than it is to, say, ambush him when he's walking through the woods 60 yards away from me. Maybe it's some luck (NOTE: I don't think so), but I have yet to cripple a bird."

Over the past half a dozen Iowa seasons, Maddy has successfully tagged eight adult gobblers with his "little" 20-gauge. All were taken at under 30 yards. Limitations? Well, until the powers that be start filing self-discipline, woodsmanship, and patience under the category called Limitations, Maddy — known as Daddy Maddy to his friends — will just have to go without. You see, his thinking and mine are about the same here, though he certainly won't admit it. It really doesn't matter if you're shooting a .410 single shot or a 105mm howitzer. Both have their limitations. And, as Clint Eastwood so matter-of-factly put it in his film *Magnum Force*, "A man has got to know his limitations."

Stan "Daddy" Maddy flanked by sons, Keane (right), and Jason, (left). One shoots a 20-gauge, one a 12, and one, an in-line Knight muzzleloader. The bottom line? Gobblers such as this incredible Iowa Eastern really need to be concerned, regardless of who's behind the trigger.

Debunking Shotgun Myths

Shotguns and rifles are different in that the rifle throws a single projectile while the shotgun fires multiple pellets. Okay, M.D., now there's one hell of an obvious statement. Obvious, yes, but I'm not done yet. Shotguns differ from rifles in the number of projectiles they fire, but they also differ in the mindset that many hunters have about these very individual firearms. What mindset? Well, the mindset that says because a rifle provides but one "chance" for success, the shooter must therefore be much more cautious in his or her presentation of that projectile. Shotguns, with their hundreds of pellets, seem to offer a much greater margin for error. Translation? Turkey hunters don't need to be as careful nor as practiced in their shooting skills simply because, well, aren't you sure to hit something with that many pellets? The envelope, please. And the answer is — NO!

This philosophy that multiple pellets guarantee success is what I refer to as one of several turkey shotgunning myths. And while I certainly don't wish to get ahead of myself and reveal too much of the forthcoming segment, The Mystery of the Miss, I do want to take a few minutes and look at and analyze a handful of these shotgun shooting myths in the hopes that by bringing them to light,

Outdoor writer Phil Bourjaily conducts his version of shotgunning research prior to the spring season. Such testing breeds confidence and familiarity.

turkey hunters will begin to place a new emphasis on marksmanship. The truth is, it's easy to miss a golf ball with a handful of sand when you're throwing in a windstorm. You'll see what I mean.

Myth #1 — Multiple pellets mean few misses. We've already looked at this one in the opening two paragraphs. It's worth mentioning again. Don't allow yourself to fall into the trap. Where are all those pellets going? And when they go, do they go the same way each time? Once you start shooting this "can't miss" turkey gun, you'll begin to see exactly how easy it can be to miss something the size of a turkey's head with so many pellets.

Myth #2 — Shotguns always shoot where they're pointed. It's true *if* we're talking general directions. Like north. What we're dealing with here is not a pellet or two. Or even a dozen pellets. What we're talking about with shotguns and patterns, as you'll see in the section on patterning, is the densest portion of that pattern. Where is that densest portion located in relation to where you were aiming? Surprisingly enough, very few shotguns will hit to the point-of-aim. That is, few guns put the densest portion of any pattern precisely behind the bead right out of the box. There are ways to correct this, as we'll discuss; however, the first step in fixing the problem is recognizing that there indeed is one.

Myth #3 — Bigger pellets equal better performance and greater range. While larger shot sizes can and do have their place in certain applications, to make an across-the-board statement such as "bigger pellets mean better performance and longer distances" is not only unwise, but incorrect. Unless I'm mistaken, turkey hunting is a sport not of distance, but of proximity; therefore, big pellets such as BBs and #2s, still legal for turkey hunting in some states, and the long-distance retained energy that they can — key word: can — provide are in most cases unwarranted. Too many of the larger shot sizes begin to falter, pattern-wise, once chokes get beyond the Full category.

Myth #4 — All shotguns shoot the same. Here, I find myself at a loss when I try to say anything other than, "It simply doesn't work that way." Even given identical shotguns tested at identical distances under seemingly identical conditions, differences in performance, including variables such as pattern density, point-of-impact, and consistency, will quickly show themselves. This is true even with factory ammunition of the same manufacture and lot number. It's foolish, then, to assume that what works in Old Joe's Model 12 is going to work in your Model 835. Oh, it might; but chances are pretty good it won't.

Myth #5 — A Super Turkey Choke is the answer to all the problems. As you'll see later, choke tubes are but one part of what we call a recipe for shotgunning success. It's a combination of things that, when used together, creates a winning team. Imagine, for instance, that your truck is running poorly. Would it make sense that changing the carburetor, and only the carburetor, is instantly going to solve all your mechanical problems? Maybe it will; maybe it won't. Maybe it's not a carburetor problem at all. Maybe it's the plug wires. The same holds true for turkey guns. Sometimes all it takes are a series of educated guesses known as trial and error.

Solving The Mystery Of The Miss

The boy was devastated. At 9 o'clock that morning, he'd missed his first-ever wild turkey gobbler, one of a trio of longbeards that had finally decided to wander on over and see just exactly what all that hen-ruckus was. The shot was only 15 yards. Maybe 12. Either way, the birds saw something they didn't quite care for, and with a quick turn and a sharp putt, the jig was up. Had it been an experienced finger on the trigger, all would have been over but the flopping and the handshakes. And while his shot was ethical and well within both range and the bounds of responsibility, it was also a clean miss.

Eleven o'clock. For the last hour and 40 minutes, I had pleaded with this old ridge-runner until finally, he too stepped within range. Seventeen yards. I held my breath. So did his father, who sat by the boy's side. But when the little 20-gauge pump went off, the gobbler — and a huge Iowa gobbler at that — turned tail and ran. Frightened he was, and a bit wiser, but unscathed..

From where I sat, some 20 feet away, I could see the boy's face get red. He didn't want to cry. He couldn't, not with men around. But he did, and I heard his father's heart break. Then his father did something that surprised me. Before the boy could even get to his feet, his father instructed him to cycle a live round into the chamber of the little Remington. "Pick a spot on that tree and shoot it." he said. And the boy did just as he was told. "Now," said his father as he slid his arm around the boy's still-slouched shoulders. "Do that the next time." And with that, I knew we'd all started back at Square One.

Ah, the Miss. Just ask any turkey hunter, and, if he's both honest and reasonably experienced in the trials and tribulations of the spring woods, he'll tell you that sooner or later, what happened to the young man in the opening paragraphs of this segment is going to happen to you. Hunt long enough, and you'll miss. No question about it.

Do I believe this old line? Well, maybe yes. And maybe no. No, I don't believe that everyone, every single turkey hunter to ever carry a sporting arm into the field, is at some point in a turkey hunting career going to whiff a shot at a big old gobbler. Some people are just flat lucky. On the other hand, I do believe that misses can occur, even to the most experienced shooters. However — and here comes the key to this entire section — misses, though frustrating and even traumatic, are not without their positive side. *Positive side*? What could possibly be positive about missing a turkey? Well, it's like this: A miss is not the tragedy it might at first seem if that miss can be explained and therefore prevented in the future. And in my honest opinion, approximately 99.98 percent of the misses that occur in the turkey woods can be explained.

Take, for instance, the young man above. He was inexperienced, far too eager to succeed, in part due to the presence of his father, and not accustomed to having something the size of a wild turkey gobbler all but sharing his front shirt pocket. This diagnosis was relatively simple. He picked his head up off the stock of his little 20-gauge in order to get a better view of this incredible bird and he was struck with a case of nerves. The cure? Problem one is easy enough to fix with range time, practice, and confidence building. Problem two? I told him that when he stops shaking at the sight of a strutting gobbler, he either needs to take up something a little more exciting, like

I hate to say it, but super-full turkey-specific choke tubes are not always the answer to a shooter's patterning problems. Only range time will provide all the clues.

bungee jumping without the string. Or he's dead.

But what else might be behind what I'm going to refer to as the Mystery of the Miss? As I mentioned earlier, a miss that can be explained can be prevented. Let's take a moment and look at some of the most common reasons behind this all-too-common occurrence.

1. **Head off the stock** — It only makes sense. You've done everything right, and now you're looking down the rib at a big two-year-old tom. Sure, you want to see the fruits of your labors. How do you do that? You lift your head off the stock. All you're doing is clearing your field of vision, right? Wrong. You're setting yourself up to throw all 2 ounces of those #6s right over that gobbler's head. Oh, you'll scare him all right, but that's about it.

Explanation and cure — *"Wood to wood," my father always told me. Wood being my head and wood being the stock of my Model 24 double. It's simple physics. In order to shoot straight, you have to be looking down the rib with your eye on a parallel horizontal plane with the centerline of the barrel. Is that difficult to do with that gobbler out there at 30 yards, and you want to see all the action? You bet; however, what you have to remind yourself — and I actually do so, silently, before each shot — is to keep your head down on the stock until the shot leaves the muzzle. Be conscious of what it is you're doing. Remember, wood to wood.*

As *Field & Stream* shooting editor Phil Bourjaily demonstrates here, it's important to develop good, head-down form while on the shooting range. Why...

2. Bird too far — Turkeys are big birds. Gobblers in full strut appear even bigger. Because they're big birds, it's very easy to underestimate the distance between you and your target. Add other variables such as undulations in the terrain, weather, or foliage, and judging distance becomes even more difficult. Oh, and nerves. Don't get into that, "He's going to see me, so I better shoot now" syndrome.

Explanation and cure — *In the past, I've used and suggested a couple different methods for improving hunters' range-estimation skills. Laser rangefinder? Sorry, but it's just not practical in a turkey hunting situation, unless you have the luxury of being in a blind. There's just too much movement involved in raising, ranging, and lowering such a device. Better is off-season practice using life-sized cutouts. Or, as we've done in the past, a full-sized wild turkey 3-D archery target. Either the cutout or the target can be placed at predetermined distances, both on open ground as well as in the timber, and those visuals used for later reference. These practice sessions, combined with simple field experience, can prove quite helpful when it comes time for "Do I, or don't I?" with that trigger. A second technique that can be used quite successfully involves placing your turkey decoy or decoys at a known distance. Does this have to be exact? No, not really, but even quickly pacing off 15 or 20 yards while that bird's gobbling in the background can help you. And it's a great confidence builder as well. Just let him step over that "line in the sand" you've drawn, and it's handshakes and a heavy walk out.*

3. Bird too close — Again, you've done all your homework. The only thing is, that longbeard isn't standing at 30 yards. Not even 20 yards. He's at 20 feet. That's less than 7 yards to you and me. The safety goes off, the gun goes boom, and the bird flies away. What gives?

Explanation and cure — *Personally, I believe that nationwide each spring, as many or more gobblers are missed at ranges under 15 yards as are missed at 50. At first this observation makes no sense; however, with a little thought and some looking back, it all becomes much more clear. Remember all that range time you spent prior to the season? All those rounds shot and patterned at 30, 35, and 40 yards or beyond? Did you ever think to put one on paper at, say, 20 feet? Ten yards? Fifteen yards? Think of it this way. Stand still. Now, would you rather I throw a golf ball at you, or try to hit you with the front of a Greyhound bus? Well, that golf ball is what you have, pattern-wise, at 20 feet, thanks to the modern ammunition and super-full turkey choke you're using. And it's a hell of a lot easier to miss something the size of a turkey's head with a golf ball than it is with the Greyhound pattern you have at 30 yards. A little head off the stock. A case of the shakes — remember, he's close enough for you to count his eyelashes. And that golf ball goes whizzing by his noggin. How do you fix this? First, take the time to know what your gun's going to do at all of the different ranges you'd expect to encounter in the field. And then some. Then practice. In some cases, hunters can help direct these close-*

Because it leads to good, head-down-on-the-stock form in the field. It's all practice. And repetition. And more practice.

range patterns through the use of specialty sights such as scopes, traditional iron sights, or other optics. Here, mastering the miss is all about confidence and knowledge.

4. **Shooting at the bird** — My goodness. How am I going to miss a turkey that's standing still at 35 yards? Hell, there are 200-some pellets in this Roman candle thing I've shoved in the chamber.

Explanation and cure — Archers know better than any other group of hunters that to be successful, one must concentrate not on the animal but on a very small portion of that target. A archer will look for a group of hairs, an odd-colored spot, or a 1-inch-square part of the whole. Then they visualize their arrow passing through that very small target and impacting the ground on the opposite side. Success! Conversely, what does the archer who simply "shoots at the deer" have? A wallet full of unfilled tags at the end of the season. Successfully harvesting a wild turkey with a hunting implement, be it shotgun, muzzleloader, or bow, is no different. The successful turkey hunter focuses on that gobbler's head and neck area, with his intent being to place the densest portion of his pattern on that very small target. Certainly, a 30-yard bird body-punched with 2 ounces of copper #5s is likely to be pronounced dead; however, for every body-hit bird that dies immediately, another makes it into the timber or into the air, never to be found except by a member of the local coyote population. And we owe the bird much more than that. Concentrate. Focus. And pick a spot.

5. **Unfamiliar with the firearm** — Why is it that some folks will work and work and work until they're shooting dime-sized groups at 100 yards with their rifle, yet believe that patterning a shotgun prior to turkey season is just plain silly? Those people will miss.

Explanation and cure — This one's simple. Spend the time on the range until you know what your weapon is going to do every time you squeeze the trigger or finger the release. Know what it does at various ranges. Experiment with different combinations of choke and shotshell and shot size to the point that you can predict the end result of each and every round. Test various shaft and broadhead weights; maybe even try several broadhead designs. And then practice to the point of boredom. Then practice some more. Too much work? Well, here's something to think about. Do you have control over any of the following: The weather? The bird? Sunrise? Sunset? How your weapon performs? With so many variables out of your hands, why not do something about the one element you **can** control?

6. **The Unexplained** — Earlier I mentioned that approximately 99.98 percent of all misses that occur during the spring turkey season can be explained. My lackluster mathematical skills notwithstanding, this still leaves exactly 0.02 percent, well, unexplained. And that, friends, is where they're going to have to stay. These are those misses that, upon close exami-

That's my turkey gun, hard at work in the November goose fields. I shoot this Remington 11-87 year-round, and have the utmost confidence in it. Do you in yours?

nation, simply defy logic and reason. Maybe the bird moved. Gremlins, perhaps. Maybe your practical joking hunting partners removed all the shot from your shotshells. Or maybe it was just a clear-cut case of accuracy trauma. Either way, the bird's gone and you're left without a clue. Me? Have I ever missed a bird? Yes, I have. It was during the Spring of 1995, just out of Gravois Mills, Missouri. Had him dead to rights, too, until an errant gust of wind altered the predetermined course of my lead pellets. Damn wind. And I'm sticking with that.

6

Chokes, Shotshells And Other Things

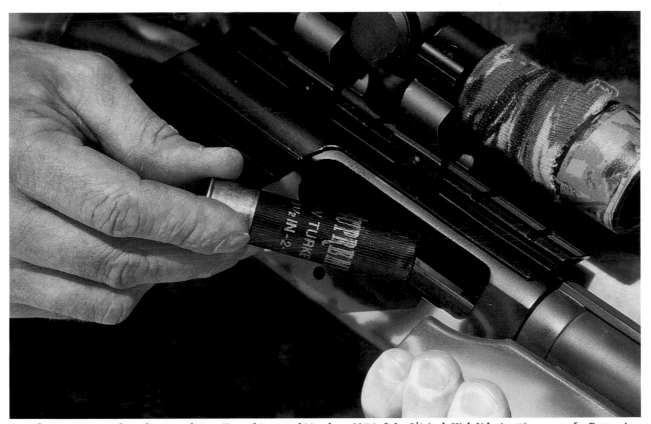

A good recipe starts with quality ingredients. Here, this scoped Mossberg 835 is fed a 3½-inch High Velocity #6 as part of a Patterning Day experiment.

An Inside Look At Ammunition

There was a time when the definition of "turkey load" could truthfully be printed as "any shotshell placed into the chamber of a shotgun while both owner and gun were in the process of turkey hunting." Maybe it was a 2¾-inch #4 buckshot, perhaps a 3-inch BB. Or maybe even a 3½-inch 10-gauge stick of dynamite, just crammed full of #6 shot. The bottom line is that back some 20 years ago,

shotshells were pretty much shotshells. Turkey loads? Ah, the old timers would say, just use the same thing you're using for ducks and geese. It was OK advice; not good, and certainly not great.

Today, it seems like we as hunters are at the opposite end of a 180-degree spin. Whereas a short time ago, shotshells specifically made for turkey hunting were simply not available, now the choices are so numerous as to be a bit confusing. Will the 2¾-inch magnums still work? What about 3-inch? Or this new 3½-inch 12-gauge? Are

Winchester's ammo guru, Kevin Howard, an avid turkey and waterfowl hunter who recognizes and preaches the connection between good ammunition and shotgun performance.

#4s a good choice? They worked on ducks. And what about shot charges? Here's one that carries 1⅞ ounces, and another that packs a full 2 ounces? High-velocity? Why high-velocity turkey loads?

Whoa. Slow down there. Yes, it can be confusing, with box upon box upon box of these new fancy turkey loads lining the shelves; fortunately, while the choices may have become higher in number, the basic fundamentals of shotshell selection hold true.

"There's been a lot of changes in turkey ammunition," says Kevin Howard, owner of the Missouri-based Howard Communications public relations firm. Howard has worked with the folks at Olin Winchester for the past 14 years. During that time he has seen more than his fair share of advancements. "I think part of the reason why you're seeing so much on the shelf is that turkey loads themselves have gone through quite a progression over the past 10 years or so. When turkey hunting started getting popular (NOTE: In states like Ohio, this wasn't until the early 1980s; in Washington, add another 10 years), most people used the high-brass, heavy duck loads or goose loads. There weren't specific turkey loads. But when people really started looking at tighter chokes and denser patterns, that's when turkey loads began to come into their own."

"Initially, the move was to simply add more shot. For instance in the 3-inch guns, you could increase the payload from 1⅜ ounces to 1⅝ ounces to 1⅞ ounces and finally, 2 ounces. Then when the 3½-inch guns came

along, they (the shotshell manufacturers) were looking at 2¼ ounces of shot. With all this, the thought was more shot and tighter chokes mean denser patterns. I think (laughs) that a lot of those shells are still on the shelf because the trend over the last several years, and Winchester really lead the way on this, was to go to higher velocities."

As Howard explains it, the folks at Winchester decided some years ago to take a closer look at velocity and its impact — no pun intended — on both pattern density and penetration. It seems that research was leading ammo-techs to the conclusion that standard 12-gauge loads of 2 ounces of #6 shot moving at muzzle velocities of approximately 1,150 feet per second (fps) were inconsistent, and in many cases, unable to penetrate a turkey's bone structure at the head and neck.

"What was happening, and I saw this a lot myself when I figured out what was going on," Howard says, "was that a lot of turkeys were being knocked down but not killed simply because (the hunters) weren't getting that penetration through the bone structure."

As a solution to this lack of penetration problem, Howard explains that some of the nation's ammunition manufacturers, with Winchester the front-runner, have made the switch from traditional turkey shotshells to a new high-velocity offering. In most cases, these high-velocity, or HV, rounds will feature both a downsized shot charge — 1¾ ounces versus the traditional 3-inch, 2-ounce loads — and a redesigned shot cup or wad, which, when combined, are providing turkey hunters with some lightning-fast, 1,300 fps choices.

"It's actually a case," Howard laughs, "where less is more."

But What Size?

All of which brings us to another ammunition topic, one fully capable of fueling both frustrations as well as arguments. When it comes to shot size, ask the hunter who delights in pulling Old Tom into spitting distance, and he'll tell you that nothing works better than copper-coated #6 shot. An hour and another sporting goods store later, and you'll have some fellow on a soapbox extolling the virtues of #5s. "Distance, penetration, and retained energy," he'll say, as he launches into yet another hour-long dissertation. Then there's the guy who thinks that anyone shooting anything less than #4 shot is a fool, except — maybe — those folks using those new-fangled duplex shotshells. You know, the ones that have #2 and #4, or #4 and #6, all snuggled into the same hull?

All discussions aside, the question still remains, is there *really* one "best" shot size choice for hunting turkeys? Well, the word "best" here makes things just a little tricky; however, let's go back to Kevin Howard and see

Modern turkey choke tubes come in a wide variety of shapes, sizes, and constrictions. Only through testing can you determine which "tool" works best for your situation.

what he has to say about the subject, size by size.

#2 (still legal in some states) — "In my opinion, it's too big. You'll get some holes in your pattern. A turkey's head and neck area is actually pretty small, when you look at it. And with something like #2s, you can develop holes in a pattern and actually miss a turkey."

#4 — "I like #4s. Most shotguns will shoot them pretty well. With a high-velocity load, you have a load that's definitely capable of taking turkeys at 40 and 45 yards very easily."

#5 — "My favorite. It has good pattern density and retained energy. I try not to take a turkey over 30-35 yards, but if I have to take a shot at, say, 40 or 45 yards, #5s still provide enough penetration."

#6 — "Great pattern density because of the pellet count (2 ounces = 450 pellets), but you're losing a little bit because of the lighter weight pellet at extended ranges. Basically, you're losing velocity and therefore losing penetration."

#7½ (again, legal in some states) — "Too small, unless you're willing to hold your shots to 25 yards or so. You're going to lose a lot of pellet energy."

Conclusive? Certainly not, but it does give you something to think about from a man who spends 12 months out of each year either shooting shotguns, talking about shotguns and ammunition, or thinking about shotguns and ammunition.

Personally, I've come to these conclusions about shot sizes and turkeys. Nothing scientific, mind you, but rather just a summation of those things that I've seen and heard and experienced over the past 11 years.

1. Approximately 99 percent of the nation's turkey hunters use #4, #5, or #6 shot. The reasons are simple — (a) shotshell choices, including gauge, hull length, and shot material, are much broader in these sizes, (b) #2 and #7½ shot aren't legal in all states, and (c) #4, #5, and #6 shot all offer, with some limitations, everything a turkey hunter needs and requires in terms of penetration and retained energy.

2. Of this 99 percent, approximately 50 percent shoot #5s. Why? Well, as Howard says, #5 shot comes closer to being that "perfect" pellet, than do any of the three most popular shot sizes. With #5s, you have pellet count (297 pellets in a 1¾-ounce load), pattern density, and retained energy, even at distances past which most turkey hunters should be shooting. Throw in the high-velocity factor, and you're now armed with an even more lethal combination of variables.

3. High-velocity turkey loads seem to be catching on, a note that only makes sense as, technically speaking, it would appear a very good thing to be able to increase energy retention and foot-pounds on target — Whoa! All that means is the force with which the pellets hit the turkey. He doesn't care, but you should. You want to hit him hard without sacrificing much in the way of pellet count. In '97, my wife and I both switched from 2 ounces of #6 shot to 1¾-ounce HV #5s and 1¾-ounce HV #6s, respectively. Why do I shoot #6s? I'm big on pattern density, something I get more than enough of with #6 shot. Also, I don't plan on shooting anything more than 35 yards away. Energy retention? Not a problem.

Believe me. Tubes can have a dramatic impact on such variables as pattern density, consistency, and overall performance; still, they're only part of the whole picture.

Putting The Squeeze On: Choke Tubes

Few shotgunners would argue that turkey hunting has done more for the design and development of the modern specialized choke tube — hunting tube, that is — than has any other event. Not satisfied with what the shotgun manufacturers touted as full chokes, turkey hunters — although many were as much inventor as they were hunter — began experimenting, most looking to determine the extent to which a shot charge could be constricted before that charge demonstrated any adverse effects such as blotchy or odd-shaped patterns.

Almost immediately, problems began to show themselves. In truth, the problem was two-fold, entailing both pellet deformation and, for lack of a better phrase, pellet alignment. The dilemma was simple. Upon reaching the start of the constriction, the soft lead pellets were violently squeezed into a much smaller area. This compacting of pellets often resulted in pellet deformation, and shot which is out-of-round displays a tendency to fly erratically. The second part of the problem, pellet alignment, had to do with the fact that a portion of the pellets in the shot charge were still jostling for position in this recently-altered package even as they left the muzzle. This movement, combined with the aforementioned pellet deformation, often resulted in patterns that looked more like a ran-

dom placement of fly specks on an old window than they did an effective harvester of wild turkeys.

Fortunately, the solution was as elemental as was the problem — constrict the shot charge more gradually and over a greater distance, *and* allow the individual pellets to realign themselves within the charge *before* exiting the muzzle. Armed with this new information, designers began to both lengthen and taper the choke's forcing cone — the point at which the choke actually begins to constrict the shot charge — in an effort to reduce the severity of what had been a sudden and very dramatic change in the shot charge. More thought was also given to that section of the choke immediately following the constriction, and it was soon found that by extending this parallel or non-constricted portion of the choke, pellets were afforded the opportunity to realign themselves fully *before* the charge left the muzzle.

In time, turkey choke tube innovators and designers would achieve that which was never before thought possible — a 90-percent pattern at 40 yards. In black-and-white terms, this translates into 405 of 450 pellets (2 ounces of #6 shot) falling within a 30-inch circle at 40 yards! To turkey hunters, these new tubes represented the Holy Grail of shotgunning. To turkeys, they meant trouble — pure and simple.

The Final Word On Choke Tubes

Not magical instruments, choke tubes, regardless of whether their inside diameters measure .730 inch or .655 inch, are only as good as is the individual pulling the trigger. To take that a step further, he who merely buys and installs one of these new special-purpose choke tubes and heads afield without spending time on the range is doing both himself and the wild turkey a great disservice. For those new to the world of specialty chokes, it's sometimes best to think of these devices as simply one ingredient in a much larger recipe. This is a list that includes, among other things, the best in modern ammunition, sights or optics, experience, patience, and practice.

Better yet, think of it more like a recipe for success.

The Importance Of Patterning

Tell me what you think about this. Let's say you've just won $10,000 in your state's Pick 4 Lottery. You lucky guy. Riding on a financial wave, you decide to treat yourself to that wonderful centerfire rifle you've always wanted. So, armed with $10,000 in your pocket, you motor on down to the local sporting goods dealer where you proceed to pick out your rifle. Oh, and you'd better have a scope. Bases and rings, too. And then there's a box — no,

Patterning begins by developing a serious, "¼-inch group at 100 yards" attitude toward the process and the end result. Assemble your range equipment, and give yourself enough time to – here's the key – do the job thoroughly and precisely.

better make it two — of your favorite ammunition. And, finally, because tomorrow is the opening day of deer season, you might want to strongly consider a hunting license and a deer tag. Can't forget about those.

Thus overloaded with loot, you retire to that corner of the basement into which your wife has long since stopped venturing. There, you mount the scope on the rifle, pile your blaze orange clothes in the corner, and, with a wistful backward glance at your latest acquisition, ascend the stairs to bed. The next morning — Opening Morning! — you take your new sporting arm, and you step into the field a deer hunter.

Ridiculous, eh? Such a story doesn't even warrant a good, old-fashioned, "Man, that's crazy." Still, every year from coast to coast, turkey hunter after turkey hunter after turkey hunter becomes the shotgunning equivalent of our oh-so-negligent friend above. They grab their shotguns from their racks. On the way out the door, they grab a handful of shells from their infamous "shell shelf," and off they go — turkey hunters. What's the difference? Easy. None.

For the sake of everyone involved, I won't belabor the point here. Yes, it's a cliché, but it's true — you can't hit what you can't see. But what turkey hunters who don't familiarize themselves with their shotguns don't realize is that it's just as difficult, if not impossible, to hit a target when you don't know what's happening once the stuff comes out of the end of the gun. Fortunately, there's a very easy remedy to this situation. It's called patterning.

Patterning, as world duck calling champion Buck Gardner is so fond of saying, isn't rocket science. It's not even close. It is time-consuming, and that is why so many turkey hunters slide right on by this step in the process. Look at it this way. What sense is it to buy the latest camouflage patterns; to practice calling until you're better than the birds themselves, to gain access to some of the finest turkey ground in the country, and what sense is it to scout until you know both the land and the wildlife intimately, IF you have absolutely no idea if you can hit the proverbial bull in the butt with that camouflaged bass fiddle you're hauling around with you in the woods? If that's the case, leave it at home.

But laziness aside, it's true that some folks either don't pattern their turkey guns at all or don't do enough of it simply because they aren't all that familiar with the process. So, let's take a look at this patterning process through the use of some of the most often-heard questions about the subject.

What does patterning do? Patterning actually does a number of things aside from the obvious. First, it provides the information that you need in order to make an accurate decision as to the right combination of shotshell, shot size, shot charge, choke, and sights (if applicable) for your particular shotgun. Without this information, you're doing nothing more than guessing that the shot you're shooting through that tube at

It's the little things like these most excellent yet very elemental target stands from Birchwood-Casey that take the hassle out of shotgun patterning, and in doing so, make folks more likely to do it properly. Or do it at all.

Many, many fine and somewhat "formal" turkey pattern targets are available; however, 8½ x 11 sheets of ordinary typing paper with a rough outline of a gobbler's head, neck, brain, and spinal column will work just as well.

the muzzle is going to provide the best in terms of performance. Why guess if you can find out for sure? Secondly, patterning provides a type of trial run for both you and the shotgun prior to the actual hunt. I think I speak for us all when I say that I'd rather have a firing pin or O-ring break on the practice range than on opening day in the field. Third, and perhaps most significantly, patterning gives you the confidence, both in yourself and your firearm, that you'll need in the field. Believe me, every pattern that prints true makes a world of mental difference when it comes time to drop the hammer on a big old gobbler. Fourth, patterning is an excellent way to practice one of the least-practiced skills in the outdoor field, range estimation. You're there, and the distances are marked, so doesn't it make sense to take advantage of the situation and really get to know what 30 yards looks like? Forty yards? Ten yards? And finally, a day spent in front of a patterning board is a great way to introduce young hunters and shooters to the fun and enjoyment that is this great sport of ours. Do we need any more than that?

What do I need? Each spring, I put together what I call a Range Bag. It contains everything that Julie and I will need for a morning's patterning. In that bag, you'll find:

- A selection of ammunition in different hull lengths, shot sizes, and charges
- A selection of after-market choke tubes
- Muff-style hearing protection, plus disposable ear plugs for anyone else
- Two pairs of shooting glasses
- A set of B-Square precision screwdrivers for making adjustments
- Black and blue magic markers
- Staple gun with extra staples
- Roll of fiber masking tape
- A small pair of needle-nose pliers
- Leather sandbag
- Model 5075 Shoot-n-C turkey targets from Birchwood-Casey
- Full-size turkey targets from Quaker Boy
- Roll of plain white butcher paper
- String and handled awl

In addition to the gear that's in the bag, I'll also include a Lohman Sight-Vise, a pair of Birchwood-Casey metal target stands, and several 30-inch square pieces of heavy cardboard for target backing. If the day we've chosen dawns chilly, I'll throw in a Coleman catalytic propane heater and a thermos of coffee. I've learned that it's much easier to stay on the range until I've completed the task if I'm warm on the outside as well as on the inside. Whether it's hunting or hunting practice, it's never a bad idea to go prepared.

You know what your shotgun does at 40 yards, but what happens at 10? Or 12? Proper testing involves ALL the possibilities. Oh, by the way, that hole below this 10-yard turkey target? That's the wad!

Where can I go? We're fortunate here in Iowa in that we have a wonderful facility just 10 or so miles from the house. The Matsell's Bridge Shooting Facility includes a 100- and 200-yard range, covered benches and seats, yardage markers, and an informal trap range. But do you need something as "fancy" as this? Certainly not. Actually, any place where you can safely — key word: safely — shoot up to approximately 50 yards has all the potential to become a turkey patterning range. Still can't find something? A quick telephone call to your local wildlife conservation officer or state department of natural resources will often get you pointed in the right direction.

How do I pattern my gun? The actual patterning process is actually quite simple. Just for grins, let's say Julie gives me a brand new Remington 11-87 Super Mag for Christmas. Wonderful girl! Come nicer weather, here's how I'm going to go about pattering that new gun.

    a. Using a Birchwood Casey target stand and a 30-inch square of cardboard covered in white butcher paper, I accurately measure out 30 yards — Wait! I'll get to the 40-yard thing in a minute! — and place my target stand at that point. In the middle of the paper, I make a golf ball-sized

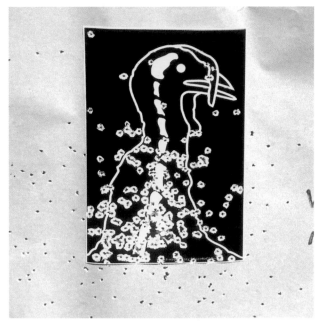

The identical combination (see previous photo), this time at 20 yards. Notice how the pattern begins to open slightly.

black dot. That's my aiming reference.

    b. Back at the bench, I decide on a shotshell-choke combination to try first. Typically, this is something that has worked well for me in the past. Today, I'll start with a 28-inch barrel — I shoot a 28-inch for both turkeys and waterfowl — a Remington Extra Full turkey choke tube, and a Federal shotshell containing 2 ounces of copper-plated #6 shot.

    c. With hearing protection and shooting glasses on, I put the gun in the Sight-Vise, aim it like I would a centerfire rifle, and squeeze the trigger. I then change the paper, make another black dot, and repeat the process. What I'm looking for in this step is the center of the pattern. In other words, where is the heaviest concentration of pellets located? If it's dead center, I'm on my way; if not, I'll have to make adjustments. Basically, this tells me where the gun shoots.

    d. Again back at the bench and with my target still at 30 yards, I'll try another combination. Maybe Winchester's 1¾-ounce high-velocity #5s through a MAD Max tube. Or a Lohman tube. Maybe high-velocity #6s. And despite the Remington's ability to handle 3½-inch shotshells, I'll also try 3-inch and 2¾-inch rounds. What I'm looking for is consistency.

    e. Once I've found a shotshell-choke combination that I believe works well, I'll replace the plain white butcher paper with one of the printed turkey targets. At this new target, I'll fire no

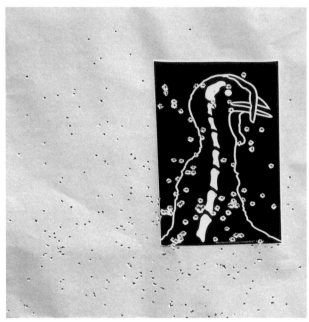

At 30 yards, pattern density begins to show an obvious change.

Here is the pattern at 40 yards. This is my personal maximum yardage. Why? Patterns are still consistent and I'm still confident, but I'm starting to wonder.

fewer than three rounds using the combination that I've decided upon. What I'm looking for here are hits in the head and spinal column, nothing else. Here's where it gets personal. If the information on the target says an effective load will result in four to five vital hits (brain/spinal column), I want eight to 10. And I want them consistently. If I get them right out of the gate, good; if I don't, then it's back to the combination drawing board for another set of chokes, shotshells, and shot sizes.

f. Finally, and once the process has led me to a combination that I'm satisfied with at 30 yards, I'll begin moving my patterning board and turkey targets in 5-yard increments, both toward and away from the bench. I want to see what the gun will do at 40 yards — my personal maximum range — as well as at 10 and 15 yards. As I mentioned earlier, each time the hammer falls, your confidence in your decision is bolstered substantially.

g. Oh, I almost forgot. Please remember to clean up and remove all your shotshell casings, targets, target stands, staples, and anything else you brought with you to the range. After all, you packed it in; you pack it out. Nothing is more disgusting or discouraging than to see a public shooting range that more closely resembles a landfill than it does a recreational facility.

What am I looking at or for? Again, that's easy. What you're looking for is consistency. You want to know,

without doubt, what your shotgun is going to do every time you pull the trigger. There are, of course, certain stages in the patterning process where you're looking for other variables, such as pattern density, point-of-impact (where the gun shoots), and specific hits in the vital areas. All of these, once the right combination is found, will eventually lead you to Nirvana, also known as the state of consistency.

It's not shooting where I'm aiming. What can I do? Surprisingly enough, a lot of shotguns won't place the densest portions of their patterns dead center in the middle of your patterning target. The reasons behind this "inaccuracy" can be many, and might include stock length, comb height, barrel-eye alignment, or improper shotshell-choke combination. Or it may be something as simple as — sorry — operator error. Just ask the fellow who owns the Mossberg Model 835 pump gun and who has experimented with 3½-inch high-velocity turkey loads, and you'll soon enough learn what recoil and flinching can do to your accuracy. However, we're talking about shooting where you're aiming. If you find aiming to be a problem with your shotgun, a relatively easy remedy might be to employ some type of sighting device such as a scope or iron sights, or perhaps even an Aimpoint or HOLOSight system, and essentially sight the shotgun in as you would any scoped or sighted centerfire rifle. Instead of adjusting the sights to correspond with a single projectile, you'll move the crosshairs or other device into alignment with the densest portion of your pattern. Doing so will allow you to "move" that center of concentration right, left, up, or down as necessary.

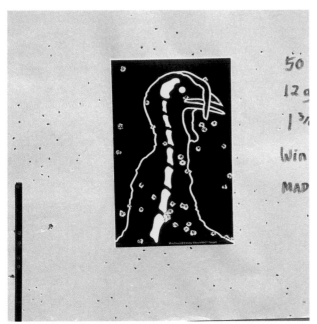

Fifty yards. Sure, it looks all right, but how often are you afforded the luxury of an enclosed shooting position, a bench rest, hearing protection, and a normal heartbeat in the turkey woods? Just too "iffy" for me.

Ouch! This gun hurts! Is there something I can do?
I'll never forget the day the young man brought the pump gun to the house. Man, he was proud of his new Mossberg 835. Chambered for the latest and greatest, the 3½-inch 12-gauge shotshell, the fellow was certain that this was THE turkey gun. "Let's go out back and shoot it," he said. I didn't have to be asked twice. Okay, long story short. If I remember correctly, the first round out of the muzzle elicited something that to me sounded like, "Man, that was rough." The second, however, came with a grunt of mixed pain and surprise. Oh, and a bloody nose. "Youth wanna thoot this," the young man asked. I declined. Okay, so here's the scoop. No one feels the recoil in the field when there's a longbeard standing 30 yards away. Adrenaline takes care of that. Shooting at the range is totally different. Here, there's no turkey to help soak up some of that recoil. So, what can you do? Without changing the gun itself, you can do what outdoor writer and Field & Stream shooting editor, Phil Bourjaily, does, and that's to place a partially filled shot bag — sand will work, too — between the butt of his shotgun and his shoulder. Big, heavy loads like the 3½-inch candles are still tough, he says, but it's a lot better at the end of the day with the bag than without. Another method is simply to wear a padded sweater or jacket. In some cases, one of the specialty shooting sweaters that come with a padded shoulder will work well, too. Anything that puts some padding between you and the gun will absorb some of the punch.. If you don't mind altering the gun somewhat, there are additional options available that can have an effect on felt recoil. Ports, small angled holes, can be

drilled near the muzzle. They serve to both to reduce recoil and soften muzzle jump. High-tech recoil pads can be used on the butt and recoil-reducers can be installed directly into the stock. For more information on how to reduce recoil, I'd strongly suggest talking to your local neighborhood gunsmith. Chances are he or she will have several suggestions on how you can take the pain out of practice.

Do I have to do this every year? Let me ask you this. Is the hour that you'll spend on the range before the season worth the four weeks of confidence that you'll get knowing that that shotgun in your hands is going to do exactly what you programmed it to do? I thought so. For me, nothing changes from year to year. Not gun. Not choke. Not shotshell. Not even socks. Okay, so the socks change, but my point is that even though I know what my shotgun does, I'll still shoot it every spring. I'll go through the identical process that I've outlined above, and at the end of each session, I'll say — "Yep. It's there again." That's confidence.

Camo, Slings, And Other Things

I always feel like a hypocrite when I discuss shotgun camouflage in my seminars. I'll tell you exactly why. Typically, my outline reads that I address camouflage and all the aspects associated therewith. Then, I talk about shotguns. No problem so far. The problem lies, however, in my in-depth approach to camouflage. Remember, there is no such thing as an insignificant detail when it comes to hiding from two of the sharpest eyes in the field. I then tell them that I, at least for the past five years or so, haven't bothered to camouflage my shotgun in any way. Inevitably, and with good cause, someone will raise a hand and say, "But M.D., you said…." Sure, I know what I said. It's a case of, as Jim Schoby used to say, do as I say, and not as I do.

Now, just what in the hell am I talking about? What I'm talking about is this: Should you, or should you not camouflage your shotgun for the purposes of turkey hunting? Some folks do; I personally do not. Still, let me summarize shotguns and camouflage in one, easy-to-remember statement. If you think, even for an instant, that the fact that your shotgun is *not* camouflaged may play some role in your success or failure in the field, by all means camouflage it. A camo shotgun is just another variable that you have some degree of control over, unlike the weather, that you have absolutely no control over. Why not take advantage of the situation? The bottom line, and I say again, is elemental — If you have to think about it, do it. In fact, if you have to second-guess or reconsider any

This Mossberg Model 835 came from the factory with a coat of Woodland camouflage paint, an excellent all-round choice for the multi-season turkey hunter.

Roger Kiely opted for the "no-camo" option; however, this Iowa longbeard, Kiely's first, didn't seem to mind.

aspect of your camouflage system — I hate that word, system, but it's rather appropriate here — tend to it. It's just that simple.

Fortunately, and thanks in part to modern technology, camouflaging your pet turkey gun is about as easy as saying the words "paint it up." Some of the more common options include —

From the factory. Many modern turkey guns come from the factory wearing a layer of camouflage paint, and all the buyer has to do is decide from among the several different patterns available.

No camo. This has been my personal option as of the past several years. However, I do currently shoot a Remington 11-87 Special Purpose with a matte black (non-glare) barrel and receiver, and a dull finish stock. Even the bolt's black. The only thing that shines on that gun is the bead, and if a gobbler's close enough to be spooked by that, well, he's close enough to have his day ruined.

Tape. It used to be that you could tell a turkey gun that had been camo-taped because it always looked like a cow with a cold had sneezed on it. Only it was twice as tacky. Today, though, companies such as Hunter's Specialties and others market a type of "no-mar" tape. Available in several different camouflage patterns, the

tape adheres well yet doesn't leave that awful sticky residue behind once it's removed.

Paint. Just say the word "paint" around the man with a Benelli Super Black Eagle, and instantly he'll go all wild-eyed. It doesn't matter that it comes off, he'll tell you. He doesn't want it on there in the first place. Still, his reluctance notwithstanding, paint certainly does have a spot in the shotgun camouflage lineup.

Socks. Until I went the no-camo route, I was a huge fan of the slip-on gun socks. All you do is slip one on, trim it up, and you're ready to go. At the end of the day, you take it off and polish Old Betsy up. Rain? Not a problem. Simply remove the sock and throw it in the dryer along with your soggy camo clothes.

Adhesive camo kits. These became popular two or three years ago. Sure, they look fancy, but they're actually little more than three or four die-cut pieces of camouflage tape that can be molded to a shotgun's stock, receiver, forearm and barrel.

Chaps. Initially, most folks bought gun chaps as a means of protecting a firearm from scratches and dents; however, it wasn't long before some enterprising individual realized — "Hey. If I make these things in camouflage, then everyone will want one." And

Gun socks, like the one Julie uses here on her 11-87, are a fine choice for those wishing a temporary solution to the camouflage issue. TIP – Pattern the gun both before and after installing the sock to ensure the action works freely.

On the subject of slings, get one. Nuff said.

while I won't go so far as to say that has indeed been the case, these zippered covers for stock and forearm have their followers.

Let me talk for just a minute about shotgun slings. Get one. It's just that simple. Truth is, you're going to be carrying that smokepole around in the woods a lot more than you're going to be using it. You're just a mode of transportation for a shotgun. That's what it boils down to.

Longbeards And Muzzleloaders

POP!

Beside me, I could feel my wife look at me. She knew that sound as well as I did. It was a percussion cap. Typically, the pop is followed almost immediately by a big BOOM! Where was the boom?

We heard our hunting companion walking through the leaves long before we saw him. When we did see him, it was head was head down, feet dragging, camouflaged muzzleloader drooping unceremoniously from one hand. Silently, he sat down next to us. "Of all the people that had to be with me this morning," said Jason Maddy. "It just had to be you." Behind my headnet, I grinned an invisible smile. This was going to be good.

"Where was the boom, Jay?" I asked. "Wasn't there supposed to be a boom?"

To make an hour-long story tremendously short, the whole thing went something like this. The gobbler, a big old bruiser that both Jason and my wife, had dealt with in seasons past, had come enthusiastically into our morning set-up; unfortunately, he came from the opposite direction we had planned. Even after using all the strategies and secrets in all three of our playbooks, the big tom refused to budge.

"Can you move on that bird?" I asked Jason. Without a word, the young man slowly got to his feet and cautiously began to circle around the end of the small rise that separated us from the still-gobbling longbeard. One minute. Five minutes. Ten minutes. Then, the dreaded POP!

"He started to walk away," Jason said. "When he started to walk back up the hill, I gave a couple low yelps. Man, he just turned and headed right for me. Couldn't have been 20 yards. Man, I wish you hadn't heard that. I'm never going to live this one down."

Later, Jay would determine the culprit to be a far-too-heavy film of oil in the nipple. This prevented the flame from the cap from reaching the main powder charge with sufficient heat to ignite it. The remedy? "I should have unloaded the gun yesterday, popped a few caps this morning, and used a fresh charge," Jason said as we made our way out of the field that afternoon. "Don't worry, man," I reassured him. "I won't say anything." Good thing he didn't hit that gobbler with the look he gave me following that remark. It's a shame to shoot them up too bad.

There's just something about wild turkeys and muzzleloaders that, well, fits. I think the word I'm looking for here is tradition. Or rather traditional. Yes, there are few things as traditional as hunting wild turkeys with black-powder firearms. Nothing quite as frustrating nor as challenging either. Just ask Jason Maddy.

More and more turkey hunters each year are accepting this one-shot-is-all-you-get type of undertaking. And with good reason. In its simplicity, muzzleloading is just plain enjoyable. For many it is a chance to break away from the technology and gadgetry that has in recent years invaded the tradition of hunting. Here, one has to develop the load, putting together a combination of powder and shot, wads and cushions, in much the same way as a baker assembles the ingredients for an award-winning dessert. Then there's the time on the range — the patterning, the analyzing. And, yes, the back-to-the-drawing-board. There are ramrods and possibles bags. Okay, so from a "stuff" standpoint, muzzleloading may have nothing over modern firearms; however, some of this so-called stuff is just pretty neat to look at and even better to use.

Finally, there's that one shot. Have you done everything right? Is the gun ready? Is the load up to the task? Are *you* ready?

An occasional misfire aside, Centerville, Iowa's Jason Maddy is an experienced and enthusiastic practitioner of the black arts; black powder, that is. Over the years, the 27-year-old has tagged many fine southern Iowa longbeards while afield with a favorite front-stuffer. It is an outdoor activity he became involved in strictly for the "thrill" of doing something just a little bit different. "It's that one-shot deal that gets me," says Maddy.

But where to start? For the turkey hunter looking to delve into the world of muzzleloading shotguns, there's an almost infinite number of choices and decisions to be made. What gun? What load? Do I need this? What about that? Fortunately, black powder and turkeys can be as simple or as complex as one wishes. So let's take a look at the simple side, with a little of the advanced thrown in. Of course, we'll get a little help from the man who knows how to make a smokepole go "POP!" (He's going to get me for that one.)

Firearms

I shot my first black-powder gobbler in Washington state in 1997. The gun? An antique double-barrel 12-gauge that a dear friend of mine had traded me for a chest freezer. "Just look at that right barrel," Norman said, handing me my new fowling piece. "You can't get a dime in there on edge. Now that's tight."

Yes, it was tight; however, in order to place the better part of the somewhat erratic pattern on a gobbler's head and neck at 25 yards, I found it necessary to put the brass bead some 4 inches to the right and 4 inches above the tom's skull. You just try "guess-timating" 4 inches here and 4 inches there with a gobbler strutting around just beyond your bead. It's tough.

Today, I still shoot that old gun using 100 grains of FFg black powder, a felt cushion wad, and 130 grains by volume of copper-coated #6 lead shot followed by a thin over-shot wad. Sure it kicks like the devil, but boy it does the job on those longbeards. I just have to make sure they're within 25 yards and remember about the 4 inches.

But what if you're not into freezer-trade guns? This day and age, there are muzzleloading shotguns aplenty. Such a list might include:

Connecticut Valley Arms (CVA) offers The Trapper and The Classic Turkey Double. Both 12-gauge, and both very pretty little muzzleloaders. Also available from Mountain State Muzzleloading in Williamstown, West Virginia. See either *www.cva.com*, or *www.mtnstatemuzzleloading.com*.

Cabela's sells three blackpowder shotguns, a 10-gauge (30-inch barrels), a 12-gauge (28.5-inch), and a 20 (27.5-inch). Need muzzleloading stuff? Look no farther for wads, shot, powder, and all the bells and whistles. See *www.cabelas.com*.

Thompson/Center gives fans of traditional muzzleloaders the 12-gauge New Englander, a double-duty turkey and waterfowl shotgun.

Fans of more modern guns may want to consider T/C's Encore, which offers a wide selection of drop-in barrels, including a 12-gauge tube with interchangeable chokes. See *www.tcarms.com*.

Knight Rifles serves up the TK2000. Sounds like a Terminator model number? That's what it is for turkeys. Super-full load-through choke, camouflage finish, sling, fiber optic sights, and an in-line ignition system make the TK2000 a step ahead of many modern shotguns. And the patterns? Devastating. Oh, and make sure you get a supply of the 3.5-inch shotshell wads. See *www.knightrifles.com*.

Bass Pro Shops carries Thompson/Center and CVA muzzleloading shotguns, along with every conceivable piece of gear and gadget for the purpose. See *www.basspro.com*.

Certainly an afternoon spent roaming around on the Internet will reveal additional possibilities in terms of muzzleloading shotguns, including complete start-to-finish kits for the do-it-yourselfer. Still, the list above should prove a good jumping off point. If you are still confused, just ask. Both Cabela's and Bass Pro Shops employ knowledgeable folks who will be more than happy to help answer all of your questions, either over the telephone or, in some cases, on-line. The same is true with Knight Rifles, Thompson/Center Arms, and Connecticut Valley Arms. And there's always your friendly neighborhood sporting goods dealer.

Still looking for a bottom line? The truth of the matter is that any muzzleloader, be it made in 1902 or 2002, is only as reliable as the individual behind the buttplate. Keep it clean, feed it well, and learn it thoroughly.

Powder, Shot, And The Load

If there's one thing that makes folks stutter-step when it comes to muzzleloaders and turkeys, other than the thought of being limited to only one shot — But isn't that our goal regardless? — it would be the seemingly infinite list of things that must be carried into the field and pushed into the firearm in order to make said firearm go boom. While it's true that he or she who would choose a black-powder shotgun will have a bit more in the way of necessities, it's not nearly the conglomeration of stuff that, say, fishermen haul around in their tackle boxes or golfers carry in their golf bags. Sorry, Tiger, but I'm right on this one.

"Myself, I take a little bit of Pyrodex Select granulated powder. Why Pyrodex? Personal preference, I guess. And it does make cleaning my shotgun a little bit easier," says Jason Maddy, "A few 3.5-inch steel shot wads from Knight Rifles, and 2 ounces of #5 lead shot. I'm thinking about trying that new Hevi-Shot material. Oh, and some Knight over-shot wads, too."

Maddy doesn't carry a possibles bag per se, but rather just totes his muzzleloading supplies in his turkey vest. "Typically, I'll carry two extra loads or shots," he says. "Knight Rifles has red speedloaders out now that go all the way through. They're not separated into two compartments. I'll load one up with powder and one up with shot. That's one load. I'll have four speedloaders altogether. I'll also carry my capper with me and a couple extra wads and over-shot wads. And that's all I carry. Basically, it boils down to the fact that you have one shot and you have to make that one shot count."

One shot. That's all. But it's not like picking a clearly marked box of modern 12-gauge ammunition off the store shelf. Those who shoot front-stuffers have to create the load on their own.

"Basically it's (load development) been a process of trial and error," says Maddy. "My brother, Keane, and I have always been messing around with muzzleloaders. In the beginning, I was doing what a lot of folks were doing, that was using the same amount of shot as powder by vol-

I had the pleasure of watching hunting partner, Phil Bourjaily, tag this Iowa Eastern with a Knight TK-2000 muzzleloader. A tremendous piece, the TK has revolutionized black powder turkey hunting, perhaps forever.

ume. Finally, we decided that we could get better patterns with something other than this old rule of thumb. So we started backing off on the powder charge and increasing, slightly, the shot charge. We started with 1¼ ounces of #5 shot and worked up to 2 ounces before deciding that 2 ounces worked the best for us. That's on top of 110 grains of Pyrodex Select. That's what I shoot now. Keane shoots 120 grains and 2 ounces of #4 shot. He likes #4s. That's the load that works best for him out of his gun. It's all in finding what works best out of your personal shotgun."

To emphasize. That's *your* personal muzzleloading shotgun. Load development is not about what works for your buddy or the guy down at the bowling alley, although those loads may prove a worthwhile place to start your research. Each muzzleloader, like each shotgun, performs differently, even with identical fodder, be it modern ammunition or pellets on top of Pyrodex. The only way — and, yes, I'm repeating the essence of Chapter 5 here — to know how that muzzleloader performs and how best to feed it in order to achieve its highest potential is to experiment. Just like you did with all those different makes and models of modern ammunition, choke tubes — oh, yes, let's not forget the choke tubes — sights, distances, and other variables. Try Maddy's 110 grains of Pyrodex and 2 ounces of #5 shot. If it works, good; if it doesn't, change something. Take notes. And by all means, take your time. After all, you have to figure that every

My "traded for a chest freezer" double-barrel 12-gauge muzzle-loader, was a gift from good friend, Norman Johnson, and is a proven turkey-getter. Inside 25 yards, that is.

That's Walt Ingram on the left, the man who started me down the road to turkey-related self-destruction. Thanks, Walt.

Just a little off the top. And a trim, please.

hour you spend on the range prior to turkey season is going to come back ten-fold once you've sweet-talked that old longbeard inside of 30 yards. Doesn't it make sense to do everything you can to ensure that the time you didn't spend on the range doesn't come back to haunt you?

7

Find Them First: Scouting

"I see nut-ting! I hear nut-ting!" Sgt. Schultz of Hogan's Heroes fame describes a turkey hunter's worst nightmare

There's no sense hunting where the turkeys aren't. Scouting is only part of the battle. But it is a big part.

Turkey Scouting 101

"There's no sense fishing where there's no fish."

That's my father. A man with two degrees, a Phi Beta Kappa key, and an elementalist's view on the world of hunting and fishing. Okay, on life in general. Truth is, though, he's right. His sage advice, his thoughts on the process known as spring crappie fishing, can also be applied to spring turkey hunting. "Success," he'd say

when expounding upon his worldliness, "begins with locating potential."

Unfortunately, where turkeys are concerned, locating that potential can sometimes be easier said than done. These difficulties often change with the place a person hunts. Out West, for instance, the distances between gobblers or groups of birds can be great and the terrain some of the most physically demanding in the country. East of

Landowners can prove themselves excellent sources of information when it comes time to start the scouting process. Understand, though, that they have their own responsibilities, and schedule your time with them accordingly.

Mental Scouting: Using Your Head

Say the word "scouting," and most hunters will immediately think of two things: time and physical effort. Similarly, ask those same individuals why they don't do the scouting they think they ought to, and there's a good chance they'll come up with an identical set of responses.

The truth is, effective turkey scouting actually begins long before you ever step foot in the field. In this regard, I like to tell folks to start scouting smarter, not harder. Yes, I know it's not original, but it certainly does get the point across.

Essentially, this mental portion of the scouting process relies on your having access to two things. The first is people. Not just any people, but folks who are willing to spend some time with you and answer the questions you're going to have concerning these first steps in locating your next gobbler. The second element is paper. In the past, these reference materials most likely included maps, brochures, magazine articles, and other publications; however, with the proliferation of the Internet and the availability of such incredible research tools as aerial photography and topographic software programs, this reference category has expanded practically to the point of being limitless.

But first, people. Traditionally, "people" in regards to turkeys and turkey scouting meant landowners. Certainly landowners are a very real and very vital part of the entire scouting puzzle. However, they're typically not the first inning in this mental ball game. So if not the landowner first, who then? Over the years, we've asked for and obtained information from a long list of individuals. Many of the tips provided eventually paid off in notched tags and hook-spurred gobblers. Personally, my list includes the following:

Rural mail carriers and UPS drivers — Just think. These people are driving the back-roads right at the break of day *and* at dusk for at least five or six days each week. They see the birds that cross the gravel roads, and they see the birds feeding in the roadside fields. Chances are good, too, that not only will they know where the birds are, but because their business revolves around addresses, they'll likely know who lives in such-and-such a house or who owns a particular plot of ground. They're busy people, and to them, time is of the essence, so don't try to keep them too long. Still, they're fantastic contacts.

School bus drivers — See the explanation above.

the Mississippi River, though, it might not be distance that proves troublesome when trying to locate turkeys, but rather the number of people sharing the woods with the same end result in mind. Most translate this to read—hunting pressure can make getting a bird to gobble, let alone come into the call, a Herculean task. The fact remains, you have to find them before you can tag them.

There is a way of answering the question of "Where's the gobbler?" That's through a process we hunters all know as scouting. Now wait. Before you turn to the next chapter thinking this is all going to be old hat, hold on. Certainly, I realize that I personally did not invent the word nor the process called scouting. And, no, I don't know all there is to know about every intricacy involved; however, what I do know is this: If a turkey hunter puts himself or herself at a disadvantage prior to opening day, chances are it's going to have something to do with scouting. Or more precisely, a lack thereof. It's not going to be calling. It's not going to be camouflage. It's going to be scouting. And while scouting at first might seem an elemental process, many folks nonetheless go about it rather inefficiently. Not necessarily incorrectly, mind you. Just not very efficiently. The bottom line here is that the more efficient a turkey hunter is in his scouting, the more prepared he's going to be come dawn on opening day.

That all said, let's take a few minutes and look at what I'll call the two principle components to effective scouting.

Now is NOT the time to strike up a conversation about turkeys and permission to turkey hunt. It's just common sense, that's all.

Wildlife conservation officers — Some know them as game wardens. Regardless of the title, these men and women have their collective fingers on the pulse of the local wildlife scene as well as anyone. Many are turkey hunters, so don't be surprised if they're a bit guarded with their information. But, I've never known a wildlife officer who wasn't more than happy to help point someone in the right direction. These folks are excellent sources for items such as public hunting opportunities, special tags or permits, and specific wildlife regulations.

State fish and wildlife biologists — In Ohio and during my formative turkey hunting years, it was Bob Stoll. Washington? Dan Blatt, Sr. Here in Iowa, the man to call is Dale Garner. Maybe in your home state, the title is Upland Game Bird Program Manager. Stoll's business card read something to the effect of Forest Game Research Biologist. Here again, regardless of the title, these wildlife professionals are often a wealth of information on topics ranging from the state of the state's turkey flock to the latest scoop on an area's "sleeper" turkey hotspots. They're not hard to track down; the biologists, that is. All is takes is a telephone call to your state fish and wildlife agency, and the question, "Who's in charge of the turkeys?"

Conservation organizations — Sure, it makes sense to think National Wild Turkey Federation. After all, the topic is the wild turkey. And, yes, the good people at the Federation are always ready and willing to help out a fellow turkey hunter or huntress. What a lot of folks don't realize is that the members of non-turkey conservation organizations such as Whitetails Unlimited, Pheasants Forever, or the Ruffed Grouse Society can all be extremely helpful when it comes to answering turkey-related questions.

District Foresters — Let's face it. These folks spend the better portion of their lives wandering around in the woods. Who better than they to see turkeys? Can't locate your district forester? Many state natural resource agencies will include a division or department of forestry in their network. Not there? Check out the United States Department of Agriculture at ***www.fs.fed.us***.

Landowners — Really couldn't leave them out, now could I? There are few better individuals to speak with regarding the turkey hunting on a particular parcel of ground than the person who owns that ground. Now I'm not saying that in every case the landowner is going to know the whereabouts of each and every longbeard on his place. But there's a good chance that he will have

In many parts of the country, maps are as important a part of hunting success as are turkey calls and shotguns. Just a little bit of public ground here in Washington state? You betcha!

some information which will, in the long run, help make the time that you do have to scout much more efficient.

Farmers — Another tremendous source of information. They're out there with the birds darn near on a daily basis, so it only makes sense that they would know the straight skinny. Too, these hard-working folks can often point you toward a piece of unrelated ground where you might find a bird or two. Like the young corn and bean man we spoke with in the spring of 2001 in Iowa. "I don't mind if you hunt that piece," he said to our request. "But I think you'd be better off up there off of Cherry Grove. That's where I've been seeing the birds all winter." They were still there come mid-April. Just ask Julie. Or how about Jimmy Carlson, one of the hardest-working individuals I've ever had the pleasure of meeting. "I saw about a dozen of 'em up there on the (Can't say…sorry) farm last night," said Carlson during one of our impromptu meetings/scouting sessions. "And a couple of 'em were those big, fat, puffy ones." Puffy ones? Well, let me just say that one of those "big, fat, puffy ones" weighed exactly 28.3 pounds, and came through the three-strand barbed-wire fence right where Carlson said he would. Success through scouting? You betcha.

Other hunters — Last, but certainly not least, there are other hunters. Here, I like to tell the story of my first Washington state elk scouting trip. It was October 1993, and Julie and I were up along the Little White Salmon River in Klickitat County. We'd met a nice young man, a river raft guide as it turned out, who in what little spare time he had absolutely loved to hunt elk. Learning this, I was quick to ask what I thought was a perfectly normal question. Normal, that is, for a boy from Ohio. "Where are the elk around here?" I said. Shocked, Julie grew silent, a look of combined amazement and horror on her face. Unfazed, the young man smiled. Then, slowly, he pointed at 400,000 acres of national forest and said matter-of-factly, "Up there." I was learning. "You ever see any turkeys while you're up there," I volleyed back. "Turkeys? Yeah. You have a map?" Did I have a map? Duh. My point is this. Turkey hunters, understandably, will be a bit reluctant to give out much in the way of specific where-to-go information. After all, the chances are good that they worked hard for that information, and they figure that you should work hard, too. But there are other hunters out there — elk hunters, deer hunters, grouse hunters, and the like — who may have the turkey details you seek, and may themselves not be interested in turkeys and turkey hunting. Such was the case with our tight-lipped elk hunter. He lost his tongue on the subject of bulls, but was more than obliging on the topic of beards.

Now for the paper part. Like the "people" aspect of turkey scouting, this element that I'll refer to as "paper" is almost without limits. At no time has this statement been any truer than the present, thanks in large part to a combination of technological advancements and the Internet. But what are these so-called paper products that can be of assistance to the turkey scouter? My list would include:

Maps — The trick with using maps as a scouting tool is to get the most detailed, the most recent, and the most specific maps available. For the past several years, I've been using a set of maps produced by the Delorme Mapping Company (***www.delorme.com***) of Yarmouth, Maine. Known as the Atlas & Gazetteer Series, these incredible collections of topographic maps are available for each of the 50 states, and put the whole of your hunting area right at your fingertips. Most of the gazetteers include a section which lists that particular state's public hunting properties, along with a chart detailing the types of game species found there. Telephone numbers, GPS coordinates, camping facilities — it's all there, and all in one easy-to-use format. Is this an important part of scouting success? Well, my Washington Atlas & Gazetteer, which includes five years of turkey scouting, hunting, and sighting information marked and highlighted, was deemed significant enough by the members of our NWTF chapter that as I was leaving the state in 1997, they asked if they could auction it off at the next fund-raising banquet. Let's just say I still have it.

Mapping software — Don't care for big, bulky maps? Fortunately, many of the same folks currently manufacturing high-definition paper maps also market electronic versions, which can be used on any personal computer. At present, we're using Delorme's TopoUSA 3.0 software, a six-CD set covering all 50 states and broken into half a dozen different regions including the Pacific West, Great Lakes/Plains, East, Southeast, Southwest, and the Mountain States. Personally, I find the CDs practically as easy to use as the traditional paper versions. The software is nice in that I'm able to use the CDs with a laptop, even out in the field. GPS user? Simply install the software with the hand-held option, and you're interfacing in no time.

Aerial photography — With recent advancements in topographic mapping and related software, the need for aerial photography as it pertains to scouting has diminished somewhat. It has not gone away. Off-the-ground photos of any hunting area can prove themselves indispensable when it comes to locating potential; however, such images can be costly and in some cases may not be as up-to-date as you might wish.

Turkey-specific publications — These useful tools run the gamut from state fish and wildlife agency brochures and pamphlets to magazine articles printed in such popular periodicals as *Turkey & Turkey Hunting, Fur-Fish-Game,* and the National Wild Turkey Federation's *Turkey Call Magazine.* Typically, publications and periodicals provide good jumping-off points. They'll put you in the ballpark. From there, you'll need to resort to a combination of maps and perhaps people contacts in order to narrow the choices down.

Global Positioning Systems, or GPS, can prove helpful when it comes to relocating pre-souted areas such as roosts or strut zones. Too, they can really come in handy when it's time to find the truck!

The Internet — Okay, so maybe if you're the owner of a dot-com business, the Internet is bad. But for turkey hunters looking for information, the Internet is a good thing. It is a very good thing. Here, web surfers can find everything from the NWTF on-line to current turkey regulations and everything in-between. With little more than the click of a mouse, you can apply for or purchase non-resident turkey tags, receive harvest statistics for the past 10 seasons, or download printable maps of selected public hunting areas or state or national forest lands. And then there are the chat forums. Ah, the forums. The truth is, some of these electronic meeting places can be quite useful as data collection sites. There is an art to sifting through the chaff — sounds a lot like crap, doesn't it? — in order to get to the wheat. It's there. You just have to dig a little.

And finally, learn to use those things on the sides of your head. Here's an example. In the winter of 1993, Julie and I were taking a photography course together at Clark College in southwestern Washington. On the final day of the course, the instructor allowed us a sort of show-and-tell period — a "here's what I've learned over the past eight weeks" kind of thing. Julie opted for a brief slide presen-

For many turkey hunters, scouting is a never-ending process. Here, I spend some time with hunting partner, Dave Fountain, as we do a little informal reconnaissance on a recently-acquired parcel of turkey ground.

tation. As she went through her show, she paused on a photograph of several live Eastern wild turkeys, including one full-strut longbeard, which she had shot not far from our home in northern Clark County. "What are those?" said a young lady seated in front of me. "Those are wild turkeys," said the older gentleman in the next seat over. "I've got those all over my place in Klickitat County." Before my wife was finished with her piece, I had introduced myself to this gentleman, and was receiving written instructions on how to get to his place along the Columbia River. Over the next four years, Julie and I would tag six beautiful Merriams gobblers while hunting his ground. Julie's first turkey, a five-bearded tom, was among them. What's the moral of my story? Mouth shut, ears open, and listen, listen, listen.

Physical Scouting: Legs And Lungs

Now, reality sets in. Yes, people and paper products can certainly be helpful scouting tools, but there's no getting around the need to actually strap on those hunting boots, grab a pair of binoculars, and hit the trail. Think of it as having the chance to put all that information you've collected by talking to different folks, poring over maps, and surfing the Net to work for you. I also like to explain to those attending my seminars that scouting is more, much more, than simply going out and looking for the

birds. It's not only the turkeys you're scouting, but more importantly, it's the topography of the hunting area. What I mean here is simple: The better you know the lay of the land you're hunting, the more likely you are to do the "right" thing in the "right" way when the longbeard finally does gobble from two ridges away. How are you going to get to him without being seen? Is there a fence between you and him? A creek? In-the-field scouting gives you the chance to see and know these things far in advance of the season. Want another example? Every time he gobbles and you have to move from your present location, it's a guess as to what to do. Scouting makes that an educated guess.

But what exactly should you be looking for as you go about this field research? Well, let's look at these various scouting clues, all of which could be rather accurately placed under a heading known simply as "sign."

The Significance Of Sign

Before I get started, let me ask a question. Have you ever hunted with a guy like this?

"Yep. He's a big one," he'll say, all the while poking a short stick at the deer track in the dirt in front of him. "I'd say 175 to 200 pounds. That's live weight, of course. Eight-pointer, I reckon. Three, maybe four days ago. Been eating well. Just look how the tips of these toes are sunk

Turkey tracks like those being studied here are just one clue among many, saying simply – the birds were here at one time. The question is – where are they now?

A dusting area. In many cases, dusting areas such as this one will be visited on a regular basis, and a blind situated nearby can at times be very effective.

into the ground. A 150-class buck, if he's an inch. Slightly jaundiced left eye. Oh, and…"

You know him? We all do. The thing he doesn't realize is that unless that deer, be it buck or doe, was actually standing in those tracks he was analyzing, the only information our hunter's going to know for sure is that at some time in the past, a deer walked through that little patch of bare ground. My point is this. Tracks are just one indicator that game, in our case turkeys, are in the general vicinity. Feathers are the same. So are droppings. But when we look at all these things collectively, we're able to start putting the pieces together until finally the picture that is the puzzle becomes clear. What follows, then, are several pieces of this puzzle.

Food and water sources — Food, water, and shelter. Just as is the case with humans, turkeys share these same three basic requirements for survival. Of these three, water is the most significant to the scouting process. Why? Turkeys can fast, if necessary. And with few exceptions, adequate though hopefully short-term roosting areas can be found just about anywhere along the birds' daily path. But water is something turkeys need every day. Essentially, if you find the water, you're well on your way to finding the turkeys. True, in some places, water isn't a concern; still, in places such as the arid West or Southwest, water sources, prove an excellent starting point.

Tracks, feathers, droppings, and the like — All of these physical signs can prove helpful, not only in determining that turkeys are present, but can provide clues as to the numbers of birds in a given area as well as the sex of those birds.

a. **Tracks** — The rule of thumb reads that if the middle toe of a turkey track measures less than 4 inches, it's a hen; more than 4 inches, it's a gobbler. Remember, though, these are merely guidelines.

b. **Feathers** — Turkeys are constantly losing and replacing feathers, and turkey hunters are constantly picking these things up. But what do these feathers tell us? Well, black-tipped breast or body feathers point to a gobbler, while light-colored tips mean a hen. Lengthy primary or wing feathers, some measuring up to 18 inches long, can also help identify a bird as a gobbler.

c. **Dusting areas** — Because feathers are often lost at random, finding a reliable field source of them can be difficult. Fortunately, turkeys make locating these clues a bit easier, thanks to the birds' habit of dusting. Dusting areas, or bowls as they're often called, are nothing more than shallow depressions made as the birds thrash and

When a gobbler struts, he drags the tips of his primary feathers on the ground. Under ideal conditions, such "strut marks" show up quite clearly. Yet, they only indicate that a gobbler was here – once. More information is necessary.

A turkey hunting generalization. Droppings in the shape of the letter "J," like this one, were left by a gobbler.

wallow about in a patch of bare dirt or sandy soil. Basically, it's the turkey's way of taking a bath. Feathers are often dislodged as the birds dust.

d. Strut marks — Take two small garden-style hand rakes and duct tape them 30 inches apart on a yardstick. Now drag the rakes along the ground for, oh, about eight to 10 inches. A couple feet away, do it again; however, this time, pivot the stick a few degrees off straight — right or left, it doesn't matter — as you drag it. There. You've just made a reasonable facsimile of strut marks. Gobblers make these interesting marks by dragging their three outer-most primary feathers on the ground as they strut. Sometimes they strut while walking straight; other times, they turn and spin, thus creating the curved marks. Understandably, these marks are best seen on old logging roads, sand patches, or even snow.

e. Droppings — Here is another rule of thumb concerning physical evidence. If the dropping is straight or J-shaped, it's a gobbler; if it looks like a soft-serve ice cream cone — sorry, folks — or simply appears as a blob, it's a hen. That's generally speaking, mind you. As former turkey owners, we've seen gobblers pass blobs and hens have arrow-straight movements. And both sexes will on occasion leave shapeless black masses resembling tar or roofing cement. What you do know without question upon finding turkey droppings is that at one point in the past, there were turkeys in the area. Chances are, they're still in the area — somewhere.

Roosts — One of the questions we hear most of all concerns roosts and roosting areas. "Will the birds use the same roost night after night, or will they just use anything that's handy?" It's a good question, and certainly one that the person scouting should keep in mind. But I must answer in general terms. It's been my experience that the Western subspecies — the Merriams and Rio Grande — are very likely to roost in the same area, often the same tree, night after night. Some folks believe this is because of a lack of suitable roosting areas. Others, myself included, think that it might have to do with that particular roost's proximity to a physical requirement, water being the most frequent candidate. Easterns, on the other hand, will often have several favored roosting areas scattered throughout their square-mile or 2-square-mile daily home range. Where they are in that range come fly-up time is where they're going to roost. The exception to this, and one which I've seen frequently in Iowa, can be seen in some of the smaller woodlots, where, like in the West, suitable or

Conversely, twisted or curly droppings are, generally speaking, signs left by hens; however, I've watched gobblers leave curls and hens produce "Js." Both sexes, too, will leave shapeless black masses which resemble tar.

Bob Grewell photo.

There he is! Better yet, you have permission to hunt that very piece of ground. Scouting done? Not by a long shot.

favored roosting areas are at a premium. Here, even Easterns can be found roosted in the same big red oak on a nightly basis. But how does all this information affect the turkey hunter? Well, finding a roost or roosting area is a good thing. Disturbing that roosting area, perhaps by getting too close or visiting just out of curiosity or excitement, can be a bad thing. Instead, tuck this information away. Better yet, use it in conjunction with #4.

Strut zones — Think of strut zones as the disco dance floors of the turkey world. Gobblers head to these areas like kids to the Good Humor truck. All strut zones are different, but they do share one characteristic. They're typically in a relatively open area where the hens can actually see him strut and prance. Strut zones do come in various sizes and in a variety of topographical locations. I've seen zones as large as a football field and as small as a countertop. I've also found them on logging roads and in hidden meadows

Sounds — Here you get right back into using those things on the sides of your head. Listening to birds, whether it be right off the roost first thing in the morning, the almost constant babble the birds make as they travel and feed, or as they prepare to fly up in the evening, is not only an excellent method of obtaining valuable scouting information, but also

provides one of the world's finest instructional calling sequences available. Listen, and learn. But what if the birds aren't making any noise? Is it all right then to pull out your turkey calls and start trying to instigate something? Well, sure it is, but only if you're scouting your best friend's favorite turkey hunting ground. If that's the case, then by all means, play away! Seriously, though, turkey calls really have no place in pre-season turkey scouting. I mean, why start the game if you're really not prepared to play? Locator calls? That's a little bit different, as you're really not trying to attract attention but rather elicit a reaction. You'll still want to go "light," even with the locator call. Again, there's really no sense in causing that gobbler to think there's anything out of the ordinary until opening day.

And finally, there are the birds. This part is actually quite simple. When you see them, watch them. If you're patient — and we all know how difficult that can be — there's a good chance that the birds will reveal everything you need to know. They will give away things like where they roost, where they go in the morning, and how they get there. They'll show you where they water, where they feed, and where the boys like to hang out in hopes of meeting the girls. The trick here is to practice this type of avian voyeurism *without* getting caught. And

81

Mark Drury of MAD Calls claims that effective scouting contributes 90 percent or more to the overall success of any turkey hunting venture.

Wise, old gobblers, like this longbeard waiting to wear Drury's tag, don't come as a result of luck, but rather a combination of in-depth scouting, patience, and persistence.

that's just one of the many things we're going to look at a little more in-depth in your next course. Class dismissed.

Turkey Scouting 201

Most turkey hunters, even the inexperienced, are familiar at least to some degree with those aforementioned elements that constitute scouting. Things such as turkey tracks, feathers, dust bowls, droppings, and actual visual encounters with the birds are oftentimes too obvious to miss. They're also aware of the benefits that can come from scouting, the most positive being a notched turkey tag carried not in a wallet or shirt pocket, but around the leg and just above the hooked spur of a 23-pound gobbler.

But what many hunters don't realize is that there is a second course in successful turkey scouting, a program that for simplicity's sake we will call Turkey Scouting 201. This program takes what turkey hunters have learned or experienced, or both, in the introductory course and builds upon it in much the same way a carpenter builds a mansion on a foundation of concrete. Here, the concrete lends all the support and basic strength for the structure, while the house, from rough beginnings, is transformed into something more substantial. Simply put, Scouting 201 is a way by which hunters can add firepower to their turkey hunting arsenal.

For many, the man behind this arsenal, figuratively speaking, is Mark Drury. Currently the general manager of MAD Calls, a subsidiary of Outland Sports, Drury lives with his wife and young daughter in the turkey-rich hills near Columbia, Missouri. Now 33, Drury began turkey hunting in the early 1980s while still a sophomore in high school.

"I started turkey calling in order to become a more proficient turkey hunter. I felt that if I called better, I'd have a better chance of killing one," said Drury.

And call he did. Since entering his first calling competition in 1984, Drury has amassed six world calling titles, three of which were won in the natural voice calling category. Drury's list of accomplishments also includes a world title in the two-man team calling championship, the King of Calls, and the World Championship in 1992.

Recognized more today for its fine line of turkey calls and hunting products, the company known as MAD Calls originally started as an outdoor video venture.

"People kept asking why we didn't make our own brand of turkey calls, so I started that (MAD Calls) in 1993. And we've had a great deal of success since then, both with the videos and with the call company," said Drury.

In 1997, his company joined forces with Outland Sports, whose holdings also include Lohman Calls, Feather Flex, Blue Ridge, API Treestands, and others.

And now, having met the professor, it's time to open those spiral-bound notebooks. Class is in session.

Don't leave home without 'em, says Drury. Binoculars, that is.

Me: What are the most common mistakes turkey hunters make when it comes to scouting?

Drury: Number one would have to be doing too little scouting, and not spending enough time out there. The second mistake would be not scouting effectively. I think that a lot of guys like to go out and rather than paying attention to what the birds are doing, they like to go out and call one in. They want to see that turkey and get the "pump" before the season. I think that's a big mistake — to try to call before the season at all.

Me: Like with whitetails and the scent/disturbance factor inherent to scouting, is it possible to scout too much for turkeys?

Drury: I don't think it's possible to scout too much, if you do it wisely and effectively. So long as you're not bumping them off the roost or bumping them out of their strut zones. You really need to sneak around and make sure you're unseen. Obviously a turkey's not going to smell you and smell where you've been, and if you're quiet, he won't hear you, but if he sees you, that's how you're going to screw up an area.

Me: When do you personally start your most intensive scouting?

Drury: As soon as they start gobbling. That's also when these birds begin their initial (flock) split-up. I like to know where the birds are when they're in their full flocks. And then when they split up, I like to know where those 2-year-olds get pushed off to because those are the birds that I like to key in on personally.

Me: Maps. Obvious, but often overlooked. How important are maps in pre-season scouting?

Drury: I think maps are important just so you can remember what you've learned. I like to overlay aerial maps with a transparency, or just laminate the aerials themselves. Then you can mark on them where birds are roosting or where the strutting areas are. You can also make different marks on there for where you've found dust bowls or the highest concentration of tracks or where your food sources are. This way you don't forget what you've already learned. And I do use aerials, not topographic maps.

Me: Will you scout a piece of public ground differently than you will a private piece?

Drury: I probably hunt more public ground each spring than I do private. And yes I do scout them (public areas) different because I'm trying to find areas that I think are least likely to be hit by hunters. So I'm trying to find, using aerials, those places that are the farthest away from any

Awesome!

access points or roads, and that's where I'll concentrate my scouting.

Me: We're taught not to use turkey calls prior to the season. Is there a time when it's wise to use a turkey call when scouting?

Drury: Personally, I don't use turkey calls at all (when scouting). If I do call, I'll use a locator call like a coyote howl, an owl hooter, or a crow call.

Me: In your opinion, what's the single most important piece of equipment when it comes to scouting successfully and effectively?

Drury: A good locator call, a good set of shoes, and a good set of binoculars. And by shoes, I mean a good hiking boot that will allow you to cover a lot of ground. I always carry a pair of binoculars with me because I'd rather observe the birds from a distance as opposed to at close range. I'd rather see where they're at from a quarter-mile as opposed to 40 or 50 yards. I don't want to be anywhere close to those turkeys because I'm afraid I'm going to bump them. So I listen from a distance and I look from a distance.

Me: A lot of hunters think that once the season starts, scouting's over and done with. Is this the case?

Drury: I don't think so. I think you're constantly scouting and learning how to become a better hunter. And that all falls into scouting. What you've learned while hunting one day is oftentimes what helps you kill that bird the next.

8

Turkey Calls And Calling: The Heart Of The Matter

I almost hate to use the cliché, but it certainly is appropriate when it comes to learning the nuances of turkey calling – Practice makes perfect. Or at the very least, it makes you better.

Now here's the part where this whole thing starts to get interesting — turkey calls. I kind of look at it this way. If all you do to improve your turkey hunting skills is learn to call turkeys, it's like paying to see the entire ball game, but showing up only to watch the bottom of the ninth. Hell, you've missed everything. The opening pitch. The bench-clearing brawl. The seventh-inning stretch. Well my gosh, you've missed the beer man, the peanut guy, the brat dude, *and* the nacho cart. Make that two nacho carts.

Yes, turkey calling is an important part — note that word "part" — of turkey hunting. And no, I certainly don't want to downplay the role of turkey calling for the part it plays in the success, or the failure, of any turkey hunt. But my goals in this particular chapter are three:

Photo courtesy of Outland Sports

One of the country's most respected and knowledgeable authorities on the art of turkey hunting, Lohman Game Calls', Brad Harris, has dedicated a major portion of his life to learning to "talk with the animals."

1. To emphasize what David Hale says, and that is that turkey calling is but five to 10 percent of turkey hunting.

2. To debunk some of the myths and misconceptions surrounding turkey calls and calling by taking the mystery out of these often mysterious and quite frequently frustrating "implements of destruction." (NOTE — My sincere apologies to Mr. Arlo Guthrie and his legendary tune, *Alice's Restaurant*.)

3. To demonstrate that anyone capable of using a pencil, making a whistle using only a blade of grass pinched between his thumbs, or rubbing two sticks together CAN operate a turkey call.

To follow up on the last point first, anyone can operate, or "run," a turkey call. The difference rests in the varying degrees of ability and, of course, desire. Simply put, if you want to become a better turkey caller, you can become a better turkey caller. It's that easy.

For a lot of folks, it's easiest to think of turkey calls as musical instruments. And essentially, that's exactly what they are. They are things to be practiced and played and played and practiced. Granted, some players are better than others. Some players, and I honestly believe in this theory, are just naturals. These are the people who can play the notes or throw the ball or paint the picture the very first time just as though they'd been doing it all their lives. But even with this so-called natural talent, these folks still must practice before they can actually create music. Or turn a double play. Or create a beautiful painting.

Let's jump right into the various types of turkey calls that are available to today's turkey hunter. Before you begin, toss intimidation and ego out the window, and invite self-confidence in the door. When it comes to turkey calling, you write your own report card. Certainly you can and should ask for assistance in the form of constructive criticism. But it's not perfection to the human ear that you hope to achieve, rather consistency in the field. Turkeys are not perfect. Just remember that.

Subject: Locator calls
Speaker: Brad Harris
Hometown: Neosho, Missouri
Occupation: Vice-president of public relations for Outland Sports; turkey hunter
Interests: Hunting, game calling, and spoiling his grandson
Titles: 2001 NRA Great American Game Call Challenge; many, many others
Key word: Versatility

Before we get started with Mr. Harris, let's take a real quick look at just what locator calls are and why a turkey hunter might use them. To begin, think about two things. First, consider the phrase, "locator call." In the Latin, if there were such a thing, I'd assume that the phrase meant simply a call used to locate something. In our case, that something is — no surprise — a turkey. A close second is the fact that as a good friend of mine, Jim Schoby, used to say, "The game doesn't begin until he gobbles." True, sometimes he gobbles on his own with no instigation whatsoever. That's a good thing. But, quite often, he *doesn't* gobble on his own, and we must take it upon ourselves to yank a gobble out of an otherwise silent turkey. Enter, the locator call.

In their most elemental form, locator calls are those calls that imitate a natural sound the turkeys have heard in the past, and to which they will respond with what's known in the turkey hunter's dictionary as a shock gobble. A shock gobble is easy to define if you think of it this way. You get up in the middle of the night to answer the call of nature. It's dark, and you're stumbling your way down the hallway. Unbeknownst to you, your 4-year-old son left his all-metal TONKA front-end loader parked in the middle of the hallway. There in the dark, big toe meets TONKA truck, and before you know it, you're doing a pretty reasonable rendition of Lord of the Dance while

Bob Grewell photo.

Just a few of the many, many locator calls available to today's turkey hunter. Clockwise from upper left – MAD Calls' cherry coyote howler, the Palmer Hoot Tube from Hunter's Specialties, and Lohman Game Calls' Gold Series crow call.

What comes when called? It only makes sense, seeing as you just howled like a coyote moments earlier.

coughing up a series of muffled obscenities. Those exclamations? Those are shock gobbles. They came out before you even realized what it was you were doing, and all as a reaction to something abrupt and very unexpected. That gobbler, already high-strung due simply to the season, hearing a loud explosion of sound, reacts with the avian version of your profanity.

As many turkey hunters already know, the list of sounds capable of tearing a gobble from an otherwise quiet longbeard is quite lengthy. Ideally, the sound chosen is as mentioned earlier, a natural sound. It is one that in no way tells that gobbler — "Hey. There's something odd going on around here. Since when does the Ice Cream Truck swing 'round this ridge?" A crow call is a good one, and probably one of the most commonly heard locator sounds today. So, too, is the pleading cry of the barred owl. Or a coyote howl. A goose honk. Duck quack. Elk bugle. Well, you get the picture.

Still, there are those who believe that that best locator calls include things such as truck doors slamming or car horns honking. When I first moved to Washington in 1993 and began presenting turkey hunting seminars to a then greatly inexperienced turkey hunting population, I can't tell you how many times I heard the — "Oh, just slam the truck door. Works every time." Finally, I got to thinking that maybe these Western folks had something. After all, my crow call didn't work every time, and that old

Midwestern standby, the barred owl, failed miserably in the Pacific Northwest. After a year, though, I came to the conclusion that perhaps my more traditional methods made just a bit more sense. A truck door, it seems, gets awful heavy awful quick, especially when you're trying to pack it up and down some of those Washington hills. And besides, it's a son of a gun to get in your turkey vest.

So here's what Harris has to say about locator calls.

Me: Simple question, Brad. What's your favorite locator call?

Harris: No doubt about it, the coyote howler is my favorite evening roosting call. It's also one of my all-round favorite locator calls to use throughout the day, just because of the sheer volume and range you have with it. Especially if I'm hunting real big territory like mountainous country or wide-open prairies. You need every bit of that range and volume. There are a lot of situations where it's just my favorite locator call.

Me: But aren't coyotes a natural predator of wild turkeys? Won't a coyote howling cause the birds to clam up?

Harris: I assume that it could do some harm. And it might make a gobbler a little bit cautious if you were to howl at him from too close before he flies down. *But,* I've done

Tag-team locating can be very effective as one member calls and the other listens. Here, I attempt to strike a southern Iowa gobbler while my able assistant, my Pop, lends an ear.

Surprisingly enough, owl hooters aren't just for daybreak anymore, but, as Harris claims, can yank a gobble out of a longbeard at any time of day.

quite a bit of testing with wild turkeys, and I've intentionally blown the coyote howler at gobblers that I've called in to 40 and 50 yards, and I've never had a turkey just duck and run. I've had 'em stop, pick their head up, and look. They'll pay attention, but in no time, they're back to doing whatever they were doing. If these turkeys ran for their lives every time they saw or heard a coyote, they'd be running constantly.

Me: What's the number one mistake you see folks make with locator calls?

Harris: Certainly, volume. Sometimes folks either immediately blow way too loud and drown out everything around them. Or they don't practice enough to where they can control the call. In other words, they can't reach the optimum volume of that call and have it perform for them as a long-range locator. Second, a lot of folks will blow a series too long. Maybe a turkey will respond on the first note you make, but if you're blowing a long sequence on a hooter or a coyote howler or a crow call, you may miss that gobble. I like to hit 'em a short burst first and try to get that quick response from that gobbler. And if that doesn't work, then I go into some more aggressive calling.

Me: If you're locating with a partner, how do you do it?

Harris: Put a little distance, say 20 yards or so, between

you and the caller, and you should hear more turkeys than the guy doing the calling. Under windy conditions, I like to put a caller/listener well downwind of me. A lot of times, I'll call and the guy listening downwind will pick up gobblers that I'll never hear.

Me: Is it all right to mix and match your locator calls in the same sequence? Won't this just confuse or alarm a bird?

Harris: I think it's a good thing. It's like turkey calls. I'm constantly switching calls because turkeys are, well, they're just turkeys. There are certain things that will trip their trigger. Sometimes it's that basic call that you're using. Maybe a box call or an owl hooter. And that's great, but there are some days when they just won't respond to that. To me, it's like running your fingernails down a chalkboard. That sound just infuriates some people, whereas with other people it doesn't bother them at all. So that's what you're trying to do with that turkey. You're looking for that chalkboard effect. And that very well may be an elk bugle in Missouri where there's no elk. It doesn't mean that they won't respond to it. Different sounds will trip different turkey's triggers. You have to be versatile.

Me: Isn't an owl hooter a early morning or late evening kind of thing?

TIP – Late-season greenery has a way of soaking up sounds, including locator calls. A good word is to lessen the distance between call stands. Say from every 100 yards to every 50.

President of New York's Quaker Boy Game Calls, Chris Kirby, pictured here with a Texas Rio, is one of the most well-versed turkey hunters in the business today.

Harris: I use an owl hooter all day long. There's a big misconception that the owl hooter is an early morning and late evening locator. And there are a lot of days when I'll make turkeys gobble in the middle of the day strictly with an owl hooter when they wouldn't respond to a crow or a hawk or a peacock or any of the other traditional calls. I'm constantly using a variety of sounds throughout the course of the day because you never know what is going to make that turkey gobble. So if you stop using certain turkey calls, you're missing a lot of opportunities throughout the day.

Me: Can there be any such thing as too much crow calling? Won't the birds simply stop answering?

Harris: I think that's possible with any call. You just get immune to it. It's like people living next to a railroad crossing. Twenty times a day, the train comes through and hits the whistle. Well, the people living there hear that and don't even notice it. But when you go to visit, it just drives you crazy. So, yes, just like that, turkeys can get tuned into certain sounds that eventually they'll just write 'em off. That's why you're using a variety of (locator) calls to try to find something that he isn't accustomed to.

Just as an aside before we get into the topic of those implements designed to create turkey sounds. Surprisingly enough, I cannot tell you how to operate a turkey call. Oh, let me take that back. Given enough space, say, an additional 60,000 words, I might be able to get you started on the path to turkey calling success. But, for now, let it suffice to say that it would be extremely difficult for me to *tell* you how to run a turkey call. Now I, as well as countless thousands of callers across the country, can *show* you how to run a turkey call in just a couple of minutes. Will you be considered "good" after those 120 seconds? Maybe, but I doubt it. What's my point in all this? My point is this: Go on out and buy yourself a turkey call. Better yet, buy yourself a box call. You're going to buy one anyway, so I'm not coercing you into doing anything that you weren't going to do on your own. Okay, so you didn't know you were going to buy a box call at this point in your turkey hunting education. Just trust me. You were. Now, between the instructions that came with the box call and the words that follow, you'll soon find yourself making sounds of some description. There, you're on your way. Just keep reading.

Subject: Box calls
Speaker: Chris Kirby
Hometown: Orchard Park, New York
Occupation: President, Quaker Boy Game Calls
Titles: Four-time U.S. Open; Two-time Masters Invitational; World; Grand National
Key word: Confidence

The box call. Why is it so popular? It sounds like a turkey. It's easy to use. And it works. That's why.

Me: Why a box call, Chris?

Kirby: It's easy to use, number one, and when you have something that's easy to use, the individual that's using it then has a tremendous amount of confidence in it. And the only way you're going to be successful in the field is if you're confident in the sounds that you're producing out of the calls that you've chosen. The evolution of the box call has come a long way. Every turkey hunter has a box call because every turkey hunter learned from someone, usually someone who's older than him or her and has been around a long time, and everyone's grandfather out there started with a box call. They're extremely effective.

Me: There are so many kinds out there. How do I choose one?

Kirby: When you're trying to choose a box call, the first thing that you have to have in your mind is the sound that you're trying to get. Do you want a higher pitched clear sound? Do you want a lower pitched raspy sound? Do you want a loud box call, or do you want a soft box call? Let's look at the Little One-Sider. It's a compact call made out of furniture-grade mahogany. Mahogany is a fairly tight-grained wood, so you're going to get a higher pitch out of the call, first, because the box is so small. And secondly, because the wood is so dense. When you get into, say, a 10-Sider that has poplar on the bottom and cherry on the top, that longer and bigger call is going to deepen

the call a little bit and give you that "older" sound. I'd start with a more traditional box call, and once you have a good feel for how much down pressure you need and how much angle you need to play with, then you might get into the boat paddle-type calls.

Me: When I "test drive" a box call, what am I listening for?

Kirby: Let's talk about consistency for a minute. In my experience, 99.9 percent of the box calls out there are purchased at 3 feet away. It's no different than camouflage. And if I were to say that my camouflage at 3 feet looks really good — well, I'm not really concerned about how my camouflage looks at 2 or 3 feet. I want to know what it looks like at 40, 50, or 60 yards when that turkey first looks at me. That's when the camouflage has to work the best because when he's at 20 yards, he's already in range and the camo has already done its job. With consistency of sound, it's the same principle. I'm not too concerned with how my box call sounds right here, right next to me. It's at 200 or 300 yards where that turkey might first hear that sound is where I need it to be good.

Me: Is it a good idea to take an experienced caller with you when you go out to purchase a box call?

Kirby: Absolutely, but you've got to like it before your buddy does. Even though your buddy tells you it sounds great, if you're not totally confident with it, chances are you're going to be a little apprehensive before pulling it out when you've got that turkey gobbling in front of you. Hunting is such a personal sport. You have to have confidence in everything you're doing from the boots you're wearing to the camo you're wearing to the gun you're shooting to the call you're using. It's got to be something that *you* like and *you* have confidence in.

Me: Advantages and disadvantages to a box call?

Kirby: Biggest disadvantage to a box call is movement. I've had people tell me that they were running their box call and the turkey turned and ran the other way because he saw their (light-colored) box call. Well, if you're running a box call, there's movement involved. That turkey isn't seeing the box call, he's seeing you move the call. The biggest advantage is that you can go really loud with them, and you can tone them down. You also get a consistent yelp every time you open and close that box call. The ease of use is probably the biggest advantage.

Me: What about practice?

Kirby: A lot of time in my seminars I'll ask, "How many people here practice their calling?" And some of them raise their hands. And then I'll ask, "How many people practice their calls enough that they'd like to stand up here and run their calls in front of everyone?" And everyone's hand goes down. It's a first impression. A lot of people practice with the TV on and they think, "Ah, yeah. That sounds fine." But they don't really listen and they don't really practice. Although making a sound on a box call is very easy, making the *right* sound at the right time is the trick. And if you don't practice making those right sounds, it's not going to work for you.

Me: Should someone attempt to tune his or her box call, or is this destined to be a "do over/buy over" kind of deal?

Kirby: You certainly don't have to be Tim "The Toolman" Taylor to fix a box call. First, understand that chalk IS NOT the ultimate fix to a box call. It does help in the end. What happens with a box call is this: You're relying on the grain of the wood to create the friction that will then create the proper sounds. Over time as you use that call, the grain of that wood lays over flat and things begin to slide. You lose your friction. All you need to do is take a little 100-grit sandpaper. You don't need a belt sander. And you don't need to reshape the call. All you're trying to do is to open the grain of the wood back up. Clean it up. Get the dust off of there. Get the oils off of there. That's on the lid (NOTE — The top part). The rails (NOTE — The sides) are the same, but because the rails are so thin, you don't want to use sandpaper. You want to use a piece of Scotch-Brite scrubbing pad.

Is the fact that your hands are "tied up" with a box call a legitimate complaint? It's all in knowing when to trade the call for that piece of wood and steel in your hands. And that, friends, comes with experience.

If I can interrupt here, I'll say a couple things about chalk and box calls. As Kirby mentioned, chalk in and of itself is not a cure-all. In fact, I heard Chris say years ago that many of the calls he sees being brought back into the shop or into the local sporting goods store, calls that "don't work right," simply have too much chalk on them.

The type of chalk you use on your box call can and does make a different. Today, most manufacturers market a line of box call chalk. The common denominators here are that the material is of a moderate degree of hardness and, most importantly, contains no oil. And as Kirby just explained and we all know by now, it's oil that defeats the way a friction call works.

But back to chalk. Manufacturer-supplied chalk will work, as will the carpenter's chalk found in most building supply and hardware stores. Blackboard chalk will work in a pinch, but such material is often too hard to be very effective and can in some cases contain those nasty oils that we're trying to steer clear of. Another very traditional chalking material is fiddle rosin. This stuff is a hard wax-like substance used by fiddlers and violinists to, as Charlie Daniels is fond of saying, "rosin-up their bows." Here, experimentation is certainly not a bad thing. But it might be wise to practice just a bit of moderation when it comes to chalk and box calls.

Here, Julie runs a box call along a Texas creek in hopes of yanking a gobble out of a mid-morning longbeard. Box calls are perfect tools for the "prospecting" hunter.

Me: Does rain or damp weather really spell the end for all box calls and those who might use them?

Kirby: Unless the two friction surfaces, the underside of the lid and the rails, get wet, the box call is still going to work. What if you drop it in the creek? Well, then, it's likely not going to work, and the only choice you have is to dry it out. You can let it air dry, put it in front of a small heater, whatever. But a box call that gets wet is not done. It's not time to throw it out and buy a new one, although as a manufacturer, that would be fine with me.

Me: Push-button yelpers. They're only for new folks, right?

Kirby: There are people out there who say stuff like, "Ah, I don't want to tell 'em I used an Easy Yelper to call him in because that's for a beginner and I'm not a beginner anymore." Well, we're all beginners. The day we stop thinking that we're beginners is the day we stop learning about wildlife and what we can do better in the woods. And that call right there (push-button yelper) has been effective since the day it was made, and I carry one with me every time I'm out there.

Me: What's up with these gobble tubes? I can't say as though I've ever had one work.

Kirby: I'm going to compare it to rattling for deer. How many times, percentage-wise, are you out there rattling and actually going to have a deer come in to the horns? It's a pretty low percentage in most cases. Gobble tubes are no different. There's a situation and an attitude that you have to "feel" coming from that gobbler. There's not a doubt that you can call a bird in with a gobble shaker, but it takes a very aggressive bird to come into a gobble call.

Me: How can I become a better technical caller?

Kirby: First, I think you have to have a sounding board, whether that sounding board is an instructional (calling) video or just a hunting video that has live hens on it. What I mean is that you can sit in your living room and call all you want and sound good to yourself, but you have to have something to compare it to. When you're practicing your hen yelps, dissect those sounds into two distinct parts: the front half and the back half. Think about both the clear part and the raspy part. Experiment with your calls. Use different ways of holding your calls and different pressures. Don't always run a call the same way.

Me: Okay, how about becoming a better, well, field caller?

Kirby: To be a better caller in the field, you have to be a good caller in the living room to begin with. Let's assume you've done that and you're confident with your three different calls. You can cut. You can yelp. And you can cluck and purr. All you need to take into the woods are those three sounds. Pay attention to the area you're hunting. Applying calling to a turkey hunt is actually the last ingredient. If you can't find a turkey, or if you can't read sign, or if you can't read the land, it doesn't matter how good a caller you are, it's not going to work.

Kirby's Final Answer

Apply this principle to your turkey hunting, and it will always, always help: Don't get into a situation where you call to a gobbler and he responds. Get him into a situation where he gobbles and *you* respond. What's going to happen during that conversation is this — you call, he answers. You call, he answers. You call, he doesn't answer. Now you don't know whether he's coming or going. You call a little louder. He doesn't answer. Now you try a different call. And before you know it, you're thinking all these thoughts that you don't need to be thinking. Instead, put that thought process in his mind. Let him gobble. Answer him. Let him gobble. Answer him. Let him gobble once or twice, and don't answer him. Remember, he only has 30 or 40 days in the year to mate. He knows there's a hen over there, but he doesn't know whether she's coming or going. At some point, he's going to have to break and come in.

That's Mr. Kirby's input. Personally, I'm still a big fan of the pot-and-peg style turkey calls. Yeah, I use a variety of diaphragm calls and, from what folks say, sound at least as good as the average bear with those little pieces of tape and metal and rubber. As for a box call, I don't know why but I just don't have the confidence in myself with that particular instrument. It could have something to do with the fact that I don't practice with a box call as much as I should. It could also be the rather common situation where success in the field with something other than a box call has led me to leave that particular call behind.

Still, it's the pot-and-peg calls that always have and continue to attract my attention. Maybe it's a success thing. Or the fact that they are relatively easy to use and become proficient with. Therefore, I seem to practice a bit more with such calls as opposed to other types. As the kids would say — whatever.

For Mark Drury, though, pot-and-peg calls are much, much more than a "whatever." This Missourian has turned the study of wild turkeys and their reactions to a wide range of pot call-produced sounds into a science. It is a revolutionary science dealing with pitch and frequency, wavelengths and distance, and a host of other invisible — or should I say inaudible? — variables known only to the avian ear. But all this note-taking and data collection has not caused Drury, who I'll call Father Frequency, to wander off the path of the traditional turkey hunter, for as he's fond of saying, "You make the right sounds at the right times, and something's going to happen." That's what I like about Mark. He's a black-and-white guy living — and hunting — in a world that's gotten, well, gray.

Subject: Pot-and-peg calls
Speaker: Mark Drury
Hometown: St. Peters, Missouri
Occupation: Manager, MAD Calls and Drury Outdoors
Interests: Hunting, gold, and competitive turkey calling
Titles: Six world titles; over 150 state, regional, and national wins
Key word: Frequency

Me: Pot call? How do I choose from among the dozens there on the wall of my local sporting goods store?

Drury: Versatility is the key. When I go into the field, I carry two or three calls. Today, I'm down to my 4x4 Mag and a separate Aluminator because I want as many sounds in as few calls as possible. You just never know what that turkey is going to want. If I had to give you one call to start with, it would be an aluminum call. They're easy to run, they're super high-pitched, and year in/year out, I get more turkeys to respond to that aluminum call than anything else.

MAD Calls' Mark Drury, a pot-and-peg virtuoso.

Photo courtesy of Mark Drury and MAD Calls

Me: Mark, I'm going to say a call material. That is, the material that the surface of a pot-and-peg style call is fashioned from. And you tell me the first thing that comes to mind. Slate.

Drury: Purrs very well and yelps pretty good. A con might be that it's very difficult to get above 10,000 or 11,000 hertz (international unit of frequency equal to one cycle per second) with it. It's hard to get real high-pitched with a slate call.

Me: Glass.

Drury: It runs well. It's very easy to scratch up and it yelps well. But there again, it's hard to get above 10,000 to 12,000 hertz with glass. A second con might be that glass glazes over very easily. It gets slick, and takes a lot of care and maintenance.

Me: All right. Let me break away for a second. Talk about glass call maintenance?

Drury: You can put it in a case or use a lid on it, but in my opinion, glass calls just don't stay scratched up very well.

Me: Back at it. Aluminum.

Drury: It's easy to use. And it's easy to scratch up and

For soft purrs and sensuous yelps, nothing beats good, old-fashioned slate.

maintains its surface very well. I don't know of a con for aluminum. The only con I might think of is that on cold mornings, the aluminum contracts and it just doesn't run as well. That's the only thing I can think of. And when I'm talking cold, I'm talking below 35 degrees.

Me: Breaking away again. You've taken all this time to camouflage yourself from head to toe, and then you take a piece of shiny aircraft aluminum out into the field. What's with that?

Drury: (Laughs) Turn it upside down. You're not going to be running it when the turkey's in sight anyway. If a guy's not smart enough to hide that aluminum, he doesn't need to be out there with a gun in his hands.

Me: Fair enough. Titanium.

Drury: Titanium doesn't contract in cold weather. Moisture, heat, cold weather. Nothing affects titanium. Other than that, there's no difference between titanium and aluminum. It runs well, it holds its surface extremely well, and it's capable of some really high pitches.

Me: Crystal.

Drury: It's an awesome call. Unlike the glass, crystal will get you 15,000 hertz. It runs well. Turkeys gobble at it readily. If there's a con, it slicks up pretty easily when it's

rolling around in your vest.

Me: Glass. Crystal. Isn't it the same?

Drury: Crystal is glass in its purest form. If you look at crystal on edge, you can see all the way through it. Glass will have a bluish tint. There's a lot of sand and silica and iron and all kinds of elements in glass.

As I did with Kirby, I'm going to interrupt Drury's lesson here to talk for a minute about strikers. A pot call without a striker is like a guitar with no strings. In fact, a pot without a striker — I'm fond of calling them "sticks," just so you'll know — is really nothing more than a neat paperweight. Without a striker, a pot could be used as a $20 coaster on which to set your beer. Strikers are the bat to the ball. The shell to the shotgun. The apple to the pie. It's the thing that makes the call work.

Today, strikers come in a variety of shapes, sizes, and materials. Why? Well, maybe it's easiest if I describe it like this. Have you ever seen someone playing music — I'll call it music for definition's sake — by tapping spoons on water glasses? Each of the glasses is filled with a different amount of water, and each water level produces a different tone. Some are high-pitched; some are low. Others are flat sounding, while still others are clear and crisp. The same principle can be applied to strikers, with maybe a twist. The materials that the strikers are made of correspond to the various water levels in the glasses. A

Pot-and-peg calls are versatile things, performing well under a wide range of climatic and environmental or terrain-related conditions.

heavy or dense material, such as rosewood or purple heart (a type of wood), produces a lower pitch than does a lighter, less dense material such as carbon, graphite, or a wood such as pine.

But why is this important? Perhaps the most notable factor involves versatility. Simply by changing strikers, a caller can make a single pot call sound like several different turkeys — some high, some low, some raspy, and some clear. The various materials are, how should I say, climatically versatile; that is, a wooden striker isn't going to be worth a darn in a downpour, but an acrylic or carbon stick — read: waterproof — will keep on going and going and going. Yes, just like that little drum-playing rabbit. So, all that behind us now, an idea should be forming. The idea that a turkey hunter armed with one pot call and a handful of strikers is not only able to more fluently speak "turkey," but has saved a bunch of money. Let's see; buy a $20 call, or $2 striker?

Me: Give us the bottom line, Mark. Friction calling depends on what?

Drury: Successful friction calling is based on the hands of the user. If the guy's a good friction caller, he can make damn near any pot-and-peg sound good. But when you're dealing with a novice or someone who doesn't toy around with this stuff all year long, you have to get him the best peg you can in combination with the best pot. To be honest with you though, I've seen guys who just cannot run

one. And they're never going to get better at it. I don't know why, but some guys just have trouble running a pot-and-peg. They generally squeeze the life out of it and suck all the sound out. Guys have a tendency to smother the sound simply because of the way these types of calls were traditionally made, that being with the body forming the sound chamber. Today's pot-and-peg calls are designed to be run with as little skin contact as possible. The pots do the work. All you have to do is hold them on your fingertips. And that's why women who generally have a softer touch are quicker to learn it.

I'm going to break in here again with another analogy. Congratulations. You've just purchased a new aluminum pot-and-peg call. But what the hell, it must be broken. You can't get anything out of it but some muffled shufflings and draggings. What gives?

First, it's not broken. There's really nothing to break. But your new call does require a little breaking-in. Think of it like an old vinyl record album. Remember those? Before a record album actually became a playable record, it was nothing more than a round piece of vinyl, flat and smooth as the proverbial baby's butt. The music you hear coming from that album is actually created when the needle of your record player makes contact with the thousands of grooves carved into that once-smooth surface by the manufacturer. In a nutshell, vibration equals music. The same thing happens with a pot-and-peg call. But it's you, not the manufacturer, who puts the grooves into

There it is! That instrument of the Devil. The diaphragm call.

Drury: There's really no wrong way. Scuff the hell out of it. The more you scratch it, the better off you are. Avoid skin contact with the striking surface. You don't want any oil on there. It's a friction call based on friction between the peg and the striking surface, so you really have to decrease the amount of oil that's on that striking surface.

Me: Since the mid-1990s, you've done extensive research on the relationship between call frequency and turkey response. The Dead Silence locator call. The Super Aluminator. The Super Crystal. All 15,000 hertz or higher. What's the bottom line on frequency, Mark?

Drury: Higher pitched sounds travel farther and faster and are more clear when they get to where they're going. Bottom line? If you're higher pitched, you're going to be heard at the greater distance and you're going to be heard more clearly.

Ah, yes. We're finally there. Diaphragm calls. Those instruments of the Devil. Guaranteed to get your gag reflex going and aggravate to violence even the Pope. Ah, diaphragm calls.

Let me say first that I am by no means an expert on diaphragm calls and their use. True, the first gobbler I ever called into gun range, a fine 2-year-old Ohio longbeard that became my father's first wild turkey, was seduced with a double-reed Quaker Boy diaphragm which I, after the fact, had to physically pry from the roof of my mouth. Looking back, I remember it all now. Wow! I sounded bad. Real bad. Still, that bird didn't seem to mind.

Today, if you run into me in the turkey woods, I *will* have a diaphragm call in my mouth. Tucked into the right side of my face between my molars and my cheek, the call will be used from time to time throughout the course of the day, often in conjunction with the ever-present pot call I carry in my vest pocket. Mine is a fairly typical history in regards to the diaphragm call. I tried, I gagged, I spit it out. I was then coerced into trying again. And again I gagged and spat it upon the ground, this time with curses and complaints. But I didn't give up, though there were many times I longed to do just that. Finally I began to make sounds that didn't make my skin crawl. Certainly, I had help. Cassette tapes, videos, and live presentations all helped. One-on-one "lessons" from those well-versed in the ways of the rubber horseshoe helped, too. And over time, I got better. I did not become great. Some would say not even good. I just got better. During that time, I've learned quite a bit about these mysterious pieces of tape and metal. Here's some of what I learned:

surface of the call. And the record player needle? That's your striker.

To prepare your new call or to keep your current pot call in fine working order, it's necessary to scuff it up. Some will call it scratching. Others, roughing it up. Still others refer to it as conditioning the surface. Whatever you call it, it's important. And fortunately, it's very easily done.

Conditioning your pot call requires little more than an abrasive substance of some sort be rubbed over the surface of the call. The softer the call material, the less abrasive the conditioner. For instance, slate, a relatively soft material, is often scuffed with a piece of scouring cloth. Titanium, at the other end of the hardness scale, calls for something a little more aggressive such as 80- or 100-grit sandpaper, or even one of the new conditioning stones available from several of those who manufacture turkey calls. Simply scratch it up, blow off the dust, and you're ready to go. If there is a rule to conditioning a call, it might be this: Scratch from top to bottom. Play from side to side. Essentially, all that means is that some of your best sounds are going to be achieved when you run the striker at a 90-degree angle (perpendicular) to the scratches. I scratch my calls from 3 o'clock to 9 o'clock. I'll then hold the call so I can move the striker from noon to 6 or 1 o'clock to 7, give or take a half hour. The key is to experiment.

Now, back to Mark.

Me: Is there a "wrong" way to scuff up a pot call?

1. Typically if you can make a sound, any kind of sound, with a diaphragm call, you *can* be taught or learn how to use one to call turkeys.

2. The advantages to using a diaphragm call are many. These include —

   a. No hands required. This means you can keep your mitts on your shotgun where they belong.

   b. Rain isn't an issue. Hell, the call should be wet already. If it's not, he's in range.

   c. Diaphragms offer the whole of the turkey's vocabulary, including the gobble.

   d. They're light, easy to carry, and relatively inexpensive.

   e. They have no moving parts.

3. The disadvantages are few. In fact, there's only one. And with apologies to my now-retired English teacher Mother — "They ain't no easy-to-use box call."

4. My theories on diaphragm calls —

   a. It's easy if you think of a diaphragm call just like that blade of grass you pinched between your thumbs and whistled across. Just turn your thumbs sideways and slap 'em up in the roof of your mouth. Put your tongue on the grass and blow. It's that simple.

   b. Always remember that the wild turkey's "yelp," that sound from which all other turkey sounds come, is a two-note call. There's a high first or front-end sound followed by a lower back-end sound. Tongue pressure high gets the high note; tongue pressure low gets the low note.

   c. Start slow. First, practice making the high note, and only the high note. Press your tongue against the rubber and blow from your chest. Then —if you visualize it happening in your head, it's easier — take some, but not all, of the pressure off the rubber with your tongue until the sound changes and gets lower. Phonetically, it should sound something like — KEE (high)…YOKE (low).

   d. Again, start slow. KEE (one, two, three) YOKE….KEE (one, two, three) YOKE. Gradually, then, build up speed until the two notes sound as one. Always, always, always, though, you should hear the two notes.

Hell, there's another one! But just think – there's no moving parts, and only one way it can work. Frustrated? Give one to an 8-year-old. He'll show you how it's done.

   e. Call fit and practice. It's all about call fit and practice.

   f. Unfortunately, some folks simply cannot use a diaphragm call. Usually, this inability stems from physical reasons, such as my wife's very high and very narrow palate, or my father's full upper dentures. Both, however, use box or pot calls, and both regularly kill turkeys. No problem there.

   g. And finally, never ever give a diaphragm call to a kid under 10. In less than 60 seconds, that kid will be light years ahead of what it took you 12 very painful months to achieve. And you're still bad. Oh, there is one exception to the "no-kid" rule. Don't like his folks? Give him two, just in case one rips. They'll love you for it.

Still afraid of diaphragm calls? Well, you shouldn't be. And you won't be, *not* after reading what Ricky Joe Bishop has to say on the subject. Yes, Ricky Joe's won more turkey calling competitions than most of us have hair follicles; still, he had to start somewhere. And today, when he's not hunting spring gobblers, Bishop spends the vast majority of his time teaching people how not to be afraid of this inch-square irritation known simply as the diaphragm call.

A member of the Lohman Gold Staff Team, Georgian Ricky Joe Bishop, here working some diaphragm magic on a Missouri longbeard, is as much turkey call innovator as he is turkey hunter.

Subject: Diaphragm calls
Speaker: Ricky Joe Bishop
Hometown: Warm Springs, Georgia
Titles: Grand National (94-95); US Open (2000); 4-time Georgia State Champ
Hunting experience: 24 years
Key words: Frame fit

Me: First, Ricky Joe, why do folks have so much trouble with diaphragm calls?

Bishop: I think a lot of guys have trouble just tolerating them in their mouths and just getting, well, a normal sound out of them. They just don't take the time to practice with them like they should. To get comfortable with them. You say "diaphragm call," and most guys will say, "I can't use those! I can't use those!" But the main thing is just getting to where you can tolerate 'em in your mouth. My little boy picked it up pretty good to where he can go with it.

Me: That said, what is it about kids and diaphragms?

Bishop: They (adults) may have tried it before and they couldn't do it, so they put it down and went on to something else. Kids just don't take "no" for an answer. They seem to just be able to stick it in their mouth and get a sound out of it.

Me: One reed. Two reeds. Four reeds. Three with a notch. Where's a guy to start?

Bishop: A lot of guys jump into a call that has too many reeds. Too many thick reeds. You want to start out with a thin single-reed or a thin double-reed call. It takes less air to flex that rubber.

Me: Why the different reeds?

Bishop: Basically it's to get different sounds and different tones. A single reed will give you a real clear sound. You go into a double, and it's gonna give you a little rasp. For beginners, I'd suggest sticking with a single or a double. As you graduate from that, go into a triple. What a triple-reed does is it gives you a more raspy sound. You're getting all these crazy cuts now, trying to get a little bit higher pitch or a certain tone because you know that on any certain day, you're never going to know what a turkey's gonna like. Me? I'll just go with a 3½-reed cutter. That's all I carry in my bag, but I've got buddies who'll take 10 different calls with 10 different reed configurations and they'll say, "Well, he wasn't liking this one today, but he sure was liking this one here."

Me: Getting back to choice, Ricky Joe, is there anything else in terms of picking one or two from among the dozens that are out there?

Bishop: Get something that's simple. Maybe get a couple different reed designs and see what you're most comfortable with. And there's something else that's worth mentioning. Everyone's palate (the upper part of your mouth) is a different size. And sometimes you can find calls that are made with different sized frames. There are four or five different sizes. There's a youth, and then small, medium, and large frames. Thing is, most of the calls on the market are a standard small frame but they come with a large piece of tape. And it's hard for some folks, me included, to tolerate that large piece of tape in their mouth. So what I'll do is I'll take a pair of scissors and cut off, say, an eighth of an inch at a time until it fits my palate just the way I like it.

Me: You say that the call has to fit. Is fit really that important?

Bishop: It's kinda weird. When I used to turkey call, I used a medium-sized call and trimmed that tape all the way down. Now there was a section in the roof of my mouth that that thing would pop into. And after a contest, I'd have to reach into my mouth with my finger and actually pop it loose outta there because it would be pressed in there so tight. I've seen some guys who got into calling who at first didn't know there were different sized frames, but once they started getting 'em to fit, it was like night and day with their calling. It (frame fit) does make a lot of difference. It's like buying a pair of shoes. You want something that's gonna fit.

Me: In a nutshell, what's the secret? That first step?

Bishop: Getting that sound is just a matter of getting your tongue positioned right, getting the right pressure (on the reeds), and blowing the right amount of air.

You want to know what the worst part is about talking with these veteran turkey hunters? Well here it is

Lohman Game Calls' new Pump Action Yelper was the brainchild of calling champ, Ricky Joe Bishop, pictured here, and the answer to the prayers of thousands convinced they could never use a diaphragm-type call.

October, and I'm only now figuring out, thanks to folks like Kirby, Drury, Bishop, and Harris, exactly where I made all my mistakes in the field last spring. They just reminded me of all the times I was far too anxious. And when I called too often. And when I moved at the wrong time. And when I was too loud, or too soft, too this and not enough that. But have each of them been there at one time or another? Again, to quote the Minnesotans, "You betcha!" And that's why they're good at what they do.

9

Turkey Tactics

"This calls for a little strag-a-tee."
Bugs Bunny

I just love it when a plan comes together. Truthfully, this gobbler wasn't the one we had set up on originally; still, he was the one that reached our decoys first.

You know, I'm really going out on a limb here — and no roosting-related pun intended, honest — by calling this chapter, Turkey Tactics. To be completely truthful about the whole thing, I should have called it "A handful of things that may or may not at any given time lead to success in the turkey woods." Or maybe "Things I've tried over the past 12 years which haven't been complete failures."

I hate to sound elusive here, but the truth of the matter is this: For every so-called turkey tactic that's been tried, there are a dozen waiting in the wings to be experimented with. Quite fortunately for those who would chase this most noble bird during the spring of the year, there are a handful of tactics — strategies, if you will — that have proven themselves time after time after time. Are they foolproof? Certainly not, particularly when you look at the man in the mirror who, at 3 o'clock in the morning, is once again dressing in odd clothes and going out to, as he says, "do battle" with a bird whose brain is the size of a black walnut. And that's a walnut without the hull.

Here in this chapter, we're going to look at several things ranging from how it should happen to why it often doesn't. Through it all, I'd like you to keep one very important biological fact in mind. Several million years ago, Mother Nature decided that this spring turkey thing was going to work like this: The gobbler would gobble, and the hen would slowly yet purposely wander over to him, calling quietly as she goes. She would then throw herself at his feet, literally, with the result being baby turkeys.

Enter Man. Being the bossy sort that we are, we decided to rewrite all these years of gobbling and wandering to where they now read — I, the hen, will wander and

100

call quietly, and you, the gobbler, will alter all those many years of evolution and come running to me. You see? We haven't attempted to rewrite a book; we've tried to author *the* book. Still, on occasion, we're successful.

Over the years, I've learned a lot of turkey hunting tactics. While I'd love to say that I've retained and actively practice every one of these on a regular spring basis, I'd be lying; however, here's a list — and I'll try to make it as complete as possible — of those things that I've come to know as helpful hints. These include:

1. Turkey hunting is little more than a collection of generalizations. Generally speaking, turkeys won't cross creeks to get to your calling location. Generally speaking, older, mature birds are much more difficult to persuade than are their younger, more eager counterparts. And generally speaking, rain will cause gobblers to become silent as church mice. Generally speaking, there's always that one rebellious fellow that will do everything the book says he shouldn't. The trick is to find him. Or at the very least, anticipate the generalizations, and then be prepared to roll with the many punches these birds are known to throw.

2. From the very instant you first put a striker to slate, you're creating an illusion in that gobbler's small mind. Anything that you can do to round-out that illusion, using a decoy, scratching in the leaves, walking away, or sounding like several different turkeys as opposed to one, the closer you come to recreating or reproducing reality. That's turkey reality, mind you. In other words, the more you think like a turkey, the better prepared you'll be to present a believable illusion. Just say to yourself — "I'm an actor. And the woods, my stage."

3. For you, a turkey hunt is recreation. For the turkey, it's pure, unadulterated survival. That said, it's easy to understand that this "game" is a bit more serious for him than it is for you. That's not to say that you can't take the game a bit more seriously. How? Learn everything you can about your quarry. What he likes. Where he lives. Where he goes. And most importantly, why he does what he does. It's like we tell folks in our seminars; the moment you begin to educate yourself about the wild turkey as a wild creature, you'll also begin to answer each question you'll ever have regarding strategy. Knowledge, it's true, is power.

4. Again, back to the illusion thing. This is the ultimate game of playing hard-to-get. You, the hen, want to appear willing, but not too willing. Go just so far, and then reconsider. Bat your eyes, wink from a distance and then turn your back and go back to talking to

It's all about creating an illusion. A complete illusion, one that will get that gobbler to thinking that it's just another day. Just another girl. Just the way Mother Nature intended it to be.

your friend. Oh, yes, it's difficult not to throw yourself at this feathered version of Mel Gibson or Tom Cruise, but resist. Use the Force. Anything.

5. A lot has been said about set-up. Where to sit. When to sit. All that's fine and in many cases worthwhile, but remember this: Your goal is to make it as easy as possible for that gobbler to get from where he is to where you are. Period. That's it. No creeks. No fences. No brush. Roll out the red carpet and see what happens. Are you going to make mistakes regarding set-up? Sure. Are you going to sit down only to wish 30 seconds later that you'd sat somewhere else? Absolutely. Are these irreversible blunders destined to throw you and your entire bloodline into the realm of being forever without a turkey? Certainly not, but only if you learn — LEARN — from these experiences.

6. And finally, there are the three words — 33 letters and a hyphen — that in and of themselves are the only things you need to know in order to be successful in the turkey woods. Eventually. Maybe not today, but eventually. Those three words? Patience. Persistence. Self-discipline. Practice those, and the rest will come easy.

Roosting 101

In Utopia, all turkey hunts go something like this:

Roosting a bird – that is, enticing a bird to gobble on the roost the evening before a hunt – helps tip the scales in your favor. Ever so slightly, mind you, but in your favor.

The evening before the opener, right about dark, you hoot on your owl hooter. "Who cooks for you? Who cooks for you all?" you ask. About 150 yards away, a gobbler responds. You know about where he is, and how to get there. You then go home, double-check your gear, and get a good night's sleep (yeah…right!).

The next morning, you're in position a good hour before sunrise, and a full 30 minutes before shooting time. Below you and approximately 100 yards away stands the oak where you believe your bird to be roosted. Right at shooting time, and right on cue, the bird gobbles. You wait. He gobbles again. You wait. He gobbles. You call, oh so softly. He double-gobbles. Five minutes and two dozen gobbles later, you hear him fly down. Again you wait. Then, a yelp. He gobbles. He's maybe 75 yards away. You yelp again. His response comes before you're finished. You put the call down and put the gun to your shoulder. At 50 yards, he breaks out of the timber and starts, full-strut, to walk toward your decoy. Forty-five. Forty. Thirty-five. He never notices the "click" of the safety. At 30 yards, you "PUTT" on the diaphragm call you've held in your mouth. His feathers slick down, and his head shoots up. The bead wavers, then stops as you begin to pull the slack out of the trigger. The rest is history.

Does it work like that? Sure it does. Sometimes. But believe me, there's 1,001 things that can happen between the time your lips touch that owl hooter to the moment that safety is pushed off. Brad Harris points out that many

of these things actually begin the night before the hunt, during a phase of the event known simply as roosting.

For those of you out there who aren't familiar with the terminology, the act of roosting a gobbler can be compared to stacking a deck of cards. In other words, you're swinging Fate or Luck, whichever you choose to call it, more into your favor. You're increasing your odds of success, to put it bluntly.

How's it work? Actually, roosting relies on two turkey habits. The first is the birds' natural characteristic for spending the night in trees. And the second has to do with the gobbler's inability to keep his beak shut, particularly during the waning moments of the day when, for whatever reason, he finds it absolutely necessary to tell the world, just one more time, how rough and tough he is. Many hunters believe that these twilight gobbles are the tom's way of gathering up his harem of hens, thus ensuring that daylight will find him surrounded by female company of the most attractive kind. Regardless of the reason and barring any strangeness — winged predators, a raccoon or bobcat, or maybe that proverbial tree that falls in the forest with no one to hear — it's almost certain that that gobbler will be in the same tree, maybe even on the same branch, come morning. Therefore, roosting gives you a place to start in the morning. Is it a guarantee? When it comes to turkeys, there's no such thing.

And now, ladies and gentlemen, Brad Harris.

Me: Simple question, Brad. What are the top two mistakes folks make when they're trying to roost a gobbler the night before a hunt?

Harris: I think that the biggest mistake guys make is getting too close to the roost. Or getting in that bird's line of travel. I mean getting between the bird and his roost in the evening. I think you have to roost with caution. You have to sneak around. I like to get on high points back away from where I think the birds are going to roost. That way, I can hear well but I'm not taking as great a chance at getting caught. You just need to be real careful and cautious in your approach when you're roosting birds at night. And second, you may find you're trying to use your (locator) calls a little too early. You know, before the birds actually fly up. To have your best chance of roosting a bird, you want to make sure you've given them a chance to fly up or at least be relatively sure they're up before you cut loose on your locator call.

Me: You mentioned it when we talked earlier about locating and locator calls, but I'd like to hear it again. Your favorite call to roost?

Harris: I always have an owl hooter, which is a very traditional type of (roosting) call, but I'll always have my coyote howler, too. I have more success with my coyote howler, percentage wise, than any other roosting call. Why? Part of it's the high pitch and high frequency. It's a loud sound, and one that's very natural to the turkeys. It just seems to trigger 'em a little bit different. I don't know what exactly it does to 'em or why they seem to respond more aggressively to it, but they do. They just seem to hit that howler. Plus the howler is two or three times louder than the traditional owl hooter, so you're covering a lot more ground (with the howler) and you're triggering gobblers from farther away.

Me: What about volume? Because what you're looking for is essentially a shock response, so to speak, doesn't it make sense to up the volume?

Harris: Roosting is like any other calling in terms of volume. Generally when I start roosting, I'll start with a yip and a short howl in a moderate volume and see what that triggers. But it's like progressing when you're locating any other time of the day. If that first scenario doesn't work, well then you generally start picking up the volume and length of your routine hoping to trigger a bird. Sometimes they'll gobble at the first sound you make, but sometimes you'll have to get into a whole lot of aggressive yipping and yapping and carrying on like coyotes do as a pack in order to force a gobble out. Yeah, so overall you're generally starting out soft and easy and gradually getting into the louder and more aggressive scenarios.

Me: Time, Brad? Right before dark? At dark? After dark?

Harris: The key to roosting is the fly-up. Being there when they fly up to roost is of utmost importance. So depending on how far you have to go or how much trouble it is getting into an area *and* keep from boogering birds is going to dictate what time you need to be there or what time you need to leave in order to get to that spot. What I like to do is to slip in there (the roosting area) about 30 minutes or so before fly-up. Then I put myself in a position to where I can hear well and I'll actually listen for those turkeys to fly up. Once I think the birds are roosted, then I'll proceed into my locator calls.

Me: Sounds like hearing those wings is as important as hearing the gobble?

Harris: Hearing the fly-up can be as important as the gobble. Many times, especially with older gobblers or gobblers that just aren't fired up, these birds just won't gobble in the evening. A lot of times, they won't gobble during the day either. So hearing 'em fly up can be extremely critical. But you do need pretty ideal conditions for that. You need to be able to hear well. It has to be a relatively calm evening. And you need to be relative-

After finding a bird on the roost at first light, Jason Maddy and my wife, Julie, plot the bird's potential downfall. Key word here? Potential.

ly close to the roost area, so you're going to take a few more chances getting into close proximity to the roost area so you can hear those wings. But on a calm evening, that sound (wingbeats on fly-up) carries a long way. You can hear 'em breaking branches and things like that, so, yes, those sounds are very important and you want to listen for these things. A lot of people don't do that. We all seem to listen for the gobble, but there are other sounds there that can certainly help you pinpoint your turkey.

Me: To roost, or not to roost. Is there a time when it might be better to leave the birds be in the evening? Weather maybe?

Harris: There are a lot of factors that play into that. You know, if you're in wide-open terrain or you're in big open bottom fields where you can use binoculars to spot turkeys moving to the roost, then wind or weather aren't going to be a factor. You'll be able to use the visual in order to help you find turkeys. But when you're in dense timber like we are here in the Missouri Ozarks, and you have all that wind and rain and all that, the chances of the birds gobbling and you hearing that gobbling are extremely slim. So then you weigh the odds of spooking a bird. It's the lesser of two evils. I'd rather go in there the next morning kinda freelancing it than taking the chance of boogering a bird I never heard because of those adverse weather conditions the night before.

Decoys. A much debated subject. How to use them? When to use them? When not to use them? My Pop's a believer. So, too, was this big Iowa Eastern he's admiring.

Me: Does it make sense, Brad, to do any roosting well in advance of the season?

Harris: Some turkeys are habitually attached to certain roost areas, and they'll go back to roost there night after night after night. So if you can develop a pattern like this, it's certainly going to help you in the long run. Where I find roosting to be especially important is when you're hunting new areas or you're hunting birds that aren't gobbling well or you're hunting birds that move a lot. You know, you have some birds that will traditionally roost in the same areas, but you also have birds that are nomadic. They just travel all around and may have two or three different roost sites spread over a one or two-mile area. And if that's the case, it's to your benefit to try to pinpoint those particular birds.

So you see, successfully roosting a bird the night before your hunt can improve your chances come morning. At the very least, and as I mentioned earlier, it gives you some place to start.

But what if it doesn't work? What if the Utopian scenario described above never unfolds? Is it over? Time to go home? Absolutely not.

Let me see if I can explain this way. Good turkey hunters are like skilled auto mechanics. Sure, Ford's "Better Idea" requires you to have a wee little special tool with a really big price tag in order to remove that irritating bolt. You know, the same one that then drops

the entire engine block off the motor mounts. If you have it, great. If you don't, well, it's time for a trip to the local NAPA store. A good mechanic, though, *has* that special little tool, even if the opportunity or need to use it arises but once every five years. A *better* mechanic, however, may not have that special little tool, but he'll sure as hell know where to borrow one, or how to improvise with something he does have in order to achieve the goal. Now, the question — What are you talking about, M.D.?

Simple. Good turkey hunters go afield armed with all the tools they'll need in order to be successful. Here, tools can mean both physical equipment and knowledge. Better turkey hunters, on the other hand, are also similarly armed, but when confronted with a gobbler that doesn't play by the rules — and many don't — the better hunters will take the time to analyze the situation before modifying both themselves and their equipment. How do they perform this modification? Enter Bugs Bunny's "strag-a-tee." Strategy begins with tools of the trade.

Decoys: The Art Of Deception

Let's jump into the subject of decoys. Everyone wants to know about turkey decoys. Without fail, the first-time turkey hunters that we work with in the Pacific Northwest every winter will pipe up and say — "I think I have everything I need. A dozen calls, a gun, and 4,325 turkey decoys." Truthfully, it still pains me when I have to advise them that during their first spring, it's often best to leave the decoys at home and spend more time concentrating on the birds. Decoys, I tell them, will come in time. Still, it's tough to see grown men pout.

There's no denying that turkey decoys can be very effective tools when used both correctly and safely. Essentially, turkey decoys do nothing more than help flesh out the illusion you're creating with your turkey call. Think of it from the gobbler's standpoint. He hears a hen. Doesn't it make sense that he sees one?

Although an entire book could be written on turkey decoys and their use, let's take a look here at just a handful of methods, some well-known and some obscure, that have proven themselves over the past few seasons.

Decoy types — The choices include silhouettes, blowups, foam bodies, and full-sized hard bodies, to name the most common. All have their good points and bad points.

   a. Silhouettes — Light and realistic, but still two-dimensional. They can't, for the most part, be folded, and therefore can be troublesome to pack around.

b. Blow-ups — Plastic decoys that can be inflated/deflated. Some folks love them because they're light and easily carried; however, I have yet to see any that are very realistic. And, well, I do feel kind of funny blowing up a turkey's hind-end. Is someone watching?

c. Foam bodies — My personal favorites. New paints make them very realistic; they're light and compact, and move in even the slightest breeze, which can prove problematic. Set-up is quick and quiet, and the new materials don't take a "set" and crease like the old stuff. Good all-round choice.

d. Full-sized hard bodies — They look good, I can't argue with that, but they're heavy and cumbersome. Good choice, perhaps, if you're hunting out of a blind where transporting decoys isn't an issue.

Decoy set-ups — Every turkey hunter has his or her favorite decoy tactic. Here are some of mine:

a. Jake alone — If I were made to choose one decoy for the rest of my turkey hunting days, I'd choose a single jake decoy. Why? First, gobblers of all ages are always spoiling for a fight, even if one isn't really called for. A jake decoy simply serves as an instigator. Secondly, few mature gobblers (2-year-olds and older) will shy away from a jake decoy; however, I've watched mature gobblers damn near run from hen-only set-ups. What gives? They're scared, that's what gives. They've had their tail feathers kicked by the local bully, and they're not about to go messing with what they're sure is "his girl." TIP — Set your jake decoy where you want your shot, and remember that most gobblers will confront a jake decoy chest-to-chest.

b. Hen alone — Probably the most commonly seen decoy set-up is the hen alone, and for good reason. It works. It's a case of boy hears girl, boy sees girl, boy meets 2 ounces of copper-plated #6 shot. You hope. TIPS — Don't hide the decoy from the gobbler. Gobblers don't like surprises, even female ones. Place your hen in plain view, and well within shotgun or bow range.

c. Jake and hen — A confrontational set-up. No adult gobbler likes to see a young whipper-snapper fooling around with his girls. Even if they're not his girls. TIP — Again, put the jake decoy where you want the shot to occur. That gobbler

The solo jake. If I were limited to one decoy and one set-up for the remainder of my turkey hunting days, this would be it.

knows he's going to get the girl; the jake is just the appetizer.

d. Jake and two hens — Another rig of choice. Typically, I'll set the jake as though he were breeding one hen (see below) at a quick-paced 20 yards, and the single hen some 20 feet to the side and five yards beyond the pair. This set-up gives me my yardage markers and the confrontational set-up needed to trigger those reluctant longbeards. TIP — Jakes seem to prefer the single hen, while adult birds tend toward the jake/hen pair. It's a macho thing, I guess.

e. The breeding pair — It's one thing for a gobbler to see a jake with a hen; it's something altogether different for a gobbler to see a jake mounting a hen. This is another good confrontational set-up. TIP — Make your own "breeding pair" by short-staking (use one-half of one stake) the hen with her belly on the ground and placing the jake directly behind her.

f. The half-strut gobbler — Here's a case of "How dare he strut when I'm around?" Still another good confrontational set-up, especially when used in conjunction with a single hen. Or better yet, a short-staked hen.

The hen alone. Probably the most popular decoy set-up, coast to coast. Why? Simple. It works.

Here, outdoor writer, Phil Bourjaily, arranges the tried-and-true jake/hen decoy set-up. The addition of the jake to the lone hen creates a confrontational type of setting, sure to enrage any jealous longbeard.

Stakes, movement, and other things — It's all about making it look real.

a. Stakes — Most turkey decoys come with stakes, and in most cases, these will work just fine; however, after-market stakes such as the Buckwing Expander are available, and are worthy of a look. That the Buckwing Expander, with its umbrella-like arms, helps "poof" a foam-body decoy out to its fullest is a good thing, certainly, but where the Buckwing really shines is in the stake itself. First, the stake is adjustable height-wise, which means that you can use it the first week of the season in the chisel-ground and the last week of the season when the May apples and pasture grass are knee-high. Second, the Buckwing uses a small stud on the top section of the two-piece stake to prevent the decoy from swinging more than 90 degrees one way or the other. This eliminates the possibility of your decoy spinning like Linda Blair's head in *The Exorcist*.

b. Movement — Does your turkey decoy really need to move to be effective? Personally, I don't think so. Oh, a little wind activation might not hurt, just as long as your hen isn't looking like she's riding the Tilt-a-Whirl. Do you need strings and things? There again, they might help in some instances, but don't you have enough to concern yourself with without pulling on a cord running out of a plastic bird's butt?

c. A final tip — Walt Ingram, the man who led me to my first gobbler, told me about this one. One morning, Walt was set up on an Ohio longbeard that pitched out of his roost and then proceeded to parade around in the field some 80 yards in front of the shooter and his plastic decoy. Ingram, resourceful man that he is, went back the next morning; however, this time, he turned his hen decoy to face in his direction. This time when the old gobbler flew down, he walked the edge of the field until he was right in front of that decoy's face, where he strutted and got shot. Coincidence? Maybe, but then again, if you're as handsome as a big old gobbler, doesn't it make sense to strut around *in front* of your prospective girlfriend where she can see you?

Working The 10 'Til 2 Shift

You ask 100 experienced turkeys hunters, and a buck says that 75 of those folks will say that they've tagged more spring gobblers between the hours of 10 a.m. and 2 p.m. than they have birds right off the roost. Okay, maybe only 60 percent, but still, the "yes" replies

Feather Flex's "Breeding Pair," as set by MAD Calls' chieftain, Mark Drury. Another confrontational decoy arrangement designed to appeal to a dominant gobbler's territorial sense.

Photo courtesy of Mark Drury and MAD Calls

Pennsylvanian and five-time national friction calling champ, Matt Morrett, runs a box call behind a single hen decoy. Morrett uses a decoy as an impromptu yardage marker, quickly stepping off the distance between his "hen" and his set-up location.

will be in the majority.

Sure, we all like to work that old gobbler out of the tree and right into our set-up; unfortunately, it doesn't always work that way. In a lot of cases, that same gobbler will have plenty of female friends around him, all of whom look and sound much better than you. I'm sorry, but it's true. So what now?

Now you simply bide your time and watch the clock as there's a really good chance that come 9, 9:30, 10 o'clock, that gobbler will find himself all by his lonesome. Depending upon the time of the season, some of those hens may have gone off to tend to a bit of nest building. Or maybe even to lay eggs. And some of them may have just simply wandered off, perhaps to a favored bug-eating area, watering hole, or dusting spot. Whatever the reason, he's alone. And, well, anxious.

A couple notes here. First, it might not be a bad idea to wander back to the spot where you worked that bird off the roost at daybreak. Believe me, he remembers that sweet-sounding hen he heard first thing in the morning, and there's a good chance that he'll mosey on over that way just in case she's still around. And secondly, be ready. Often when a 9 o'clock bird gobbles, he's already on his way over to check out that beautiful young lady. Stay on your toes, and take a minute to look around for a potential set-up location *before* you make that first call. You'll thank me later.

The Old Front And Back

Typically, a two-hunter team can best perform the tactic that I call "the old front and back." But there's more than one version. The front and back is often in order whenever a gobbler hangs up. What I mean is, he's come as far as he's going to, and not a step more. Remember, that's how it's supposed to work. He gobbles, and she goes to him.

Well, the front and back takes advantage of just one of a gobbler's many weaknesses. He just can't stand the thought of a prospective date walking away. With that notion in mind, a two-hunter team works the front and back as such. One hunter, the shooter, stands pat at the sight of the original set-up location, while the second hunter, using all the available cover at his or her disposal, moves 50 to 75 yards away from the gobbler's last known whereabouts. In that bird's mind, the "hen" he hears is growing disinterested, and has decided to wander off and try her luck elsewhere. He won't have any of that, so he takes a few tentative steps toward the sound of the now-departing hen, and — BAM! — walks right into the lap of the waiting shooter.

A couple variations of the old front and back are available to the solo hunter.

Working in teams of two, hunters can play the old "front and back" – a shooter forward, while the caller, or "hen," walks away from the hung-up gobbler. Sometimes it's irresistible; sometimes, a gobbler can resist it.

Sure, it's hot, but the hours between 10 o'clock and 2 o'clock can also be the best time of day to arrange a meeting with a lovesick longbeard whose hens have left him in order to tend to more maternal matters.

1. The loner can physically move some distance from the original set-up, and hope that the bird will overcome his reluctance once he thinks "his hen" is walking away.

2. Instead of moving himself, the solo hunter can "move" his hen simply by throwing or directing his now low-volume calls in the opposite direction of the tom's last gobbles. Again, this tactic relies on the gobbler thinking that the hen is leaving.

3. Finally, the hunter can simply shut up and allow the gobbler to grow weary of the game and himself wander away. Quickly, the hunter advances to the spot where the tom hung-up earlier, waits, and then resumes calling with quiet clucks, purrs, and the occasional short yelp. Here, the gobbler thinks — "Ah, she's going to meet me halfway" — and returns to his former strutting ground, only to discover that the "hen" is 6' 3" and weighs 200 pounds. And is armed.

Cutting And Running

This tactic is also known as "running and gunning." In its most elemental form, running and gunning entails little more than moving silently through an area you've chosen to hunt, and stopping to call every so often. Walk

Cutting and running. Walk and call and walk and call, but take your time. This isn't a foot race.

Julie's bird (24.2 pounds) came to a three-decoy set at 6:40 a.m. My bird (25.8 pounds) fell at 9:30 a.m. to a jake-and-hen rig. We then picked 35 pounds of morel mushrooms. Was it a good day? It was indeed.

and call. Walk and call. Personally, I love this tactic, partially due to the fact that I'm able to sit still only about four minutes before I begin to fuss and fidget; however, there are some factors to be considered before hunters throw themselves full-force into this particular strategy.

1. Running and gunning usually requires you have a reasonably large expanse of land available to you. How much? Well, that's difficult to say; however, the smaller the parcel, the more likely that you moving around through the bushes, stopping every 100 feet to pound on a box call, is going to at least temporarily alter the natural flow of things. Some problems can include but aren't necessarily limited to negatives such as squirrels barking, blue jays screaming, deer snorting, and turkeys shutting down completely. If you do this every second or third day for three weeks, things change. Turkeys move. And the woods become quiet.

2. Just because you're moving doesn't mean you're not hunting. Stealth, man. Just a little stealth. And even with stealth, the tactic known as running and gunning opens you up to discovery and disclosure. For instance, it's a known fact that for every turkey you actually lay eyes on as you're moving about in the timber, there are 57 that you *don't* see. The thing is, they saw you. Choose your path wisely. Use folds and

creases in the terrain as a blanket to cover your progress. Probe around each bend and corner with your call *before* you walk out into the open. Glass fields and field edges. Think of your call as if it were a blind man's cane — tapping and testing and reaching into every corner. And go slowly. This isn't a race. He's in no hurry; why should you be?

3. Change as the season, the conditions, or the terrain changes. Here I'm talking about the distance you travel between calling locations. Early in the season, while the foliage is still slight, maybe you stop every 100 yards. Later, as both the season and the greenery progress, 100 yards may be too far based on how well or how poorly sounds such as your calls and his response travel. Maybe 50 yards between stops would prove more effective. Climatic conditions can also play a role in how far you walk between stops. A calm day? One hundred yards, give or take. A windy day with brief bouts of showers? Fifty yards might be more than enough.

The Reverse, Or Play It Again

I've heard this tactic also referred to as Following your Echo Trail, and with good reason. The Reverse assumes two things. One, it goes hand-in-hand with running and gunning. And second, it depends on the fact

Here, I give Julie's middle son, Casey, some last-minute instruction before I back off and resume calling. Confidence in your shooter plays a major part in a successful "one up/one back" strategy.

that, well, turkeys can hear a hell of a lot better than humans can.

That said, I'll explain. Let's say it's 8:30 in morning. It's been an hour or so since you've heard your last gobble, and you're slowly and silently walking a two-track road, stopping every so often to crank out a few yelps on your old trusty box call. A mile and a half later, you find yourself at the property boundary. Total responses? One flicker, an irate gray squirrel, and — you think — a chipmunk. With no other option, you turn around, or reverse. Get it? You slowly begin to retrace your steps. A mile into your retreat, you stop and throw out a short series of yelps. And get a gobble in response. Quickly, you're mind does the math. Seventy-five yards. Maybe. But where the hell did he come from? Weren't you just through here a few minutes ago?

Well here's what happened. On your initial run down the two-track — the silent run, remember? — that two-year-old that right now is hell-bent on running you over, heard you. What's more, he gobbled. The bad part is that from 250 yards away, you didn't hear him. In other words, he was running at you while you were walking away from him.

The bottom line is it always pays to retrace your steps. Follow your echo trail, so to speak. Once it works, it'll make you think about how many times you left a nice but very lonely gobbler standing in the middle of that two-

track road while you walked, dejected and empty-handed, back to your truck. Ouch!

Setting A Pattern

In high school math, Mr. Gene Zorn taught us, among many things, this postulate — If $A = B$ and $B = C$, then $A = C$. Okay, now how does this apply to turkey hunting? Here's how:

Turkeys (A) are creatures of habit (B).

Creatures of habit (B) by being habitual are vulnerable (C).

Turkeys (A) are therefore vulnerable (C).

What's it mean? It means that wild turkeys, like whitetail deer, are repetitious in their routine; that is, they have a routine. And short of anything changing that routine, that routine will take place presumably on a daily basis.

Welcome to the wonderful world of patterning. Patterning a gobbler is nothing more than establishing a bird's routine through in-depth and very careful scouting. Done correctly and, most importantly, without altering the bird's routine, this scouting will reveal such vital information as where the bird roosts, where he goes immediately upon fly-down, and his travel routes. Other very important information includes the location of preferred strutting areas, watering holes, and food sources. Once the scouting is complete, it's now a matter of placing yourself at one point or another within that particular gobbler's daily routine. Blinds and decoys can certainly help, as can periodic but very low-key calling. Each situation, once examined as it should be, will dictate the equipment and specific method necessary. Perhaps it's little more than a seat cushion and a healthy dose of patience.

In some circles, killing birds using the patterning method is, how shall I say, looked down upon. "You didn't call him in," says one traditionalist. "You just ambushed him," says another. Is it controversial? I don't think so. There's no fair chase issue here. There's certainly no ethics violation. And is there any difference between patterning a bird and tagging him that way, and watching a big whitetail buck for months prior to the season, hanging a tree stand, and slipping a 125-grain broadhead into his ribs on opening day? Nope. It's every bit the challenge; perhaps more so. You've located your bird. You've done your scouting. You've plotted and schemed. And sometimes you've failed. That's hunting. 'Nuff said.

Blind Luck

There's a lot to be said for turkey blinds. Sure, their use can prove an extremely effective tactic should you be confronted with a do-nothing, mind-his-own-business gobbler. But they have much better uses. Shade, for instance. Cool shade. And certainly concealment. Both concealment from a gobbler's razor-sharp eyes, and cover should you decide it's time to stand and stretch, do aerobics, turn the page of your magazine, deal another hand of solitaire, or make another corned-beef and Swiss on rye. With spicy brown mustard, of course.

All fooling aside, there's no question that blinds of one form or another do have a place in the turkey hunter's arsenal. Most turkey blinds take one of three basic forms:

Portable — These are blinds such as the lightweight, set-up-in-a-second hides made by Hunter's Specialties, and appropriately referred to as portable ground blinds. Available in a wide variety of camouflage patterns, the blinds are easily adapted to most any hunting environment or condition. APPLICATION — Perfect for the mobile hunter, kids, or those prone to fidgeting. They can be used anywhere, and can incorporate bits of native material for a more three-dimensional look. Cost is usually under $30; less for the do-it-yourself type armed with half a dozen 30-inch pieces of fiberglass staking, a few feet of camo netting, and 25 zip-ties.

Semi-portable — The popular "Black Hole" or Ameristep's "Outhouse Blind" are just two examples of what I'll call semi-portable blinds. Most will weigh between 5 and 11 pounds, and can accommodate two to four hunters, depending on their size, relationship, and whether or not they had the chili special for lunch at the local diner. These pieces typically require a bit more skill and time to assemble, but not much. APPLICATION — Perfect for archers or — finally! — those hunting from a wheelchair. Set-up choices are a little less free than are those with the smaller portable blinds, but there's not a huge difference. The most notable negative, if it can be called that, is the price, which will range anywhere from $100 to $300.

Permanent — Here, allow me to use the word "permanent" rather loosely. This last category of blind is typically constructed prior to the season in a pre-determined or pre-scouted location, and is meant to remain in place throughout the whole of the season. Most are fashioned from short poles — tomato stakes are perfect — and lengths of either camouflage burlap or netting. Sticks and brush in moderation can be added for a more complete touch. APPLICATION — Permanent blinds are most often seen at field edges, strut zones, and food or water sources. They can be situated along travel routes between roosting and loafing areas. A couple decoys, a quiet approach, and

Scouting and blinds go hand-in-hand. Find an area the birds frequent, put your blind or blinds in prior to the season, get in early, and leave the call alone.

the user is often in business. Success, though, depends greatly on prior scouting and proper placement. Permanent blinds are excellent choices on small properties as they eliminate the human traffic or activity that so often disrupts the birds' established routines.

Calling The Hens

During the spring, it's your role to "play the hen" in hopes of attracting the gobbler, right? Well, not always. In some cases, you might be better off to play the hen to attract the hen. Huh?

Imagine, if you will, a gobbler with, say, six hens. Day after day, he doesn't eat. He doesn't sleep. For that matter, he doesn't do much of anything but follow those girls around, strut, and, should they permit it, pounce on them like a black widow on her hubby. Then one day, he hears another. That's you. And, sure, while another girlfriend would be nice, half a dozen's more than plenty. So he gobbles. And he gobbles. And he gobbles. But he doesn't leave his little feathered harem. Why should he? And you, Mr. Unfilled Tag, stay lonely. Do you give up? Go home? Cry? I've tried them all, believe me, and none of them feel very good.

So why not try something different? Say, leave him alone and call to the hens. You see, hens, just like gobblers, live in a hierarchical society. You have the boss hen. The

The Grand Illusion: Scratching, Flapping, And Fighting

Field edges like the one Julie overlooks here in southern Iowa can be hotbeds of activity; however, most situations like this require a comfortable seat, ample time, and a healthy dose of patience. A couple decoys can help.

Remember this one? "If it looks like a duck, sounds like a duck, walks like a duck, and flies like a duck, well, then it's a duck." You don't? Well, regardless, there's a point to be made here.

What you're doing out there in the turkey woods is creating this illusion. Your turkey calls give sound to the illusion. Your turkey decoy gives the illusion shape. For some gobblers, that's all you're ever going to need. But there are birds out there that want a little bit more. They're the ones that seem to know that real hens — real sexy hens, that is — do a little bit more than just stand there and yelp. They scratch around in the leaves. Every now and then, they'll stand and flap their wings. And even more frequently, they'll quarrel amongst themselves, complete with muted floggings and cutts and cackles and leaf rustlings and other things.

So why shouldn't you? Think back. Have you ever had a bird gobble at you even though you'd never once made anything remotely resembling a turkey sound? There's a good chance that what he was gobbling at was the sound of your footsteps in the leaves. As some of you already know and many will soon discover, a turkey walking and shuffling through the leaves sounds darn near exactly like a person walking and shuffling through the leaves. The gobbler hadn't seen you, but based on what he was hearing, he figured it'd be a good idea if he got a jump on the competition and gobbled at this "hen" that was walking through his turf.

That should tell you something right there. The next time that old longbeard hangs up, stop your calling. Scratch in the leaves instead. Slap your hat or your gloved hand against your legs as if you were a hen standing up and flapping your wings. Cut loose with a short, almost too-short, cackle. Give him both barrels. Then, give him both barrels.

Hunting Strut Zones

The number of comparisons between spring gobblers and young male humans is staggering. The tactic I'll call "hunting the strut zones" is just one of the many that takes advantage of these similarities. For instance, think of a 23-year-old single guy in a nightclub at 11 o'clock on a Saturday night. For whatever reason, his cologne isn't working as it should, and he's still dateless. So he tries another club. Same story. Another. And another. At each, he stands at the bar, drink in hand, while every so often throwing out his patented "I'm not on the prowl" look. Finally, a female 20-something wanders over his way. He says, "Hi." She says "Hi." And a few minutes later, they're

first runner-up. The second runner-up. And so on. Now that old boss hen, well, she's just like that gobbler in that, to her, the only good competition is *no* competition. So you take your sights off of him and put those crosshairs right on top of her. Good idea, but it can still go a couple ways.

Bad — She gets insanely jealous and, not wanting to have to deal with this new competition, simply leads him away.

Good — The moment you open up, she reacts in a "No interloper's gonna take my man!" kind of way. So she squares up her shoulders, if she has shoulders, and starts in your direction. Mindless drone that he is, the gobbler follows. And follows. And follows. You see where this is going to end, don't you?

The key to calling the hens is to be aggressive. Use everything at your disposal — cutts, cackles, high-pitched yelps. More cutts. And more cackles. Every time she opens her beak to make a sound, cut her off. If you're doing it right, your fingers or your jaws should start to cramp. Ignore it, and keep it up. Sometimes it works; other times, it doesn't. But, hey, what do you have to lose?

out on the dance floor.

Well, hunting the strut zones is no different. Every gobbler has his favorite dance floors. These are the strut zones, sometimes called the strutting areas. Throughout the course of each day, lonely longbeards will visit these strut zones on the off chance that a pretty young lady turkey will not only be nearby but will be attracted to him by way of his devil-may-care attitude and low-key showing off. So, can hunting these strut zones be effective? You betcha! However, there are a couple things you need to know about them.

1. Birds that use strut zones for the purpose of finding hens often will do so silently. I have a couple theories on this one. These zones are located in what could be considered the hens' backyard. Hens already know where these zones are, and they will keep an eye on any activity that takes place on and around them. Don't let anyone fool you. Girl turkeys are often as randy as are boy turkeys. My point here, though, is that on strut zones, gobbling often isn't necessary. Spitting and drumming, on the other hand, is often an integral part of the strut-zone show. Which leads me to my second theory, and it's just a theory, mind you, which tries to further explain the gobbler's silence on the strut zone. It's late in the season. The gobblers, though still willing and able, are winding down a bit sexually. The spring foliage, on the other hand, has gotten to the point to where Oprah in blaze orange could hide in most woodlots. What had been happening at 150 yards in April is now, in May, taking place at 50 yards or less. And then there's hunting pressure and predators. My theory, then, is this. The gobbler is thinking he'll just go from zone to zone, spit and drum, yet keep a low profile, and try not to attract any unwanted attention. Then he'll just pick up those girls who haven't already gone home with someone else. See what I mean? Are not similar tactics used by young human males?

2. The second thing you need to know about strut zones is without question the most elemental. Before you can hunt them, you need to find them. How do you find them? One of the most reliable methods of locating strut zones is simply through a combination of first-hand experience and repetition. To explain. Once he's settled on a preferred strutting area, a gobbler will use that area until he meets with his demise. Almost immediately, another gobbler will move onto that zone; the reason being, a good fishing hole is a good fishing hole, regardless of who's doing the fishing. Strut zones will also reveal themselves during in-depth scouting, either through sightings of the birds while they use the zone, or with the discovery of what

Trust in yourself and you will be rewarded with knowledge and experience. And perhaps a real pretty sunset.

I'll call "high-traffic areas." These will include large numbers of tracks of various ages, feathers, and droppings, as well as the distinctive three-lined marks that a gobbler leaves in the dirt, dust, or snow as he struts. Find these, and you're well on your way to setting up on your first strut zone. Then, it's just a matter of patience. But you already knew that.

The Call-Shy Gobbler

Here's what I tell folks whenever the subject of the infamous "call-shy gobbler" inevitably comes up: Turkeys don't get call-shy. They get people-shy. People in the spring woods just happen to have turkey calls.

That's it. Period. You think that just because many a turkey hunter goes afield armed with pruning shears, the reason behind the birds being tight-lipped on any given day is because they're afraid of garden tools? Personally, I wouldn't put anything past a big old gobbler, but that's stretching things just a bit.

Think about it. For the past 330 days, all of the turkeys living on any given section of ground have gone about their daily routine without interruption. Nothing out of the ordinary. A bug here. A drink there. A little fighting. A little loving. Then, BOOM. One morning, the woods are teeming with strange life forms, most of which are creating very weird and unusual sounds. Every now

A final note on Zen – Ah, yes. Important to know when to say the hell with it.

...And Now, The Zen Of Turkey Hunting

The following are truths about turkey hunting. Understand and accept them, my friend, for you are a turkey hunter.

You will set up incorrectly.

You will move when you should remain still.

If you move, he will see you.

If you don't move, he will see you.

If you think about moving, he will see you.

Learn first not your calls but humility. If not self-taught, he will teach you.

Unlike some whitetails, turkeys do not look back. Turkeys simply run away.

Turkeys are not smart. They're just afraid of everything.

On any given day you will have all the calls you own, except the one you need.

Long silent, he will gobble from where you once sat. You, however, will be 200 yards away at the time.

The path to becoming a better turkey caller begins by first learning to set one's call aside.

Toilet paper is Mother Nature's most valuable resource.

There is no such thing as being *too* ready.

Did I mention he will see you?

and then, one of their buddies wanders over to see what the action is all about. And that's it. He's never seen nor heard from again. How do the turkeys react? They get quiet and sneaky. Oh, yes, they go on about their business, but it's for the most part all done now on the Q-T. One gobble, then nothing. Should they even *think* they hear something out of the ordinary, they'll clam up. Hell, even the deer and the squirrels hide.

Folks, it's not about being shy. It's about survival. It's simple. The birds that stand and holler — "I'm here! I'm here! I'm here!" — are also the ones that have the privilege of then riding around in the back of someone's pick-up.

So how do you handle these so-called "shy" gobblers? CLICHÉ WARNING — You fight fire with fire. What do you do when the object of your attention is playing hard-to-get? You play hard-to-get. In the turkey woods, you get call shy. That is, you should shy away from the calls and calling. Put an increased effort into scouting, observation, listening, and woodsmanship. Oh, and a little bit of patience, persistence, and self-discipline can't do anything but help. It's not over when the woods grow quiet, folks. If and when gobblers do get quiet, head for those strutting areas. Spend more time trying to pattern your local flock. Get reacquainted with your rather passive and low-volume friend, the slate call. Cluck and purr. And wait. Cluck and purr. And wait some more. Build a blind. Rediscover the joys, not to mention the benefits, of looking and listening. Play hard-to-get. And be ready.

10

Traditions: Fall Turkey Hunting

Running, while screaming at the top of one's lungs, is good therapy —
Words to describe one of the many benefits of fall turkey hunting.

Tagged on a mid-November hunt in eastern Iowa, this young-of-the-year hen, or jennie, will hold a place of honor come Thanksgiving Day. Few meals are as exquisite.

Which came first — spring turkey hunting, or fall turkey hunting? B-U-Z-Z! Time's up.

If you said spring, well, you're wrong. Technically and on a calendar that runs from January through December, the spring season does come before the fall. But it was the fall hunting season where our forefathers, cousins, and uncles first introduced themselves to the wonderful world of the wild turkey. I mean, come on. Thanksgiving isn't observed in April, now is it?

Historical perspectives asides, let's take a look now at fall turkey hunting. Up to this point, I've said little to nothing about fall hunting or the techniques associated with this most fine sport. I'll tell you why. Fall turkey hunting is, with some exceptions, a relatively undiscov-

115

He's still out there – big beard, hooked spurs, American flag head. And, yes, the gobble too. But can you find him?

May. Have I heard them gobble like that in November? Yep. Fact is, some of the hardest-gobbling birds I've ever heard were down in an Iowa river bottom, just hollering their fool heads off. Double-gobbling. Triple-gobbling. The date? November 30, 1997. The temperature? A cool 18 degrees. And that's without the wind chill. But what about the strut and the gobble, you ask? My wife, killed a fine 2-year-old longbeard on the last day of November in 1999. It was one of two adult birds that came into a small decoy set-up at the edge of a cut cornfield. Both had gobbled. And both came in full-strut, heads just as red and white as if it were spring. Exciting, just like in May? Oh my gosh, yes. My point is that you have to be out there. Think of it this way. If a turkey gobbles in the fall and there's no one to hear it, does it make a sound?

Killing hens — There's not a wildlife manager, biologist, or regulatory decision-maker on the planet who would knowingly put the members of a wild population in jeopardy. As is every hunting opportunity, fall turkey hunting seasons and bag limits are established based on the state's estimated population of that particular species. Many states, Iowa for instance, use a quota system as a means of regulating and restricting potential — and that's the key word here: potential, not the actual — harvest. Once that quota is full, no more permits are available. Should that quota be met with actual turkeys brought to bag, wildlife biologists and hunters alike should be secure in the knowledge that the population as a whole as not been negatively impacted.

Killing hens, a *personal* prospective — Although wildlife biologists have via regulation told me that, based on their research, the harvesting of adult hens during a fall season will have no negative impact on the population, I as an individual — NOTE: As an individual — turkey hunter have opted not to harvest adult hens. My reasoning behind this rests in my theory that adult hens are experienced hens, and experienced hens are more likely to bring off a successful brood come spring than perhaps a less experienced, first-timer might. Is this thinking founded in scientific fact? I don't know. But I would like to say again that this is a personal perspective. Do I tag fall gobblers? Certainly. Jakes? Yes. Young-of-the-year hens, or jennies? My, they're tasty. The bottom line is that it's up to you. 'Nuff said.

Now with that all hashed out, let's take a look at some of the methods used during this exciting fall season. For the sake of both brevity and simplicity, I've broken fall turkey hunting down into two major components. These

ered activity. Other than in places such as Virginia, Kentucky, and Tennessee, states where the months of October and November mean turkeys as much as they do whitetails or waterfowl, fall comes and goes with little in the way of talk about turkeys and turkey hunting. Why?

First, fall turkey hunting — and again with the exception of several states located within that incredible region known as Appalachia — just doesn't hold much in the way of tradition for a lot of folks. Now, before those hackles start to getting raised, let me explain. In the Midwest, for example, where many of the states offer fall turkey hunting opportunities, October and November are reserved for whitetail archers and early-season duck and goose hunters. Oh, there's a squirrel hunter or two, and there's always pheasants, but turkeys, like doves in Iowa — sorry, sore subject! — just don't have the background. There's just no history of it, plain and simple.

So there's inexperience. But that's not all. For some folks, turkey hunting is all about that mighty gobble. "There's no gobble in fall," hunters will say. "Why would I want to hunt a turkey that's not gobbling? And why would I want to kill a hen?" some will ask. Well, folks. That way of thinking is just fine as long as you don't mind missing out on a fantastic outdoor experience. Let me take it one step at a time.

The Gobble — Turkeys won't often gobble in November with the same enthusiasm they had back in April or

A young Chris Kirby with a New York state fall hen. Not surprisingly, Kirby is as deadly in November as he is in May.

Pete Clare, owner of Turkey Trot Acres, calls to a scattered flock of fall birds while his able canine assistant, Cutter, remains on full alert.

are mixed flocks of young-of-the-year birds, and fall gobblers. Certainly, there is an entire list of variables for each. This just gives us some place to start. And so, onward.

Fall Hunting The Mixed Flocks

First of all, let me give you my definition of a mixed fall flock of turkeys. A mixed flock would be any number of adult hens and their individual broods. In some instances, this flock may number but half a dozen, while in others, a mixed flock may include 50 or more. Throw in a little snow and some put food sources at a premium, and these fall flocks can swell to more than 200 individuals. That's a lot of turkeys! Typically, though, fall flocks throughout the Midwest, East, and Southeast — in other words, Eastern birds — will, on average, contain from a dozen to maybe five or six dozen birds. This is a goodly number of turkeys, especially when you walk into the group in the darkness.

With the flock defined, let's take a look at the individual birds within that group. For starters, there are the adult hens. These are the matriarchs of the flocks. The same birds that gave you fits during the spring season by constantly staying within eye and earshot of your chosen gobbler. Makes you want to disregard Number Three above, doesn't it? Then there are the jakes, the young

males, and the jennies, the young females. Depending upon the dates by which your particular fall season are governed, these young-of-the-year birds will be somewhere between 5 and 7 months old, and will weigh from 6 to 10 pounds, statistics of course ruled by factors such as age, food availability, and food types.

There you have it. Those are the players. And, understandably, the next question becomes: How should they be hunted? A better question yet: Is fall hunting any different than hunting turkeys in the spring? Well, to tell you the truth, the answer to that question is a whole lot of "yes," and a little bit of "no."

Fall hunting differs from spring hunting in that where success in the spring focuses on the gobbler's vulnerability as a result of his overwhelming urge to breed, success in the fall is centered on the wild turkey's almost insatiable need to be in the company of other turkeys. Break down this social structure, so to speak, and the birds will turn themselves inside out to re-establish it. I'll explain that in a minute. For the sake of discussion, fall hunting also differs from spring hunting in that most fall seasons are "either-sex" seasons, meaning hunters can legally harvest male or female birds. This is in contrast to the traditional "gobbler-only" spring seasons, and does throw a big roundhouse punch into what many hunters have come to accept as the unconditional rules of turkey hunting safety. Again, we'll discuss that in a minute.

A jake, or young-of-the-year gobbler. Targeting fall jakes can make for an exciting and extremely boisterous hunt.

The Traditional 'Scatter And Sit' Method

Here's fall hunting in a nutshell.

Step One — Find a mixed flock of adult hens, jakes, and jennies.

Step Two — Scatter them to the four corners of the compass by any safe and ethical means possible, including, where legal, the use of a dog.

Step Three — Sit down within 100 feet of where you scattered the flock and call them back using a combination of plaintive yelps and kee-kee whistles.

Step Four — Shoot one.

Step Five — Take the turkey to the truck and start looking for fall mushrooms.

Essentially, this part of the chapter can end right here; however, that would leave hundreds, perhaps thousands of dedicated fall hunters asking themselves, "So that's it?" With that in mind, and certainly not wishing to unnecessarily agitate anyone, allow me to expound, step by step.

Step One

Locating a flock of hens, jakes, and jennies in the fall can either be the easiest thing in the world to do, or the hardest. According to Pete Clare, who owns and operates Candor, New York's, Turkey Trot Acres, and who specializes — my word, not his — in hunting fall birds, the secret to locating these fall flocks is simple: "Identify and then find the food source."

It sounds easy, but there can be a little bit more to it than that. Take Iowa, as an example. In most years, the mid-October fall turkey opener often gives birds their choice of soft mast such as fallen apples and dogwood berries, as well as others delicacies like grass, clover, alfalfa, grasshoppers, crickets, and a whole list of creepy-crawly things. By late October, though, fall frosts have reduced this bounty, and the birds will switch to one of their favorite staples, acorns. Come November 30 and the traditional close of the season, Iowa's turkeys are still scratching up and feeding on acorns — that is, if the crop was good — along with dropped agricultural grains like corn and soybeans. All in all, it's a pretty good living. So it's easy to see that as the season progresses and the birds' foods of choice or necessity change, so do their daily haunts. The fact remains, and Clare is very correct in saying, "Find and identify the food source, and you'll find the birds."

Food sources only? Certainly not. In the fall, roost sites play as important a role in success as they do in the spring. In fact, many traditional spring roosts will also be used in the fall, and can prove an excellent jumping-off point for an early morning venture, regardless of the season.

Step Two

Scattering the flock is the key to a successful fall hunt. Period. Let's say you find a flock of 20 birds. Screaming madly, you rush into their midst. The 20 birds go in 20 different directions. Good bust! Now, let's say you find the same 20 birds and run screaming into them. This time, though, those 20 birds break into two groups of 10, one going one way, and one going another. Bad bust. Good bust, bad bust? What's the qualifier? Well, those 20 lone birds are just that — lonely — and they're going to be very eager to get back together with what they think is one of their flock. That's you. On the other side of the coin, those two 10-bird groups? They're just mini-flocks, and while they will eventually regroup, there's really no hurry as they can readily see and hear their brothers and sisters all around them. Tough break. Or more precisely, poor break.

All fall hunters have their own favorite flock-scattering method, but two techniques stand out among all the rest. These are:

The run and scream. — This is my personal favorite. For some reason, I feel much better after doing this, even if I never fire the gun. Go figure. This tactic consists of little more than locating a flock of birds, and once within acceptable range (see below), running into the middle of them while screaming insanely. I prefer the "unloaded gun, run, and scream" method. You should too.

The run, scream/no scream, and shoot. — I've never personally done this one, but I've been told it's very effective. This method also begins with locating a flock of birds and careening among them. *However*, the added attraction here is that the running ends rather abruptly, and is followed immediately by the loading of one's shotgun and the firing of one shot or several shots into the air. Due to the volume of the firing, screaming in this method is optional. NOTE: Under no circumstances should you run with a loaded shotgun. Your goal is to have any screaming be intentional. Remember that.

Acceptable Range

What this means is that it's important to get close enough to a flock of birds before starting your rush that they don't just all run off in a big herd of flashing legs and bobbing heads. Trust me. It's going to take a time or two before you determine what this acceptable range actually is; however, let me say simply that it's a hell of a lot closer than you think. Start from too great a distance, and the flock will either walk off or fly off as a group. Get in there. If they kick dirt and leaves up on you when they jump, well, you've done it right!

Step Three

Following the scatter, it's traditional to sit down and set up within 100 feet or so of where the break actually took place. Why? I'm not sure exactly; however, I'll say it has to do with the fact that the birds won't have gone all that far, often only 50 to 300 yards depending on the terrain or the subspecies. It also makes sense to the individual members of the flock that there be turkey sounds emanating from the spot where this disturbance first took place.

From this juncture, Step Three can be further subdivided into three sections. First, there's the set-up location. Secondly, calls and calling. And finally, decoys. Now just wait, I'll get to that.

Set-up — As in the spring, where you set-up in the fall after the break can either make or break your hunt. Ideally, you're looking for a seat that provides good

A jennie, or young hen, weaves her way through the underbrush as she attempts to rejoin her scattered flockmates.

visibility, yet not so far as to expose you and your position for an extended period of time. A high location is better than a low one. In other words, it's better to be on a ridge looking out or down in the direction you believe the birds will come from than it is to be in a bottom looking up. You also want something that's comfortable, for although fall hunts involving young birds often happen BOOM-BOOM-BOOM, it can occasionally take some time and several different birds or mini-flocks before the hammer falls.

Calls and calling — Once I get set up, I'll usually give the woods 10 to 15 minutes to settle back down. Often during that time I'll begin to hear the separated birds start to call back and forth to one another as they attempt to regroup. That's a good thing, and time for me to jump right in with my own version of, "Hey. I'm lost! Come on! I'm lost!" I rely primarily on three turkey sounds after the break. These are the kee-kee, the kee-kee run, and the lost yelp. Prior to scattering a flock, such as those times when I'm walking and trying to locate a group of birds, I'll resort to the tried-and-true traditional yelp as well as aggressive cutting. As far as post-break calls are concerned, however —

a. Kee-kee — This is the sound made by a young turkey that hasn't learned or is just learning how to yelp. Unmistakable once it's heard, the kee-

Blinds aren't only for the spring, as evidenced by this mid-October set-up; still, success depends on proper blind placement, which in turn depends upon – yes – scouting.

kee commonly consists of two or three very clear, very high-pitched melodic whistles that sound like "pee-pee…pee-pee-pee…pee-pee."

b. Kee-kee run — I differentiate between the kee-kee and the kee-kee run; some folks don't. Unlike the kee-kee that consists solely of whistles, the kee-kee run is a series of whistles and broken, inexperienced yelps that go something like — "pee-pee…pee-pee-pee-rap-rap…pee-pee…pee-pee-pee-rap." Imagine, if you will, a 15-year-old boy whose voice insists on cracking as he talks. High, low. High, low. That's the kee-kee run.

c. Lost yelp — Your basic yelp, but drawn out and with as much feeling and emotion as you can throw into a turkey call. Think — "I'm lost. I'm lost. Where are you? Where are you? I'm lost." This often consists of eight to 12 separate yelps delivered in a pleading, very precise cadence. It's easy, but just a bit different.

As for the physical calls, again, every fall hunter has his or her favorite. Personally, I find it much easier to kee-kee and do kee-kee runs using either a single-reed diaphragm or, with some brands, a triple-reed diaphragm played upside down. Others, however, can deliver near-perfect kee-kees with a box call or by working on the outer edge of a high-density glass, aluminum, or titanium pot-and-peg call with an equally hard plastic, acrylic, carbon, or graphite striker. Regardless of the implement, remember — high-pitched, and clear. So practice.

Decoys — It's only been within the past couple of years that readers have begun seeing magazine articles about the use of decoys during the fall turkey hunting seasons. Why just recently? I'm not positive, but I think it's like this: Going out into a busy intersection to pick up a dollar bill might be a good way to make a buck, but it's also an excellent opportunity to get hit by a bus. What I mean is that a lot of folks, myself included, see decoys and fall turkey hunting as a good news/bad news kind of situation. Certainly, decoys can be very effective. I mean, what's more natural for a young bird, anxious to get back together with his flock, then to not only hear but see a buddy in the distance? Makes sense. That's the good news. The bad news is that because most fall turkey seasons are also either-sex seasons, well, decoys stand a better chance of being "harvested" during the fall than they might during a gobblers-only, spring season. Yes, I know that doesn't give safety credit where safety credit might be due. But, it's the only thing I can come up with. So to recap — Turkey decoys used in the fall can be effective, but there's an

Though a very effective tactic, the use of turkey decoys during a fall, either-sex season is something that must be approached with the utmost care and caution. My advice is this – If you're at all hesitant, leave them at home.

increased safety aspect. Am I then saying not to use them? Just read on.

a. In most cases, I'll only use decoys in the fall when I'm hunting with a partner. My theory here is that I have an extra set of eyes and ears — as does my partner — to warn me in advance of what might be an unpleasant situation.

b. I *only* use decoys in the fall when the conditions are perfect. These conditions include high visibility in a minimum of 180 degrees, a solid backstop — a large oak or hay bale, for instance — and private ownership of the land I'm hunting. Private, unfortunately, doesn't guarantee that you'll be 100 percent alone, and you'll want to keep that in mind. Personally, I never use decoys on public ground during the fall. I'm not suggesting that those who hunt public land are any less safe than those who hunt private. What I am saying is that public land, by virtue of its access and state ownership, simply increases the chance of someone seeing my set-up.

c. I *always* use blaze orange when using decoys in the fall. That might be the blaze orange patch on the back of my turkey vest. Or a blaze orange cap placed on the ground behind or to one side of

my location. Or both. Essentially, I'll use blaze orange to cover that arc that my eyes cannot. It's not bulletproof, but I don't need it to be. All I want my blaze orange to do is make someone STOP and THINK. Every hunting accident involves the absence of those two elements. Think about it.

d. Just as in the spring, use caution when carrying decoys in the fall. Make certain they're completely concealed, either in your turkey vest or in a camouflage bag or knapsack.

e. My favorite fall decoy set-up involves using from three to six plastic turkeys. This is a flock thing, remember, and the more bodies an approaching youngster can see, the better. In most instances, I'll run all hens. Sometimes, I'll use one jake or maybe two, with three or four hens. But I really neither need nor want the red, white, and blue color patterns often seen on jake decoys. And it's never seemed to make a difference to the birds. They simply see company.

Step Four

Shoot one. Pretty self-explanatory. A word of caution though. Just because your fall target may be a 7-pound

Alice in Wonderland never had it so good. My wife, a native of Washington state, says these Iowa puffballs taste a little like oysters. They will make an excellent addition to a fine turkey supper. Now to only find the turkey!

As in all hunting situations, safety is Priority One. Here, the author packs a nice young hen out of the field, secure in the fact that his blaze orange patch is doing its part.

jennie as opposed to a 25-pound gobbler doesn't make her any less tenacious. Nor does it reduce your responsibility as a hunter to do everything you can to ensure a quick and clean harvest.

Pick your shot carefully. Head down on the stock. Aim at the head and neck only.

Step Five

Chanterelles. Shaggy manes. Hen of the woods. Puffballs. Goat's beard. Regardless of what they're called in your neck of the woods, fall mushrooms can provide some of the finest wild eats available. Be careful of what you're picking though. There are 'shrooms out that there that can kill you. Or at the very least, make you see funny liquid rainbows, ride purple horses, and rediscover the words "wow" and "cool." Not good.

Targeting Fall Longbeards

It's been said that there is no greater challenge in the hunter's world than the challenge of calling into range and harvesting an adult gobbler during the fall. So why would that be so tough? Well, there are two reasons.

First, fall and sex aren't synonymous terms as are spring and sex. In the spring, you yelp, and he comes a-runnin'. In the fall, however, you yelp, and he *goes* a-runnin'. During the summer, hen turkeys, to a gobbler, go from single-minded object of lust and desire to, well, "It's okay if she's around, but she better not be eating any of my acorns or corn kernels." Truth is, come fall, adult gobblers spend most of their time either alone, or in bachelor groups that consist of several adult toms of similar ages. Yeah, they still like each other's company, with one major difference — they can also be very anti-social. Scatter a flock of youngsters, and you better stay out of their way as they race to regroup. Bust up a bachelor group of longbeards, though, and it may be hours, hell, it may be a day or two before they get back together. After all, their territory's relatively small. And they know that sooner or later, their paths are going to cross. With adult gobblers in the fall, there's just no reason to hurry. And that's the key to success right there. Don't hurry.

The sounds used to call fall longbeards are a bit different than those that bring the youngsters to you. In the fall, adult toms will respond better — if they respond at all — to infrequent gobbler yelps and clucks, which are actually nothing more than low-pitched, slow cadence versions of the familiar hen yelps and clucks. Yelp, and put the call down for 15 minutes. Cluck, and put it down for 10. Wait some more.

The best advice I can give you about hunting fall gobblers? Take your watch off. Time means nothing, for they have all the time in the world. Do you?

122

11

Turkey Hunting Safety

"You never hear the one that gets you."

It was in 1986 that I was involved in a turkey hunting accident. Actually, it was the second week of the Ohio season at that time. I had spent the first week hunting in West Virginia.

I was hunting the Mohican Memorial Forest, which is in north-central Ohio. I got into the woods early, about a half-hour before sunlight, like I normally do. I didn't see or hear a turkey that morning so I started walking the ridge tops. I was stopping and calling like you do. About 8 a.m., which was a good two hours after daylight, I stopped and made a few calls. I didn't hear anything, and stuck the calls back in my hunting vest. I took a couple steps and felt like somebody had swatted the side of my head with a ball bat.

I was knocked down. I really didn't know what happened. I sat up, and still didn't know what had happened until I put my hand up to the left side of my face. I brought my hand back and my hand was bloody. I thought, "What in the world happened?" I looked to my right. I'd been carrying my shotgun over my shoulder on a sling. My shotgun was lying in the weeds, and it was fine. I had really thought that for some reason my shotgun had blown up.

I never heard the man shoot. He was about 30 steps from me. And it didn't click that I had been shot until he got up from his seated position and started walking toward me through the leaves. I could hear the leaves crunch. Obviously, my mind was racing at that point. It had all happened in just a matter of a few seconds, but there really was a period of time there when I had no idea what had happened.

He walked within about, ah, maybe 20 yards of me because I had fallen down the backside of a small hill. I was worried he was going to shoot again, so I yelled at him — "Hey, you shot me. Don't shoot!"

He said, "Where are you?"

I told him, "Down here. Go get help."

So I heard him take off running through the woods, and all I could think was, "I hope he's going to get help." There have been some accidents in Ohio and in other states where the shooters just simply ran off and left the victims. So I lay back down in the leaves and got a handkerchief in my hand and put it up to the side of my face. It filled with blood rather quickly. Basically what he had done was hit me from about my elbow on my left side up the arm, the shoulder, the neck, and the side of the face. Unfortunately, one of the pellets had penetrated my left eye. It was a strange feeling to gradually have my left eye fill up with blood. Basically, I had to watch the sight in my left eye get darker and darker until finally, it was gone.

I'd never been hurt that bad before. I didn't know if I was bleeding to death or not. I said a quick prayer, and I lay back down. Thankfully, the shooter did come back. He had run up over the hill to a farmhouse and called the emergency squad and come back. He helped me walk out of the woods, and about that time is when the emergency squad showed up.

I had surgery that night. I had a follow-up surgery about two weeks later. And then I had a third surgery about two months later to try to save the eye. Unfortunately the doctors were not able to save it. So I ended up losing the sight in my left eye, and still carry about 20 or so lead pellets that they did not remove from my body. The doctors said it would do more damage to remove them than to just leave them in there. Luckily, the gentleman was shooting a muzzleloading shotgun that was not tightly choked. Had it been tightly choked, he probably would have killed me at 30 steps. Also, he wasn't using copper-coated shot. The pellets tended to flatten out. When I looked at the X-rays, they looked like small little pancakes instead of round pellets.

Chip Gross hunts squirrels in a small woodlot near his central Ohio home. It's been 16 years since the accident that cost him the sight in his left eye, but today, he's back in the field. Still, the events of that day in 1986 will forever be with him.

Chip Gross, 49, is the soon-to-retire special projects coordinator for the Ohio Department of Natural Resources, Division of Wildlife. He is husband to Jan; father to sons, Pete and Andy; a devout Christian; an outdoor writer; hunter; angler and a statistic.

It took two years before Chip could hesitantly discuss his hunting accident, and four years before he could once again step into the spring turkey woods, still bearing the scars and the dark, constant reminder of that day in 1986. As our talk wound down, I asked Chip, a genuinely wonderful human being who I consider both a mentor and one of my best friends, what I thought was an understandable question given the topic at hand. "What do you do," I asked, "as the injured, if you're capable?" An ounce of prevention statement was what I was looking for. What I got was not a sermon on the benefits of blaze orange. Nor was it a soapbox discussion on first aid. And it had nothing, absolutely nothing, to do with the individual who had started the machine by which this terrible chain of events had run. What I got surprised me. But then I thought about Chip's Christian beliefs, and it all makes sense. Sort of a lesson within a lesson. Within a lesson. Here's what he said:

In those few minutes after the accident, after the shooter had run off to get help, it really helped me to focus my life. And it very quickly shows you what's important in your life. I thought of my relationship with God first because I thought (laughs) that I might be seeing him real soon. I had no idea

how badly I'd been hurt. I thought of my family. I thought of my wife and my two young boys. At that time I thought there was a good chance I'd never see them again. My point is that I wasn't lying there thinking of my job. I wasn't lying there thinking of the mortgage on my house. Or my car payment. When you have an incident like that, it focuses what's important in life. And I guess that's something that I'd like you to bring out in this that hopefully most people won't have to get to that point before they decide what's important and where to spend their time.

My intent in this chapter is not to scare you. Paranoia is not my goal. My purpose is to help ensure that every son and daughter gets the chance to see Dad or Mom pull in the driveway after every turkey hunt. I want to let every wife know her husband's coming home safe and sound. And I want to prove that the phrase, "Turkey Widow," is nothing more than a figure of speech, not a reality. What, then, is my intent? Simply to make you think, even for an instant, about what's important in your life.

Getting (Or Get A) Physical

Contrary to what some may think, the subject of turkey hunting safety doesn't kick off with the onset of the hunt. Safety is a before-after-and-during kind of proposition. What's the sense in hunting defensively and taking all the precautions necessary to ensure the safety of you, your companions, and anyone else that might be sharing the great outdoors with you at the time if your body isn't up to the task at hand? If you've ever tried to blow a diaphragm call while sucking enough wind to fill a weather balloon, you know exactly what I'm talking about. Turkey hunting safety actually begins far in advance of the season.

I'm not going to say that prior to the start of every turkey season, I head off to our friendly family doctor and have a complete, head-to-toe physical examination. Sure, it would be a good idea, but I'd be lying if I said that was the case. What is the case, though, is that it's just as important to keep yourself in good shape — let's call it peak condition — as it is your favorite box call or pet shotgun.

Like many outdoor activities, turkey hunting can, at times, be a very strenuous thing. In most parts of the country, there are hills to climb, canyons to walk out of, creeks to cross, and ridge tops to reach. Combine this with late-season heat, humidity and the extra weight that a fully loaded turkey vest brings, and you have all the makings of a potentially less-than-perfect situation from a heart, lungs, and legs standpoint.

Unfortunately, it's easy to spend the winter months cultivating a belly whose sole purpose is to protect your belt buckle from the damaging rays of the sun. If you fit this description — and that might be the only thing that fits after three months of recliners and fried foods — then I'd suggest you give some serious thought to a physical exam before the turkey season starts. It doesn't take all that long to let the doctor poke and prod your every inch. Chances are it's been quite some time since you've had a thorough check-up. If you need to, drop some of those winter pounds. Before the season, spend a little bit of time on the treadmill. Weather too bad? Just drive on down to your local mall and walk a couple laps around the bottom floor. Hell, 20 million senior citizens can't be wrong. The fact of the matter is, those folks are probably in much better shape than you are. Just spend the money and go see the doc. Oh, and age really doesn't make all that much difference. I've seen young bucks, 18 years old, who fell behind during the first hours of a hunt. On the other hand, I had the privilege of hunting with a gentleman some 35 years my senior — that's 71, if my math is correct — who is in better shape than 99 percent of the folks I know and spend time with in the field. All morning long, Bud Cannoy never broke a sweat. Never got flushed. Never appeared oxygen-starved. And we walked. Oh boy, did we walk. Only after taking this wonderful man on what can only be described as a forced march did he reveal his true age, and only then at my asking. So when your 25-year-old lungs burn and your legs ache, think of Bud. And then get a little exercise.

The Case For Blaze Orange

Okay, so you've spent many, many dollars on the latest, greatest camouflage clothing available. You're three-dimensional. You've mixed and matched your colors and patterns. Hell, you're so well hidden that you can't even find yourself. All this, and now I'm telling you to incorporate blaze orange into this masterpiece. Blaze Orange? Why not stick arms on the Venus de Milo? Maybe a big old grin on the Mona Lisa? Blaze Orange on a turkey outfit?

All right, so perhaps I'm going a bit overboard with the analogies; still, doesn't blaze orange seem a little out of place in all this hide-and-seek? Does the color have a place in the spring turkey woods? For hunters in Pennsylvania, the fish and game agency has answered that question by making the wearing or display of blaze orange to some degree mandatory. Yet the question remains — Does it have a use? If you ask me, most definitely. And here's where and how.

1. When walking into or out of the field. Movement, by virtue of its eye-catching nature, makes you most vulnerable. "I saw something move," the shooter tells the conservation officer. Unfortunately, what he means to say is "I saw something move and I shot at the movement." It happens all the time. In such cases, a little blaze orange can mean the difference between being shot and not being shot. Maybe it's a blaze orange cap.

That's Bud Cannoy with his grandson, Cale. At 71, Cannoy's in better shape than most 25-year-olds. Are you physically ready for turkey season? Or is Cannoy going to make you look foolish?

Or perhaps that little swatch of blaze orange material that comes attached or as a button-on/off accessory with most modern turkey vests. Either way, it's something very visible. It is a color that doesn't belong. And when it attracts attention, it typically it draws the right kind of attention. The safe kind.

2. When moving from calling location to calling location. Again, it's the movement thing. This time, throw in a gobbling bird — maybe you're moving from one set-up to another just a little closer to that tom — and you have all the ingredients for what I'll call a movement mistake. Is that blaze orange flag buttoned to the back of your turkey vest going to be enough to make a difference? Might be. But I prefer a full orange baseball cap. My current traveling cap is a lightweight model from Cabela's *without* the white liner inside. I'll tell you why in a minute. When I'm moving, I carry my camouflage hunting hat tucked inside the front of my shirt. Say I'm trying to locate a bird. I crow call. Nothing. Crow call again. Nothing. But the instant I hit that glass call, a bird gobbles — hard — from less than 100 yards away. Fortunately it only takes a second to exchange the hat on my head for the hat in my shirt. My butt hits the ground, my headnet goes up, and I'm ready for action.

Here, Julie and hunting partner, Glenn Sapir, decide if they *really* need to go up over that South Dakota rise. Notice the blaze orange patch on the back of Julie's vest.

Don't laugh. Sure, we received some pretty unusual comments from our fellow Washington state turkey hunters concerning our "warning" sign; still, our point was made.

3. Now, back to the white liner. Ordinarily, when that bird gobbles and finds me standing with a blaze orange hat on my head, the orange cap doesn't go back inside my shirt. Rather, it gets placed, right side up — not upside-down with that all-too-common white liner visible — behind me and behind the tree that I've set up against. This way, another hunter coming in from behind me who hears my calling, or perhaps hears the gobbler I'm working and comes to investigate, has something to see. It is something that says, without question, "Hunter here. Please be careful."

4. And finally, that blaze orange rag on the back of your turkey vest. Most years, I won't take mine off. I look at it this way. If I've set up against a tree that's as wide as my shoulders are (see Turkey Safety Commandment #1), then that flag is completely obscured by bark. And unless that gobbler circles me *and* can see through trees — that's a myth, trust me — then I don't have to worry. And even if the flag isn't completely covered and the bird does circle… well, turkeys see color in the woods every day. Surveyor's tape, timber cruiser markings. All sorts of things. What I do want to have happen is for the man who slips up behind me, for whatever reason, to have that all-important something to see. I want him to think, just for an instant, *before* he pulls the trigger, "Hey, something doesn't look right here."

Can blaze orange help prevent some turkey hunting accidents? Yes, I do believe so. But hunters need to be careful not to let this wonderful accessory lull them into a false sense of security. It's just a thin piece of lightweight material, and unfortunately not a Kevlar blanket blessed with the power to stop stupidity. Still, it can make a difference if turkey hunters use it, recognize its use, and just flat pay a little more attention to what it is we're doing out there.

The Ten Commandments Of Turkey Hunting Safety

Now here's a statistic that might surprise you. According to a number of state fish and wildlife agencies across the country, as well as documentation from the National Wild Turkey Federation, it's more likely that the shooter involved in a "mistaken for game" accident — this is where one person shoots another person thinking the victim was a turkey — will have 10 or more years of turkey hunting experience at the time of the accident. Ten or more years! How can this be?

My theory is this. New turkey hunters are nervous turkey hunters. They're unsure of themselves and their abilities. Often, their turkey hunting coach or mentor intimidates them. They pass on safe and very responsible

Always try to set-up against a tree that is at least as wide as your shoulders. Take care not to silhouette yourself, or leave your head and shoulders above something such as a stump, log, or bush.

Did you immediately see the fully-camouflaged hunter at the edge of the cover beyond the decoys? Most people don't. Remember – what you see and what is real may be two different things.

shots, fearing that they'll miss. Or worse, they'll cripple a bird. New hunters are a tentative people, and that's a good thing. They want to be sure. On the other side of the coin are the veterans. With field time comes confidence. And sometimes a by-product of confidence is a relaxing of one's natural hesitancies. Some folks call it the routine syndrome. "I've done this so many times," they'll tell you, "it's old hat." For just an instant, they'll take a lackadaisical approach to what they're doing. For just a second, they'll let their guard down. Lose their edge. And, sometimes, in that instant, someone gets hurt. Or worse.

Now wait. I'm not saying that every turkey hunting accident is caused by a 10-year field veteran. Nor am I implying that newbies aren't ever involved. To say those things would be to speak untruths. What I am saying is that turkey hunting is a mental game. A discipline. And that word right there — discipline — speaks volumes when it comes to turkey hunting safety. Self-discipline. Confidence. Valuable hesitancy. And 100 percent certainty. Why so harsh? Two reasons: There are no 6-foot, 3-inch wild turkeys. Never have been; never will be. And once the wad leaves the muzzle, there's nothing on Earth you can do to change what is about to happen. That said, doesn't it make sense to be sure?

One of the ways that you, as a responsible turkey hunter, can held avoid being involved in a hunting accident is by adhering to the Ten Commandments of Turkey Hunting Safety. Most of these, like "Always identify your target with 100 percent certainty," apply globally to the whole of the hunting community. Others, like the one involving the elimination of certain colors, are more turkey-specific. Regardless, the commandments are presented to serve as guidelines and as reminders that things aren't always as they might seem.

1. **Always set up against a tree that's at least as wide as your shoulders.** No, it's not always possible. I wish it was. Sometimes, you have to make due with what you have. Still, given the choice and the chance, it's best to set up against a tree that's at least as wide as your shoulders are. Not a rock or stump or bush, all of which do nothing but help accentuate your head and upper body. A wide tree, on the other hand, provides not only protection from the rear, just in case someone decides your decoys look awfully real, but can also help hide you from those wary gobblers that opt for the circle-wide-and-come-in-from-behind tactic.

2. **Should you see another hunter, don't wave.** And don't use a turkey call in hopes of attracting his attention. In fact, don't move at all. Rather, in a loud, very clear, very human voice, say something immediately recognizable like "OVER HERE." or "HUNTER HERE." Chances are they'll get red-faced, give a half-wave, and back out the way they came.

3. **Exercise care when using turkey decoys.** Place them

A perfect example of why it's essential that you eliminate the colors red, white, blue, and black from your turkey hunting ensemble. You don't want to look like this, do you?

A light-colored box call lid coated in blue chalk moving back and forth against a dark – in this case, camouflage – background. Bad news!

in a relatively open location. Gobblers don't like being surprised by other turkeys, regardless of whether the other turkeys are plastic or feathered. Spot them so that you can see some distance beyond and to the sides of the decoys. This buffer zone provides you with the chance of seeing someone who might stalk these fake turkeys. Position them so that in the event someone *does* shoot at them, you're not in the line of fire. Finally, always carry them so that they are completely hidden from view. No red-white-blue heads sticking out of a vest bag or half-strut tail fans protruding from the sack on your back. Both are bad deals.

4. **Eliminate the colors red, white, blue, and black from your ensemble.** Take a good look at any gobbler. His body's black, and his head is a patriotic collection of reds, whites and blues. Why, then, would you want to include such colors on your person? Remember, it's the little things, too — handkerchiefs, Kleenex, toilet paper, paper towels, socks, T-shirts. Even underwear. Think subtle. Chances are your bare wrist or neck, when seen against the overall dark base of your camouflage, appears pretty light. All it takes is a little contrast to create an undesirable situation. Eliminate it.

5. **When possible, set up in an open area.** This actually serves several purposes, both from a safety as

well as a strategic standpoint. For one, gobblers are typically a bit more at ease in those places where they can see well. He can see your decoys from a distance, and while this might be a negative in that he may stand pat at 75 yards and strut, waiting for the little plastic girl to come to him, he may not. Thick cover has a tendency to make turkeys nervous. Why? Well that's where those things — coyotes, mountain lions, bobcats— that like to eat turkeys hide, and turkeys know this. From a safety standpoint, an open-area gives you an opportunity to see an approaching hunter while he's still at a safe, non-threatening distance from your location. The bigger your visual arc — 150 degrees is better than 80 degrees — the better off you're going to be.

6. **Use caution when using gobble calls.** Sure, they can be effective in a territorial or dominance situation, but do you really want that guy on the next ridge to hear you shaking a gobble call? This is what we're listening for. This is what gets us on our feet and moving in the direction of the sound. Do you want that direction to be yours? This is a case-by-case scenario; however, if there were one given here, my opinion is that it's always — ALWAYS — a bad idea to use a gobble call on public land. But that's your decision. "I had been using a gobble call that morning prior to my accident," said Chip Gross in a return telephone call

When possible, set up in such a way as to provide you a clear field of vision through as many compass degrees as the terrain allows. Turkeys don't care for thick, predator-concealing cover; you shouldn't either.

You've eliminated red, white, blue, and black from your wardrobe, and then you go and cover yourself from head to toe with those very same colors? Is that a smart thing to do?

hours after our initial conversation. "I'll never do that again during the season. Maybe for pre-season scouting. In retrospect, it was a pretty stupid thing to do during the open season."

7. **Assume every sound you hear is another hunter.** Brand-new or relatively inexperienced turkey hunters primarily attend my seminars, particularly those that we present in the Pacific Northwest. I try to keep this in mind when I bring up this assumption that everything one hears in the turkey woods has absolutely, positively got to be another hunter. I assure the folks in attendance that my goal during the safety portion of our seminars is neither to instill paranoia nor to dissuade anyone from trying this incredible sporting opportunity. However, I do want them to realize just how serious I am about hunting defensively. A turkey walking through fallen leaves and a man slipping along a ridgeline can sound very much alike. Some talented callers, can sound amazingly realistic, particularly given the variables of wind, distance, greenery, and want. In this case "want" means, "I want to hear a turkey. Was that one?" Here, experience can and does help a hunter distinguish and separate the avian from the human. In the meantime, it's not a bad thing to assume that all those sounds that you can't immediately identify as something wild might be human.

8. **Never stalk a gobbler.** Truth is, given the wild turkey's incredible eyesight, your chances of sneaking up on a gobbler aren't very good. However, the chances of you being involved in a shooting-related accident are greatly increased. "I saw something move in the direction of where the bird was gobbling, officer," is a common post-incident statement. Sitting still and attempting to call a bird to your location, a location where you're mentally prepared and physically ready to deal with whatever unfolds, is better than trying to creep up on a bird. I mean, think about it. Do you really want to dress from head to toe in camouflage and then crawl around in the turkey woods? I don't.

9. **Make sure your camouflage is complete.** Throw a Styrofoam cup in a coal bin. Can you see it? Sure, you can, and quite easily too. Well, the same thing happens with any part of your body that's not been sufficiently attended to in terms of camouflage. In other words, anything that's neglected or overlooked is going to stand out just like that Styrofoam cup in that coal bin.

10. **Be 100 percent sure of your target and beyond.** I don't care if you've hunted turkeys one year or 101 years, if you don't get excited when that bird gobbles and then walks in close, well, you're dead. That's the only thing I can figure. But while this adrenaline rush

The smart thing to do. Congratulations on a fine bird, but remember to get that bird out of the field safely. These blaze orange bags from Hunter's Specialties are a great idea.

Phil needs to find himself a tree that's a bit wider. And he really needs to address that area – the WHITE, turkey-esque area! – of his neck left uncovered and flashing. TIP – Make sure your camouflage is complete.

is certainly a good thing, it also has the ability to change our perspective on the subject at hand. Kind of like a cherry '65 El Camino — 396 cubic inch, of course — has a way of mucking up your decision between mini-vans. Here's how I personally handle target identification: As soon as I see the bird I'm working, I say to myself, "There's a turkey." Once I see the bird's beard, I say, "There's the beard." Now I've identified the object not only as a turkey, but as a bearded, and therefore legal, bird. Then, if everything works as planned and the bird comes within range, I again say to myself, "There's the beard." Sound silly? Perhaps, but with each gobbler, this little self-help sequence not only verifies, without question, what it is I'm looking at, but it gives me the time that I need to calm myself down, double-check my self-discipline, and prepare my head for the final step in the process. Why all this? Well, I still get very excited.

That's 10; however, Number 11 is probably *the* most important rule to remember — Always think, and hunt defensively. Turkey hunting, says statistics supplied by the NWTF, is four times safer than is playing ping-pong (ping-pong?), and 50 times safer than is playing a round of golf; however, the latter stat is understandable as most would agree that combining weighted metal sticks and beer is simply asking for trouble.

As I mentioned earlier, most turkey hunting acci-

dents happen during the split-second that someone relaxes too much and loses focus. The person doesn't think; however, there can be other factors that contribute to this period of non-thought. These can include:

1. **Excitement.** Anyone who's done it knows that turkey hunting is an exciting sport. Excitement, and the resulting release of inordinate amounts of adrenaline, can at time create situations where things aren't really as they appear. If, for instance, we want to see something badly enough, oftentimes we'll see it. Look hard enough, and you just might "put" a beard on that object. Stare, and that burned-out old stump grows antlers. Or wing feathers. Or a tail fan. Excitement can be a good thing. If turkey hunting wasn't exciting, few folks would do it. But it's vitally important to remember not to let excitement, or the thrill of the moment, cloud your judgment.

2. **Peer pressure.** "I just gotta get a bird," you say to yourself. "It's the last day, and everyone down at the Texaco is gonna get on me if I'm the only one who doesn't kill a turkey this spring. I just gotta get one." What we have here is an individual on the fast track to a very bad situation. Don't ever let peer pressure create in you the need to shoot something so badly that it becomes your only priority. You don't get a bird? So what. The boys at the service station will

razz you, but you'll get over it. There's always next year. And besides, this isn't a contest. The wild turkey deserves much, much better than to be relegated to nothing more than collection of pounds and inches posted for the general public to gawk at. Did you hunt hard? Did you have fun? That's all that matters.

Self-pressure, and a lapse of self-discipline. Pressure to succeed, where success is measured in terms of filled tags, from oneself can be as detrimental or perhaps more so, than is pressure from the outside. Often, self-pressure leads to a lapse in self-discipline, and a lack of self-discipline can in some cases make us do things that we ordinarily would never think of doing. Maybe it's 65-yard shot at a longbeard. Or a 500-yard poke at a whitetail buck. Such things do little but breed frustration, which in turn destroys one's confidence. It's a vicious cycle, and one best kept consciously at arm's length.

Remaining calm – or as Daddy Maddy sugests, at Peace – can be difficult under many turkey hunting situations; however, it's one of the most vital elements for constant safety afield.

12

From Field To Feast

Congratulations on your first wild turkey gobbler. Boy, that was a fantastic hunt! That bird must have gobbled 100 times if he gobbled once. And that last time! Man, he was close. It raised goose bumps on my arms and made the hair stand up on the back of my neck.

What's that you say? Now what? No, it's not a silly question at all. Relax, though, and we'll take it all step by step. Besides, you need some color back in your face.

Contrary to what some folks might believe, there's not a turkey hunt takes place that ends immediately after the firing pin hits the primer and that big old gobbler hits the grass. In fact, there's actually quite a bit to think about after the gun goes "boom," things like ensuring that hard-won gobbler doesn't right himself and start off in the opposite direction. And then there's the question of what to do with the beast once he's back at camp or roosted securely in the garage. For that matter, what's the best way of transporting him from the field to his final place of residency? Oh, and the cleaning and the cooking. Let's not forget about the cleaning and the cooking.

Fortunately, and despite what sounds like a steadily growing do-this, do-that list, getting your gobbler from the field to the cleaning shed and from there into the freezer and ultimately onto the dining room table isn't nearly as difficult as it might at first seem. Still, there are some steps, as well as a handful of tricks and techniques, that can make this field-to-feast transition go a heck of a lot smoother. Smoother than what, you ask? Well, certainly smoother than the first time you tried to separate bird and feathers, and ended up having the garage, the yard, and the neighbor's yard look like someone attached 20 pounds of plastic explosive to a Hefty Bag filled with goose-down pillows. Remember that? Yeah, I didn't think so.

A beautiful sight. And the bird's nice as well. But what to do with that big old gobbler now?

After The Shot

First, let me take this opportunity to say that in some turkey hunting situations, life should *not* imitate the movies. To explain. Think back to any turkey hunting video you've ever seen. Following the shot, the hunter/actor almost without exception immediately jumps to his or her feet and takes off at a mad dash through the pucker brush in order to claim the bearded prize. Does this follow a shot of them returning the shotgun's safety to the on-safe position? Typically not. Do they ever make mention of the dangers associated with running with a loaded firearm? There again, no.

Sure, a nice gobbler is a grand thing to have bagged; however, our foremost priority as hunters, regardless of the game in question, is safety. In fairness to the cinematographers, manufacturers, and hunters who have produced these turkey hunting videos, it's safe to assume that the task of covering the distance between the calling location and the fallen bird is done in a wise and conscientious manner; however, it's also each hunter's responsibility to remind both himself and others about topics such as these.

That said, what then does happen immediately after the shot? Well, let's take it from BOOM!

You Got One!

It's a good shot. A clean harvest. In only a few situations will a gobbler fall over at the shot and lie perfectly still. When this does happen, it's quite often the result of a multiple pellet hit in the upper chest area. Such hits typically cause a gobbler to tip over on his beak with nary a wing beat, leg-kick, or flop. In most cases, though, your bird's going to flop and twitch and kick. Relax. It's simply the result of nerve paths or electrical motor impulses being abruptly interrupted by many small lead projectiles. A short circuit on a grandiose scale, let's say. Here, experience behind the gun will tell you when that bird is anchored, or when there's reason to believe he's not. Regardless, don't take your eyes off him.

For all intents and purposes, the bird is deceased. He just doesn't understand that yet. All you know is that he's still moving. Understandably, you're in a hurry to get to him so he doesn't get away. It's human nature. Again, relax. I'm not saying dawdle around, but the truth is, he's not going anywhere. Return your safety to the on-safe position. Stand, check your safety a second time, and quickly get to your prize. There's no need to run nor wave your shotgun around like a crazy person. Once you've reached the bird and have assured yourself that he's not going anywhere, now is the time to unload your shotgun. Leaving the action open allows you and your hunting partner to immediately see that the firearm is unloaded.

Trust me, scalpels have nothing over turkey spurs when it comes to cutting down to the bone an inattentive or overanxious individual. When my wife killed the third of her three Washington turkey subspecies, thus clinching a spot at that time as the only lady in the country to have harvested the state's coveted Mini-Slam, I was not only at her side, I was ecstatic. And stupid. In a flash, I was on the big Rio and, without thinking, had reached down and grabbed the gobbler by

Photo courtesy of Mark Drury and MAD Calls

I can't say enough about spurs and their ability to do damage. Hooks like the ones that Mark Drury inspects here can inflict some nasty cuts. Care is in order.

one leg. Immediately, the bird ripped a gash across my right palm. He then hooked that same spur into my camouflage glove and commenced to beating his wings and spinning in a circle, a dying-gasp maneuver that succeeded only in tightening the fabric around the base of my index finger to the point of breakage. That was my trigger-finger. In the long run, I won the impromptu skirmish, but I had not emerged unscathed. The bottom line? Spurs hurt. Wings hurt. Beaks hurt. Toenails hurt. It's foolish to let a dead turkey beat you up. It's certainly not esthetically pleasing, to be sure, but if you must, put your boot on the bird's head, paying close attention to his wings and feet. Only when the gobbler's breathed his last should you attempt to pick him up.

What if he gets up? One of the worst things you can do immediately after the shot is to lose focus. Now is not the time to begin digging through your vest, looking at the sky, or feverishly scratching that bug bite on the back of your neck. Keep your eyes on the bird. Can't see him? Then keep your eyes trained on the spot where he went down. Either way, stay focused and ready to safely shoot again. Ideally, a second-shot situation will present itself while you're still seated; however, it may be necessary to get to your feet and, with gun ready and you mentally prepared, approach the bird's last position. Remember — it's all about safety. If you're hunting with a partner by your side, it's vital to know where that partner is the moment you get to your feet. The cardinal rule with a bird that gets up — actually, any bird for that matter — is not to take your eyes off him.

Matt Morrett and a Missouri gobbler, the bird safely housed in a blaze orange "turkey bag" made by Hunter's Specialties. Carried as such, there's no excuse for anyone to mistake Matt for anything other than a successful turkey hunter.

What if he's gone? He fell at the shot, but that bush, tree, grapevine thicket, momentary lapse of reason, whatever, prevented a follow-up. A handful of feathers, a speck or two of blood, but that's it. What now? Unfortunately, turkeys, due to a layer of absorbent down feathers, don't leave much of a blood trail. And it goes without saying that a bird that falls at the shot but flies away isn't going to leave much of anything. Still, all isn't necessarily lost. Hit hard, a gobbler will often head for the first bit of cover he can find. That might be a brush pile or rose thicket, or even something as seemingly insignificant as a fallen tree trunk; still, it's a start and an excellent place to begin a search. Search thoroughly and carefully in a circular or fan-shaped pattern beginning at the spot where you last saw the bird. Too, don't forget to stop frequently and listen while you search. A gobbler that succumbs moments after the shot may flap his wings or quiver just enough so that the rustling sound might reveal his location. Look not only for the bird, but for anything out of the ordinary — a section of barred wing feathers, a buff tail tip, a patch of scuffed leaves…anything that doesn't belong. Birds that fly after the shot are tougher. With fliers, it certainly can help if you see them land. Lacking this visual information, it's best to draw a line from the bird's last location along his flight path, and work a search pattern a short distance to either side of this line beginning at the point where he was last seen.

But let's say that he's not up, and he's not gone. He's right there. Right where he met up with 2 ounces of copper-plated #6 shot. Just like he should be. The flopping's over. The wings are still. And your heartbeat and respiration are dropping from that of a hummingbird to a somewhat more human-like rate. All that's left now is the tagging and the carrying, right? Well, yes. And no. Field tagging your prize is a good thing, and in most states, a requirement. Once the tag is notched or completed, make sure it's not going to come off in transit. Many of today's tags are self-adhesive, and come already slathered with a glue specifically designed for fastening wild game permits and repairing broken bridge abutments; however, non-adhesive tags can be securely fastened to your gobbler's leg by using the Brad Harris method (Zip-ties) or the Dick Kirby method (electrical tape). Both methods work well, and both materials are light enough and small enough to be carried easily in a shirt or vest pocket.

Now for the fun part. Hopefully your gobbler is large enough to make you grunt and groan each time you heft him from the ground. Turkey hunters go through this "just checking" process quite often following a successful hunt, despite that fact that only in rare instances does the bird's weight change after the shot. Regardless, there's still the issue of getting the bird from the field to the vehicle, camp, or home. If you'll remember from Chapter 11, one of the cardinal rules of turkey hunting safety is the elimination of the colors red, white and blue from your ensemble. You also don't want to do anything that makes you look like a turkey. With that in mind, why would you want to drape a red, white and blue turkey-shaped object over your shoulder, and go diddy-bopping through the woods? Sure it looks good on the videos and the book covers, but it's just a pose. Truth is, there will be plenty of time to show him off later. For now, pack him into your turkey vest, snap on or unfurl the blaze orange flag that came with the vest, swap your camo hat for the blaze orange one in your inside pocket, and you're off. No vest? No problem. Today, several different companies make blaze orange game bags specifically designed for successful turkey hunters. Simply slide the bird into the bag, cinch up the drawstring top, slip your arms through the shoulder straps, and — again — you're off. Such bags are nice and make packing a hefty longbeard out of the field quite easy; however, before the introduction of the big orange bag, many hunters used the same blaze orange safety vests they wore during big game seasons. It's not the fashion statement, but then again, look at the way you're dressed. Do you really care?

134

Field-Dressing, Care And Transportation

In most cases, the time between your tagging your gobbler and his subsequent relocation to your home or camp won't be that long. If that is indeed the case, then field dressing really isn't all that necessary. In fact, not field-dressing your bird may very well help to keep dirt, leaves, and other foreign materials out of the body cavity as you pack him out of the field and get him to the place where he's to be processed.

Still, there are going to be those times when field-dressing your gobbler is a good idea. Heat, the scourge of all downed game, comes to mind. As is the case with any wild meat, it's imperative that a turkey be cooled as shortly after the harvest as possible. This is doubly important, not to mention twice as difficult, with feathered game. Feathers, down in particular, are excellent insulators, and will work to retain a bird's natural body heat and temperature. Am I saying that it's necessary to immediately denude your gobbler in times of high temperatures? Certainly not, but field dressing is one of best ways, short of plucking, to release a goodly portion of the stored body heat.

Dressing a wild turkey, be it in the field or at home, is actually quite easy. To field-dress your bird, pluck just enough of the feathers — they come out very easily — around the vent and upwards to the point of the breastbone so as to provide a clear cutting area. Insert the point of a sharp knife just above the vent, being careful not to cut too far into the body cavity so as to risk puncturing or cutting the lower intestines. That would be bad. Continue the incision upwards and to one side or the other of the point of the breastbone depending upon which is most convenient for you. Now that the final 2 to 3 inches of the lower intestine at the vent are exposed, it's a simple matter cut around the vent. Here again, be careful that you don't cut the intestines or spill any of the contents on the bird. That, too, is bad.

To remove the innards, reach up into the body cavity to the point where the cavity narrows down into the neck region, grab and pull. The heart, liver, gizzard, and intestines should all come out as one. The lungs, which appear much as flat tennis ball-sized pink sponges, should be removed after the bulk of the entrails. A quick internal wipe-down with a sheet of paper towel or, lacking that, a handful of grass, makes the bird ready to be packed out of the field. If distance and heat are factors in transit and a large cooler isn't an option, it's best to stop at the first convenient store you encounter and invest in a small bag of ice. Place a few handfuls of ice in a heavy-duty Zip-lock bag — don't just pour ice into the open body cavity as partial freezing or water-soaking, both undesirable, can result — and put the bag inside the bird. This still allows for air circulation while working to lower the bird's internal temperature.

Okay, guys. Let's get that tag on that bird and get him someplace cool. Don't you know that a good wild turkey dinner begins as soon as the bird hits the grass?

A couple additional points. If you're thinking about having your gobbler mounted in the very popular full body style, it's best if you leave the task of field dressing to your friendly neighborhood taxidermist. Believe me, he or she will thank you. If, however, you plan on simply mounting the tail fan yourself, a piece of newspaper or large sheet of cardboard spread over the tail fan during the dressing process can greatly reduce the amount of clean-up after the fact by keeping any blood and bodily fluids off the feathers. And finally, there are the innards. While most deer hunters in this country would never dream of leaving a fine whitetail heart or liver lying in the leaves, few give wild turkey innards a second thought. When prepared correctly or used in the creation of soups or gravy, few things are better than fresh turkey heart, gizzard, or liver. Not into innards? Turkey hearts and livers, sliced thin, make excellent channel catfish bait.

Off With His Head: Cleaning

Veteran turkey hunters all have their own preferred method for separating a gobbler from his feathers, as well as any other parts or appendages not destined for the dining room table. Attempting to convince such hunters to try a different cleaning tactic takes me back to the afternoon I tried to demonstrate a new crappie filleting technique to my father. Oh, he watched the entire show. Politely, and

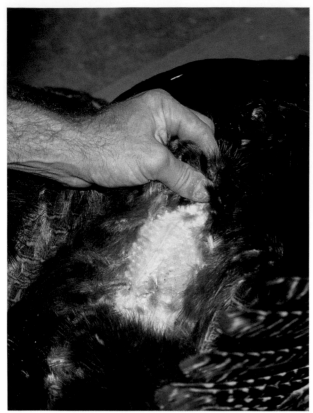

Filleting a wild turkey. I begin by plucking just enough breast feathers so as to expose the skin.

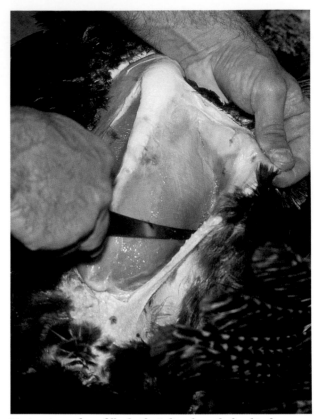

Next, using a sharp fillet knife, I slice through the skin from crop to breast point, and peel the hide back on either side.

without a single word or comment on my demonstration. Then, immediately after I had completed my presentation, he went right back to the same beheading-and-scaling method he had used for the previous 40 years. In retrospect, I believe I was the one who learned a thing or two that afternoon so very long ago; however, I digress.

Preparing a turkey, be it spring gobbler or fall hen, either for storage or the table is a rather simple task. In fact, "task" really isn't the right word at all as there's really very little work involved. Certainly, given the size of the bird, the job may at first appear intimidating; still, with a little instruction, some practice, and a bit of patience, it's all accomplished quite easily.

Dry plucking — I'm going to assume that if you've decided to dry-pluck your bird, it's your intent to prepare the bird whole. That's fine, and actually can make for a great tasting, not to mention esthetically pleasing, presentation whether baked, roasted, or deep-fried in peanut oil. And what's more, you're in luck. Unlike a December mallard whose feathers, I'm sure, were attached with a combination of epoxy, pine resin, and Wrigley's chewing gum, wild turkey feathers come out with surprising ease. Although it's possible to pluck from head to tail, it's much easier to go against the grain and pick from tail to head. The skin? Well, a gobbler's skin seems to rate somewhere between a duck and a rooster pheasant in terms of toughness; however, it's been my experience that if you're careful, particu-

larly around any shot-damaged areas, tearing the skin can be kept to a minimum. Overall, and with the exception of some mildly stubborn feathers on the legs, denuding your bird should proceed with few stutter steps. Once the bird has been picked, it's now a simple matter to remove the head, beard (if it's a gobbler), wings, tail, and feet. To remove the wings — Bend the wing away from the body toward the head to fully expose what I'll call the wing-pit, or the point where the wing attaches to the bird. Using a sharp knife, make a cut across this wing-pit. Doing so exposes the main wing joint. Cut through the cartilage at the joint. This might take a bit of practice as well as a little wing flexing. Once the connective tissue has been severed, all that's left is to cut through the remaining skin on the backside of the wing. To remove the feet, grasp the bird's leg just above the spur, or where it should be if your bird's a hen, bend the leg joint — we'll call it the knee — upwards. Make a cut at the knuckle between the upper ball of the lower leg bone and the lower ball of the upper leg bone. Believe me, you'll know it when you see it. Flexing the cut separates the joint, allowing the remaining cartilage to be severed and the leg removed. A couple words of warning here. First, it's imperative that your knife be sharp, especially when working on any joint areas such as the wings or feet. Cartilage is a tough, elastic-like material, and can prove difficult to cut. A dull blade only compounds the difficulty, not to mention raises the risk of a slip and subsequent injury. Secondly, take care when working around

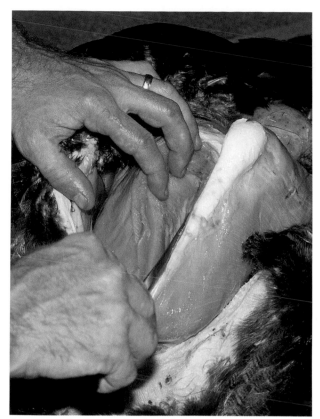

Cuts are made along each side of the breast bone or keel, as well as on the inside of both "arms" of the bird's wishbone (clavicle).

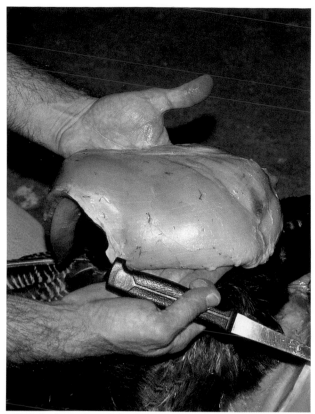

A little knife work, and the breast halves are separated from the keel and the ribs. Nothing to it!

bones, particularly the thicker wing bones that have been broken as a result of shot-damage. Typically, these protruding bones are razor-sharp and, like catfish spines, seem to seek out careless fingers and hands. These cuts and gouges will often take a long, painful time to heal.

Skinning — A second option open to the successful turkey hunter is skinning. Skinning is a skill acquired through simple experience and repetition, and while it can certainly prove a less timely method of preparing one's bird, it's not without its downsides, the most significant of which is moisture. Or more precisely, the lack of moisture while cooking. To explain. Unlike domestic turkeys, wild birds are on their own when it comes to finding food. This constant struggle to find sufficient nutrients results in a wild turkey having a far lesser fat content than does its daily grain-out-of-a-bucket domestic cousin. Because of this difference in fat content, it's important with wild birds to do everything you can to retain as much moisture as possible during the cooking process. And — that's right — skin helps seal in a large portion of what little valuable moisture a wild turkey has to begin with. Now, this fat versus no fat reality isn't said to dissuade folks from skinning their birds. It is just a culinary word of warning. For those who decide on skinning, the process is pretty simple. After removing the head, wings, feet, and fan, make an incision from stem to stern along or just to one side of the bird's breastbone. Now it's just a matter of working the skin off

the breast halves, down the back, and over each of the legs. Personally, I never skin our birds. I, like many others, like the taste of deep-fried or roasted turkey skin, and, while I've certainly used fat bacon and roasting bags with some success, nothing locks in flavor and moisture like a gobbler's own hide.

Filleting — If I don't dry-pluck our birds, I'll fillet them. This is without question the easiest and quickest way of separating mass quantities of edible turkey flesh from its former owner. There is a small amount of waste for those who don't save the back, or for that matter the whole of the carcass, to serve as the foundation for one of the finest soups on the planet. You never see Julia Child throwing away chicken backs, do you? To fillet a gobbler, I use a fillet knife simply because the flexible nature of the blade lets me work closely in and around the bones of the breast and chest. First, a shallow incision, just cutting through the skin and connective tissue, is made to one side of the point, also known as the keel, of the bird's breastbone. I'll typically make this first cut about half the length of the breastbone, top to bottom. Next, using my fingers, I slide the skin and feathers away from the breast fillets. The trick here is to fully expose the whole of each breast half. Make sure you can see the entire wishbone, and that the sides are skinned back to where the breast fillet stops and the ribs become visible. Now, slide the point of your knife, edge toward the bird's tail, into the breast to one side of the keel.

It doesn't matter which side. Keep pushing until you feel resistance. That bone you feel is the breastplate. Draw the knife down toward the bird's tail, all the while maintaining contact with the keel. Do the same on the other side. Now, turn your knife edge toward the bird's head, and make an identical cut on the outside of each half of the wishbone (see photo). With these cuts complete, it's now a simple matter to slice away each of the breast fillet halves. Just remember to keep the blade tight against either the breastplate or the ribs, and take your time. With practice, the entire filleting process should take three to five minutes; still, there's no need to hurry and do a shoddy job.

The forgotten legs, thighs, backs, and bones — As I alluded to earlier, there's not a single part of a dressed wild turkey that can't be used in some fashion. Sure, the breast fillets make for a wonderful dinner in and of themselves; however, with a little extra time and effort, both on the cutting board and the kitchen counter, there's much, much more to be had than simply turkey breast sandwiches. For instance —

Thighs — On a young bird, perhaps one taken during a fall season, the thighs can prove as tasty and as tender as that of any chicken. Preparation options are many, and include baking, barbecuing, or frying. Older birds? Well, that's another matter. Because wild turkeys spend the vast majority of their lives walking from one place to another, a big old gobbler is very likely to have thigh muscles similar to those possessed by former Olympian Carl Lewis. In other words — tough, rock-solid, and strong. Here, you have a couple choices. There's the crock pot option, which given a little red wine, a little garlic, and a whole lot of slow-cooking can be right tasty, or there's Plan B which follows.

Legs — Trust me. I've tried wild turkey legs a number of different ways. Fried, baked, grilled. And the only common denominator I've come up with is a one-word culinary summary, tough. As I mentioned earlier, wild turkeys would much rather walk or run than they would fly; therefore, they have well developed leg muscles. That's good for the turkey, but bad for the turkey hunter looking to lunch on a meal of turkey legs. And as if the musculature wasn't enough, add a series of tendons, each as strong as a tent pole, and you're rapidly approaching the inedible end of the scale. But wait! Before you throw those legs and thighs away, I'd like you to think about something — soup. Just such a recipe, courtesy of my wife, is coming shortly, so just cut those thighs off at the joint closest to the body — a slice at the socket, a quick flex, and a little more cutting is all

that's necessary — and package them up separately. Believe me, by the end of this chapter, you'll be glad you did.

Wings — Granted, there's a ton of meat on a wild turkey wing; still, what are you going to do with them? It's true that if you had, say, 50 of them, you could do up a fantastic bunch of hot wings for you and your pals during the ball game. But, and if my math's correct, that's 25 turkeys. So unless you're fortunate enough to be able to harvest several birds in the spring, each of which has two wings, and you can stockpile these tasty appendages throughout the course of the season with the intent of throwing a closing day celebration, I'd toss them into the soup pot with the legs and thighs.

Backs and bones — Two words. Soup stock.

Innards — Each spring, my garage somehow manages to get itself designated as *the* place to clean the local gobblers. Some folks are new to the art of separating flesh from fowl, and stop by looking for some direction; others, however, are simply looking for a central location at which to set up a bragging soapbox. Regardless of their individual reasons, one thing that many of these successful turkey hunters have in common is their utter disdain for turkey innards. "Now why would I want to eat those guts," some will say. "You want 'em? You take 'em." And take them I do — all the hearts, gizzards, and livers I can get my hands on. Personally, I'm a big fan of deep-fried hearts and gizzards. Too, they serve as an excellent base for turkey gravy. The neck as well. Livers, I must admit, don't do much for me. True, they can go into the soup pot or the gravy bowl. And some folks really like them just fried in bacon grease with a few sliced onions (Arg!). As for me, I'll use them either fished straight away on a treble hook or wrapped tightly in old pantyhose like a spawn bag. Channel catfish just love them. Oh, and for you newly married guys or guys with girlfriends. Make sure you explain the old pantyhose before the lady of the house finds sliced-up pairs of nylons hanging around your favorite fishing boat. Such lapses on your part could result in infrequent fishing trips. Or worse.

Washing And Storage

As is the case with cleaning, every turkey hunter has his or her favorite way of washing and then ultimately storing the processed bird. Some folks, and I have seen this, opt for the no-wash technique, claiming that if the bird's cleaned correctly, there's no need to wash it prior to freezing, and they always wash the meat before they prepare it for the table anyway.

My recommendation is this — a little bit of water never hurt anything, except the Wicked Witch of the West, and actually can help keep the bird fresh and unburned, freezer burn that is, just a bit longer. Ordinarily, all that's necessary here in the washing stage is a quick rinse under cool running water. A pick here and a pick there to remove any clinging feathers or connective tissue, and it's off to the packaging counter. Now's the time, too, to take a few minutes and extract any feather clumps, for lack of a better phrase, that had been forced into the flesh by those errant pellets that didn't hit the gobbler's head and neck. Typically these balls of feathers can be pulled from the bird using nothing more than your fingers; however, some clumps may require the tip of a sharp knife be used. Visible pellets should, of course, be removed at this point.

The final step in this washing phase is to make certain that all the blood, coagulated and otherwise, has been rinsed off or removed. Even frozen, blood is quick to spoil, and can greatly shorten the shelf life of your processed bird. Now all that remains is to pat the bird or the fillets down lightly with paper towel, and tend to the packaging.

On the subject of storage. If you plan on cooking your bird within the next two to four days, then there's really no need to go to the trouble of packaging it up tight. Whole birds need little more than a covering of plastic wrap and a stainless or crockery bowl in which to roost in the refrigerator for the next few hours. Short-term storage of breast fillets, legs, thighs, or innards is even easier, thanks to that modern marvel, the Ziploc bag.

However, if a wild turkey meal isn't in the near future, then you'll need to concern yourself with long-term storage. After years of water-filled milk containers, Ziploc bags, and the inevitable, or so it seemed, freezer burn, Julie and I have finally settled on what appears to be the perfect solution to storing wild game — the vacuum sealer. Yes, the units are a bit spendy. Our current model is a FoodSaver Professional II. Available through Cabela's (800-237-4444; **www.cabelas.com**), this particular unit will set you back about $275. Bags are likewise expensive, with a six-roll package (18-foot lengths per roll) costing right around $50; *however*, what you spend initially and in bag supply is slight when compared to the cost associated with food loss due to freezer burn, dehydration, and spoilage. Today, claims of perfect condition storage for periods of up to three years — that's three years! — are the standard in the vacuum sealer industry; still, I know of few folks, myself included, who keep wild turkey around for more than a few months. Why? It's too darn good to sit in a freezer.

But do you need, and I really mean need, a vacuum sealer? Of course not. In fact, today's thicker, heavier

Equally at home in front of a computer as he is in the kitchen, native Texan and friend, John Jefferson, handles the culinary responsibilities at our Lone Star turkey camp. TIP – Always use onions.

Ziploc freezer bags, and make sure they're freezer bags and not your basic storage bag will do a more than adequate job of storage, provided that you're careful not to extend the freezer stay of the bird or fillets for more than six to 10 months. Filling the bags, with water prior to freezing can be of some help and can extend the shelf-life; however, you'll want to be sure you (a) squeeze as much air out of the bag as possible, and (b) cover the meat completely with water, as any portion of the bird or fillet not covered by water will be the first to burn. And here's a hint for those opting to use freezer bags. Put the fillet in the bag and fill the bag completely with water. Zip the bag partially closed, leaving only about 1 inch un-zipped. Now, holding the bag by the un-zipped corner, submerge it in a five-gallon bucket filled with water. The water pressure in the bucket will force all, or at least 99 percent, of the air out of the bag. Zip it up, and the result is the Poor Man's vacuum sealer. Don't laugh. It works.

Recipes

It's one of those cases where I really do wish I had a dollar — nah, make that five dollars — for every time I had someone ask, "Well, does it taste like domestic turkey?" Or, "Is wild turkey any good? I mean, is it as good as domestic turkey?"

And while I'm not a man prone to brevity, let me answer these questions once and for all in as short a statement as I believe I'm capable of making. Once, and I repeat, once you have eaten wild turkey, Butterballs will do nothing but fall short. Period.

The problem in cooking wild turkey is much the same as it is for folks cooking wild waterfowl. Turkeys, like ducks, work for a living. No three meals a day delivered by that man in overalls carrying a bucket here. Nope, these birds pick and scratch in order to put on the pounds. Sometimes it's grass; other times, it acorns. Maybe there's corn on the menu, with a side of grasshoppers, crickets,

Nothing tastes better than a meal prepared outdoors, and wild turkey is certainly no exception. And where else, but turkey camp?

and dandelion heads. Regardless of their diet, the point remains that all this running around looking for their next meal does two things. It works their muscles, especially as I mentioned before, in their legs and thighs, and it reduces their fat content. While wild turkey may taste a bit sweeter, just a little bit more delicate than do their white-feathered domestic cousins, your oh-so-happy taste buds do not come without a price. That price? Care in the cooking. Oh, and moisture.

Turkey recipes — and I'm talking excellent turkey recipes — are almost without number; still, one thing that all recipes which include wild turkey as their main ingredient share is moisture. And it all goes back simply to the fact that wild turkeys aren't nearly as fat as are their farm-raised cousins. The recipes that follow, few though they be, are listed merely to get you started on your way through the kitchen on those occasions when wild turkey is indeed the guest of honor. They're meant to be tested and tweaked. Altered and substituted and deleted. All you have to remember is to keep it moist and go light on the spice. After all, it would be a shame to dehydrate and dilute that bird you've worked so hard to get into your kitchen, now wouldn't it?

Roasted Wild Turkey

Personally, I prefer a smaller bird for roasting purposes. Something that weighs, oh, maybe 7 to 12 pounds,

ready to go into the oven. Assuming that the bird's been cleaned, rinsed, and dried, I'll start by seasoning the bird inside and out with a combination of salt, fresh black pepper, garlic powder, and just a little touch of cayenne. If I happen to have a little fresh dill, that goes on and in as well. Next, slices of apple, orange, and sweet onion — Vadalias are my favorite — are placed in the cavity, and the cavity secured with toothpicks. The bird then goes into a roasting bag (remember: moisture retention), which is then placed, *breast down* into a suitably sized roasting pan. Why breast down? Well, why not have that wonderful breast meat constantly self-marinating throughout the whole of the cooking process instead of drying out 12 inches away from those unused juices? Finally, and using heavy-duty aluminum foil, double seal the bird in the roasting pan. Slap it into a 450-degree oven for 30 minutes, then turn the heat down to 350 and cook for about 20 minutes per pound until done. To get that eye-catching golden brown color, unwrap the bird and flip it breast side up for about 20 minutes, basting occasionally. Just keep an eye on it.

Deep-Fried Turkey

Good news. Bad news. The good news is that deep-fried turkey, and I'm talking whole turkey now, ranks among the top three greatest things in the world to eat, the other two being home-made pizza and Julie's macaroni salad. The bad news, unfortunately, is that I've only had deep-fried turkey twice. I'm going to have to work on that one.

Deep-frying your gobbler whole is a simple feat, provided you have the proper gear and a little background information. Today, turkey cookers are easy to come by. Kits, which include burners, kettles, hooks, baskets, LP hoses and connections, and thermometers can be had for just a bit more than a C-note. Add five gallons of peanut oil, the recommended cooking fluid, and a couple odds and ends such as a marinade injector and a bottle of "Holy Cow! What's that on the inside!?" liquid spice, and you're going to part with every bit of $150. After the first bite of this bird, though, you'll agree that it's worth every penny. Just follow the directions on the cooker and you'll have a bird to brag about.

The George Foreman Grill

Okay, so I'm an admitted gadget guy. I want gadgets. One year it was the Juiceman Juice Machine. Didn't get it. The next, it was the Red Devil Traveling Barbecue grill. Funny, but I didn't get that either; however, what I did get was not one but two George Foreman grills. You know, the small white Teflon-coated grills with the lid and the light that indicates something's going on inside? Well, let me tell you that for fixing a quick lunch or supper for two — I have the two-person units, but am hinting about the larger multi-burger models — this George Foreman gizmo is ideal. Here's the ticket:

Using one half of one breast fillet, slice thin (½-inch) butterfly chops across the grain of the meat. Season both sides with salt, pepper, and garlic, or use a seasoned salt like Johnny's. Either way, do both sides. Now, get the grill hot, give it a quick spritz of no-stick spray, and slide those butterflies on there. I'm giving them only two minutes total cooking time, just long enough to grate a little Parmesan on my Caesar salad and grab an iced tea. Clean up takes 30 seconds, courtesy of a damp rag and a little cold water on the grill, and you're back watching the ball game. Thank you, George Foreman. Thank you.

Bagley's Breasts

I wrote this one up in *Successful Duck Hunting* in 2001, and it still doesn't mean what you might have thought it meant then. Get your mind out of the gutter.

Like most of the recipes I use, this one is simple. Slice two wild turkey breast fillets in strips or fingers, whatever you'd like to call them. Next, take a 20-ounce jar of ordinary yellow salad mustard, and pour it into a bowl. Add pure ground cayenne pepper — yes, I said pure ground cayenne pepper — to the mustard until the mustard changes from a bright yellow to a "You know it's going to be hotter than Hell" shade of orange. Then add a little more. Taking the turkey strips one at a time, dredge them into the mustard. Scrape off the excess on the side of the bowl, and roll the strips in your favorite breading mix. I use Zatarain's, a wonderfully spicy combination of ingredients from down Texas way. Do this until all the strips have been dipped in the mustard and breaded. Deep-fry in hot oil until golden brown, and drain. Make sure you have plenty of milk, lemonade or Pabst Blue Ribbon on hand.

This recipe comes from John Bagley and his lovely wife, Michal, out of Austin, Texas. We had the pleasure of wandering around the Pedernales River Valley with the Bagleys in the spring of 2000 in search of Rio Grande gobblers. And we even found one obliging longbeard that hesitated a bit too long in front of John's .223-12 gauge over-under, his "Texas Turkey Gun," as he called it. I learned quite a bit that week in Blanco County. For instance, if you're ever turkey hunting in Texas, and a native of the Lone Star State says, "I wouldn't sit down there." Don't.

Wild Turkey Stir-Fry

Another easy one. In a hot skillet, quick-fry small strips of lightly seasoned turkey breast fillet. Be careful not to overcook the strips as they're destined to spend just a bit more time over the heat. To this, add a couple cups of water into which you've stirred a little cornstarch and a packet of prepared taco or fajita mix. Sprinkle in some Watson's gar-

A turkey stir-fry, a very simple and quick recipe that can easily be adjusted to feed two or 20.

lic oil and several shakes of House of Tsang Hot Sesame Oil. Then, if you're like me, throw in a few extra splashes of hot sesame oil, just for flavor. Once this gets to bubbling slightly, drop in your chopped celery, carrots, water chestnuts, broccoli, cauliflower, and anything else vegetarian you'd like to see in a stir-fry. As soon as the broccoli turns a wonderful shade of forest green, turn off the heat. Serve over rice or Ramen noodles. It's excellent, easy, and very quick. Plus, for you fellows who are currently dating or recently married, it'll look and taste like you spent several hours slaving over a hot stove. Don't fool yourself — she'll know the truth, but she'll appreciate it nonetheless.

Deep-Fried Turkey Strips

Again use thin breast fillet strips. Dunk the strips in a mixture of flat beer, beaten egg, garlic oil, and Tabasco sauce before dropping them into a heavy-duty Ziploc bag containing your favorite breading. I'm partial to Zatarain's, but soda crackers seasoned with salt, pepper, cayenne, ground jalapeno, garlic, and parsley and crushed with a rolling pin — or a tequila bottle — make a most excellent coating. Once breaded, lay the strips out single-file on a paper towel-line cookie sheet and place in the refrigerator for 20 to 30 minutes. This allows the breading to "set" and gives all those great spices time to invade the strips. After you've waited as long as possible, or 20 minutes, whichever was easiest, drop the strips one by one into 375-degree oil. Turn each piece once after 60 to 90 seconds, wait another 60 to 90 seconds, remove, and drain. A note here — Resist the temptation to do too many strips at once. Too many strips can lower the temperature of the oil, which in turn results in a longer and less accurate cooking time and possible — Heaven forbid — burning. Once you've learned that it is socially acceptable to beat hungry

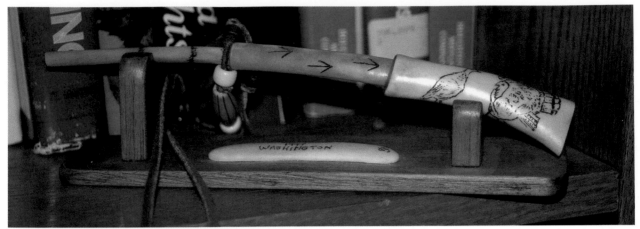

An incredibly talented man, Norman Johnson, no relation but a dear friend nonetheless, made this wing-bone call for Julie from the wing of her Washington Rio Grande – the gobbler that earned her the Washington "Mini-Slam."

guests and otherwise uninvited taste-testers out of the kitchen with a heavy stick, you'll relax and take your time. After all, you're the Head Taste-tester, aren't you?

Wrapped Breast Fillets

It might seem that we're doing a lot just with the breast fillets. And, well, you'd be right. Here's yet another simple yet extraordinary recipe.

From each of two breast fillets, you'll want to slice what I'll refer to as steaks. Cut across the grain, these steaks should be an inch or so thick; however, a little more or a little less certainly won't hurt things. And here's a tip for those of who having trouble slicing esthetically pleasing steaks from something the texture and consistency of a water balloon. Cut the steaks from the breast fillets while the bird is still partially frozen. Not only will you have something much more stable to hold on to, but the flesh, unyielding as it is in this partially frozen state, will slice more cleanly and with less hassle.

The steaks now cut, season each — both sides — to your liking. Lay each strip flat out on a cutting board or work surface covered with waxed paper. Now's the time for experimentation. In the past, I've spread the facing side of the steaks with a variety of items including blue cheese dressing, spicy brown mustard, hot Chinese mustard. Even homemade blackberry jam. The rule here is that there are no rules. Use whatever you think you'd like. Next, and because I like my meals on the spicy side, I place one ring of sliced jalapeno in the center of each steak. Are you a cheese lover? Instead of the pepper, why not substitute a hunk of good cheddar or pepper-jack? This is an open forum, folks. Just have fun.

Once you have the steaks doctored according to the whim of the moment, simply roll it up. Wrap the now-rolled steak with a piece of good, lean bacon and pin closed with a toothpick. Slap it on a medium-high, well greased grill, and cook for four to five minutes per side, or until the bacon's crispy. Don't over-do it; remember, the "no fat content" rules with wild turkey. Basting? Certainly.

A little white wine or a melted butter with garlic works well. Maybe a little lemon butter. How about orange juice? Try it; it's wonderful.

Wild Turkey Soup

After waiting in the on-deck circle for what seems like ages, it's now time for the rest of the bird to step up to the plate. Folks, I'd like to introduce — the legs and thighs. Oh, yes, and the back. And maybe assorted portions of the carcass, should you so choose. Now, onto wild turkey soup.

In a large pot filled to your liking with water, add chopped onions, celery, garlic, salt, and pepper. Bring said pot to a boil. Once boiling, add your wild turkey legs and thighs. Backs, if you wish. Cook these parts until such time as the meat can be gently pulled from the bones. Remove the pot from the heat and let cool. Don't even think about throwing the water out. It's darn near soup as it sits. As for the legs, thighs, and other things, remove them and allow them to cool.

Once the meat has cooled, pull it from the bones and cut it into bite-sized chunks. Only you know what constitutes bite-sized. Get the pot boiling again, and add carrots, thinly chopped cabbage, corn, cauliflower, broccoli, barley — anything and everything you might want in a soup. Don't forget a bay leaf, but don't eat that. They're bad. Now's the time you'll want to season your soup. Julie uses a little chicken bouillon, along with some fresh parsley, thyme, basil, and a host of other herbs that have seeded themselves between the raspberries and the start of the garden. Boil this concoction until the veggies are tender, at which point you'll want to add your turkey chunks. Simmer just long enough to heat the turkey through, but not so long that you melt the bird down into long strings of "stuff." Oh, it's still good; it just doesn't look as nice.

And as for that opening line — "...it's now time for the rest of the bird to step up to the plate." I just realized that that's probably the worst pun I've ever heard, let alone created. My apologies.

Manufacturers' Index

If Barry Manilow did indeed write the songs "that made the whole world sing," (Note to self – Hate self for mentioning Barry Manilow in a book on turkey hunting!) then the folks listed below are in large part responsible for the fact that we are able to (1) find turkeys, (2) hide from turkeys, (3) get to where the turkeys live, (4) make turkey sounds and/or noises, and in some cases (5) actually shoot turkeys.

Is it possible to successfully harvest a gobbler, called in by squawking on a swizzle stick – Don't laugh. I've seen a young Chris Kirby demonstrate just such a tactic, and it sounds pretty darn good! – while wearing a camouflage thong and armed only with a short piece of electrical conduit? Probably, but after seeing some of the folks I hunt with, exception being my wife, Julie, such a scenario is truly a visual I could live a lifetime without having seen.

That said, you might be better off to check out this list. You'll notice no thongs.

Rocky Shoes and Boots
39 Canal St.
Nelsonville, OH 45764
740-753-1951
www.rockyboots.com

Quaker Boy Game Calls
Chris Kirby, president
5455 Webster Road
Orchard Park, NY 14127
800-544-1600
www.quakerboygamecalls.com

MAD Calls, a division of Outland Sports
4500 Doniphan Dr.
Neosho, MO 64850
417-451-4438
www.outland-sports.com

Lohman Game Calls, a division of Outland Sports
4500 Doniphan Dr.
Neosho, MO 64850
417-451-4438
www.outland-sports.com

Knight & Hale Game Calls
PRADCO Outdoor Brands
3601 Jenny Lind Rd.
Fort Smith, AR 72901
501-782-8971
www.knight-hale.com

Knight Rifles
PO Box 130
Centerville, IA 52544
641-856-2626
www.knightrifles.com

Thompson/Center Arms
PO Box 5002
Rochester, NH 03866
256-463-5500
www.tcarms.com

Connecticut Valley Arms
5988 Peachtree Corners E
Norcross, GA 30071
770-449-4687
www.cva.com

Bass Pro Shops
2500 E. Kearney
Springfield, MO 65898
1-800-BASS-PRO
www.basspro.com

Cabela's
One Cabela Drive
Sidney, NE 69160
1-800-237-4444
www.cabelas.com

Maddy Brothers Guide Service
Stan, Keane, and Jason Maddy, proprietors
19274 Highway T-14
Mystic, IA 52574
641-437-1907

Remington Arms
870 Remington Dr.
Madison, NC 27025
800-243-9700
www.remington.com

Winchester
427 N. Shamrock St.
East Alton, IL 62024
618-258-3568
www.winchester.com

Federal Cartridge Company
900 Ehlen Dr.
Anoka, MN 55303
763-323-2300
www.federalcartridge.com

Hunter's Specialties
6000 Huntington Ct. NE
Cedar Rapids, IA 52402
319-395-0321
www.hunterspec.com

Feather Flex Decoys
4500 Doniphan Dr.
Neosho, MO 64850
417-451-4438
www.outland-sports.com

Bushnell Sports Optics
9200 Cody
Overland Park, KS 66214
1-800-423-3537
www.bushnell.com

Realtree Camouflage
PO Box 9638
Columbus, GA 31908
1-800-992-9968
www.realtree.com

Mossy Oak Camouflage
C/o Haas Outdoors, Inc.
PO Box 757
West Point, MS 39773
662-494-8859
www.mossyoak.com

Gerber Legendary Blades
14200 SW 72nd Ave.
Portland, OR 97223
800-950-6161
www.gerberblades.com

Pete Clare's Turkey Trot Acres
188 Tubbs Hill Rd.
Candor, NY 13743
607-659-7849
www.turkeytrotacres.com

Bug-Out Outdoorwear
901 E. Stewart
Centerville, IA 52544
641-437-1936
www.bug-out-outdoorwear.com

Beretta USA
17601 Beretta Dr.
Accokeek, MD 20607
301-283-2191
www.berettausa.com

DeLorme Mapping Company
Two DeLorme Dr.
Yarmouth, ME 04096
800-452-5931
www.delorme.com

Flambeau Product Corportation
PO Box 97
Middlefield, OH 44062
1-800-232-3474
www.flamprod.com

National Wild Turkey Federation
770 Augusta Rd.
Edgefield, SC 29824
1-800-THE-NWTF
www.nwtf.org

O.F. Mossberg & Sons
7 Grasso Ave.
North Haven, CT 06473
1-800-989-GUNS

Outlaw Decoys
624 N. Fancher Rd.
Spokane, WA 99212
1-800-OUTLAWS
www.outlaw.com

Hevi-Shot/Environ-Metal, Inc.
PO Box 834
Sweet Home, OR 97386
541-367-3522
www.environ-metal.com